PHENOMENOGRAPHY IN THE 21ᔆᵀ CENTURY

PHENOMENOGRAPHY IN THE 21ST CENTURY

Phenomenography in the 21st Century

A Methodology for Investigating Human Experience of the World

Gerlese S. Åkerlind

https://www.openbookpublishers.com

©2025 Gerlese S. Åkerlind

This work is licensed under the Creative Commons Attribution-NonCommercial 4.0 International (CC BY-NC 4.0). This license allows you to share, copy, distribute and transmit the text; to adapt the text for non-commercial purposes of the text providing attribution is made to the authors (but not in any way that suggests that they endorse you or your use of the work). Attribution should include the following information:

Gerlese S. Åkerlind, *Phenomenography in the 21st Century: A Methodology for Investigating Human Experience of the World*. Cambridge, UK: Open Book Publishers, 2024, https://doi.org/10.11647/OBP.0431

Further details about the CC BY-NC license are available at http://creativecommons.org/licenses/by-nc/4.0/

All external links were active at the time of publication unless otherwise stated and have been archived via the Internet Archive Wayback Machine at https://archive.org/web

Any digital material and resources associated with this volume will be available at https://doi.org/10.11647/OBP.0431#resources

ISBN Paperback: 978-1-80511-425-3
ISBN Hardback: 978-1-80511-426-0
ISBN Digital (PDF): 978-1-80511-427-7
ISBN Digital eBook (EPUB): 978-1-80511-428-4
ISBN HTML: 978-1-80511-429-1

DOI: 10.11647/OBP.0431

Cover image: Photo by Jason Hawke, 'A person standing on a road, surrounded by trees', November 19, 2022, https://unsplash.com/photos/a-person-standing-on-a-road-surrounded-by-trees-9QSv-09_RIQ
Cover design: Jeevanjot Kaur Nagpal

Dedication

I would like to dedicate this book to Ference Marton. A man of drive and vision, but also generosity and humour. Thank you for providing such an interesting and wide-ranging focus for my research career, and thank you for being a friend.

Contents

Dedication	v
List of Illustrations	xi
Acknowledgments	xv
Author's Biography	xvii
Foreword	xix
Paul Ashwin	
Preface	xxiii

1. Introduction to phenomenography and the aims of this book	1
Why phenomenography?	1
The purpose of this book	2
My personal involvement in phenomenography	6
Structure of the book	9
Chapter summary	14
2. Developments in phenomenography over time: From a research 'approach' to a 'methodology'	15
The focus on human experience	16
Variation and structure in human experience	19
Research examples illustrating the shift from early to 21st-century phenomenography	25
Chapter summary	33
3. Variation in understandings of phenomenography	35
Study methods	36
Outcomes—variation in ways of understanding phenomenography	38

Implications of the study for phenomenographic research	45
Chapter summary	49

4. Variation in understandings of structural relationships in phenomenography — 51

Study methods	52
Outcomes—variation in ways of understanding structural relationships	53
Implications of the study for phenomenographic research	65
Chapter summary	69

5. Epistemological assumptions in phenomenography: Implications for methods — 71

The dialectical relationship between meaning and structure in human experience	74
Awareness as inevitably partial and variable	76
Partial and varying awareness creates a figure-ground structure to experience	80
How awareness of parts combine to create a holistic experience	83
Human experience of the world as non-dualistic	84
Summary of epistemological claims and associated analytic strategies	87
Chapter summary	90

6. Study design, data gathering and the phenomenographic interview — 91

Determining the object of study	92
Gathering data	104
Selecting participants	105
Designing interview questions	108
Conducting interviews	117
Transcription of interviews	130
Chapter summary	131

7. Analysing data and reporting research outcomes — 133

A ten-step guideline for the analytic process	134
Concrete descriptions of practice	139
Research rigour	161

Transferability of outcomes	180
Chapter summary	181

8. Adding further structure to the outcome space: Structural relationships between dimensions of variation — 183

How the notion of 'themes of expanding awareness' developed	185
The traditional approach—independently constituted dimensions of variation	186
The themes of expanding awareness approach—relationally constituted dimensions of variation	191
How to constitute themes of expanding awareness	198
Not just variation in values along a dimension, but also variation in dimensions along a theme	208
Chapter summary	210

9. Phenomenography and variation theory: The development of complementary traditions — 211

Three components to the variation theory tradition	213
Development of the variation theory tradition from its phenomenographic roots	219
The relationship between the phenomenography and variation theory traditions	233
The relationship in summary—complementary theoretical, applied, empirical and educational relationships	243
Chapter summary	247

10. Phenomenography and collective awareness: The potential of phenomenography to contribute to the broader social sciences — 249

Phenomenography and collective awareness	249
Phenomenography and sociocultural perspectives on human experience	253
Potential applications of phenomenography in the broader social sciences	256
A final point	260
Chapter summary	261

References	263
Index	279

List of Illustrations

Figures

2.1	Hierarchically inclusive structure of differential awareness of legal reasoning	p. 29
5.1	Analytical constituents of experience—the referential and structural aspects of a way of experiencing (adapted from Marton and Booth, 1997, p. 88)	p. 76
5.2	Analytical constituents of experience—the internal and external horizons of awareness of a phenomenon (adapted from Marton and Booth, 1997, p. 88)	p. 79
5.3	Analytical constituents of experience—figural and non-figural aspects of the phenomenon (added to Marton and Booth's, 1997, figure, p. 88)	p. 81
7.1	Relational role of the researcher during analysis (adapted from Bowden, 2005, p. 13)	p. 164
9.1	One view of the relationship between the phenomenography and variation theory traditions, in which *Learning and Awareness* is seen as having had no impact on phenomenography	p. 240
9.2	An alternative view of the relationship between the phenomenography and variation traditions, in which *Learning and Awareness* is seen as having had a profound impact on phenomenography	p. 241

Tables

2.1	Stages in the development of phenomenography	p. 23
2.2	Critical aspects of legal reasoning discerned in the different ways of understanding it	p. 30

3.1	Critical aspects of phenomenography discerned in the different ways of understanding it	p. 42
4.1	Outcome space for 'structural relationships in phenomenography'	p. 57
5.1	Epistemological claims underlying different analytic strategies in phenomenographic research	p. 88
7.1	Example of using the 'free node' feature in NVivo to assist with Grouping and Discerning of data on 'Being a Doctor' (adapted from Yu, 2019, p. 184)	p. 147
7.2	An example of structural (part-whole) relationships between different categories in an outcome space, based on a study of the different ways in which students can experience 'price' (adapted from Marton and Pong, 2005, p. 342)	p. 155
7.3	An example of structural (part-whole) relationships between different categories in an outcome space, based on a study of the different ways in which students can experience 'information literacy when researching an essay' (adapted from Lupton, 2004, pp. 53–54)	p. 155
8.1	An example of an outcome space that constitutes dimensions of variation in the traditional way—constituted independently from each other (adapted from Marton and Pong, 2005, p. 342)	p. 189
8.2	Another example of an outcome space that constitutes dimensions of variation in the traditional way (derived from Åkerlind, 2003b)	p. 189
8.3	An alternative format for presenting the relationship between traditionally constituted dimensions of variation and different ways of experiencing a phenomenon (adapted from Åkerlind, 2003b, p. 384)	p. 190
8.4	An example of an outcome space that constitutes dimensions of variation along themes of expanding awareness (adapted from Åkerlind, 2005e, p. 18)	p. 192
8.5	Another example of an outcome space that constitutes dimensions of variation along themes of expanding awareness (adapted from Åkerlind, 2005d, p. 152)	p. 195
8.6	Another example of themes of expanding awareness (adapted from Paakkari et al., 2010, p. 944)	p. 197
8.7	Another example of themes of expanding awareness (adapted from Kettunen, 2024, p. 76)	p. 198

9.1	Patterns of variation and invariance (adapted from Kullberg et al., 2024, p. 26)	p. 224
9.2	Outcomes of an analysis of the concept of 'learning' using phenomenography (adapted from Holmqvist and Selin, 2019, p. 6)	p. 229
9.3	Outcomes of an analysis of the concept of 'learning' using variation theory (adapted from Holmqvist and Selin, 2019, p. 7)	p. 230
9.4	Complementary foci of the phenomenography and variation theory traditions	p. 246

Acknowledgments

Many thanks to the phenomenography and variation theory colleagues whose conversations have advanced my thinking for particular chapters of the book: Kristina Allberg, Jaana Kettunen, Angelika Kullberg, Terese Stenfors, Malin Tväråna, Päivi Tynjälä and Elina Wright (in alphabetical order).

My thanks also to my recent doctoral students who have allowed me to refer to their work in this book: Suet Voon Yu, Laura Killam and Lance Eaton. Talking through issues with research students always clarifies my own thinking, so you have also helped me in ways that are not so obvious.

I very much appreciate the input of the anonymous research colleagues who participated in the surveys I refer to in Chapters 3, 4 and 9, and thus contributed to my research and thinking about phenomenography. Researcher workloads are so high these days that making time to contribute to someone else's research (and the greater good of building collective human knowledge) is a hard ideal to maintain.

Lastly, I want to acknowledge John Bowden, who does not think he has contributed to this book, but whose collegial interest at a key point helped me make the commitment to writing the book. It is one thing to have many things one wants to say about phenomenography, but it is another thing altogether to commit to the many months it requires to do that in the form of a book. One does not always lead to the other, so thank you, John.

Author's Biography

Gerlese Åkerlind, PhD, is a professor emerita at the Australian National University (ANU). She was previously Director of the Centre for Educational Development and Academic Methods at the ANU, Director of the Teaching and Learning Centre at the University of Canberra, and a long-term honorary Research Associate of the Oxford Learning Institute at Oxford University. Gerlese has particular expertise in the phenomenographic research tradition, with numerous publications on phenomenographic theory and methods. In addition, her empirical research has primarily used phenomenographic methods, investigating the nature of academic practice, including university teaching, research, research supervision and academic development.

Foreword

Paul Ashwin[1]

It is a great honour to write the foreword of 'the' definitive text on phenomenography and undertaking phenomenographic research. For anyone conducting phenomenographic research, as I have done for the last twenty years, the work of Gerlese Åkerlind has been an indispensable source of wisdom and insight into the underpinning concepts, processes, significance and meanings of phenomenography. To have this seminal work brought together in a single book is a great service to the research community and an outstanding scholarly achievement.

I first met Gerlese when I was being introduced to phenomenography by Keith Trigwell in the early 2000s. During this time, I was increasingly drawn to the power of phenomenography to offer insights into the variation in the ways that different people experience the same phenomenon. For me, the distinctive power of phenomenography is the way in which it focuses both on variation and collective groups of people. Since learning about phenomenography and conducting phenomenographic research, I have introduced many doctoral students and co-researchers to phenomenography and examined many PhDs that have claimed to have taken a phenomenographic approach. As this book recognises, not everything that claims to be phenomenographic is recognisable as phenomenography. It is wonderful to now have a beautifully and accessibly written text to which to refer those who are struggling to understand phenomenography. For, as is usually the case with powerful and important ideas, it is an ongoing and productive struggle to understand phenomenography. Indeed, in reading this book, I gained rich new insights into aspects of phenomenography that I

---

1   Professor of Higher Education, Lancaster University.

have struggled to grasp (for example, 'themes of expanding awareness') and developed a much better understanding of how my own work is situated in the broader body of phenomenographic research.

This book offers a rich resource for both researchers who are new to, and very experienced in, engaging with phenomenography. For the novice, it provides a clear sense of what phenomenography is, what undertaking research from a phenomenographic perspective involves, and the range of phenomenographic work that has been produced over its fifty-year history. For the more experienced researcher, it gives a deep insight into the variation in the ways that phenomenography has been approached, the relationship between phenomenography and variation theory, and the similarities and differences between themes of expanding awareness and dimensions of variation. A major achievement of the book is that it does this with both clarity and precision and in a collegial and inclusive tone. Analytical, historical and philosophical asides beautifully draw the reader into supportive conversations about some of the most challenging aspects of phenomenography and underline Gerlese's commitment to recognise and address the variation in readers' experiences of reading the book. There are so many impressive aspects to what the book achieves, but the way in which it consistently adopts a phenomenographic sensibility to every aspect of the research and reading process is the one that impressed me most. The reflexive consistency of phenomenography is one of the aspects that first drew me towards it. I have always hugely valued the way in which it understands the research process in the same way as it understands the experiences of those who are researched and this commitment is brilliantly enacted in this book.

Phenomenography has so much to offer the troubled, divided, unequal and unsustainable world that we are experiencing in the 21st century. I want to highlight two that are elegantly encapsulated in this book, which reflect the distinctive power of phenomenography that I mentioned earlier. First, phenomenography's focus on the collective rather than the individual experience is a crucial step in moving away from a narrow focus on individual experiences towards understanding more inclusively the rich diversity of experiences that exist in relation to all the important questions we face in the world. Second, we urgently need to include this diversity of perspectives in decision-making processes. Not just because it is the right thing to do, but because the more diverse the range of perspectives we include in decision making, the better the decisions are. Phenomenography is an amazing way of not only mapping the diverse range of perspectives in relation to a particular phenomenon but also of supporting us to develop an understanding of the structure and meaning of the variation in these perspectives.

Reading this book has helped me to understand how my own research is deeply informed by a phenomenographic sensibility and how it draws on fifty years of phenomenographic research. However, it has also enabled me to see how what I am trying to do in my work is different from what is focused on in mainstream phenomenography. I have no doubt that this book will inspire a whole new generation of phenomenographers but it also has the power to open up much more inclusive and productive conversations about how a phenomenographic sensibility can inform a greater diversity of research with a greater diversity of aims. In doing so, the book has the potential to extend the contribution of phenomenography to understanding human experiences of the world in the 21st century. Reading this book is a wonderful invitation to consider how we might play a role in realising this potential.

November 2024

Preface

For me, phenomenography is more than just a methodology for conducting research. Although I have certainly found phenomenographic methods very fruitful for both my empirical research and my applications of that research in my professional role in university educational development, it is the epistemological insights phenomenography has given me into human understanding of the world and human communication and miscommunication in the world that has been the most appealing part of phenomenography for me.

Often in my life, in both professional and personal situations, I have been struck by the fact that the same situation was later described quite differently by the different people involved. My early academic training in psychology provided some explanations for this (e.g., confirmation bias, primacy and recency effects, motivations, attitudes, beliefs), but phenomenographic epistemology provided a much more integrated explanation. My study of phenomenography has helped me reframe many miscommunications as due to having discerned different aspects of the topic or situation. This reframing reduces frustration and confusion, by explaining such interactions in a non-blaming way, where people's way of thinking about a phenomenon are but a logical consequence of their way of seeing it, and ways of seeing it will inevitably vary.

So, phenomenography has not just provided me with a research focus in my career, but a lens for viewing the world, in particular human interactions in the world, and I carry that lens with me through all aspects of my life—personal as well as professional. Both the theory and empirical outcomes of phenomenographic research help me understand why and how people see the world, and phenomena in the world, differently. It helps me make sense of miscommunications between people, and why one person may literally be unable to see another person's point of view. My background in phenomenography means that, whenever I am in discussion with others, I am sensitive to the potential for different ways of understanding the topic of conversation, and actively listen for indicators of how the other person may be understanding the topic in a different way to me, or to each other.

This has been of great value professionally, especially when accompanied by the outcomes of empirical studies in relevant areas, such as studies of variation in academic teachers' understandings of teaching and learning. The outcomes of such studies have enabled me to design postgraduate courses on university teaching and learning with the knowledge that academics attending my courses are likely to be entering the course with this range of perspectives on what teaching and learning consists of. I am then able to use that knowledge in my course design, with one of the key goals of my courses being to expand participants' understanding of the nature of teaching and learning itself (not just help them become familiar with educational theory, research and methods).

This is because, as described by phenomenography, one cannot act outside one's way of thinking and understanding. In other words, the way in which teachers will understand educational theory, research and methods, and their ensuing decisions and actions as a teacher, are inevitably constrained by their understanding of the phenomenon of teaching (and learning) itself. So, to make sense of 'progressive' ways of teaching and facilitating students' learning, teachers first need to understand the nature of teaching and learning in a 'progressive' way.

Another way in which phenomenography has helped me professionally is that, when providing advice or support to individual teachers, I could listen to their description of the educational issues facing them with a sensitivity to how they may be seeing the nature of teaching and learning underlying those issues, and tailor my advice accordingly. There is no point, for instance, in suggesting student-centred educational methods to teachers who think that student learning consists of simply absorbing the information provided by teachers.

So, phenomenography has had a strong impact on the type of questions I ask in my research, the way I think and act within my academic or professional role, and the way I think and act in my personal life. Although I have conducted other forms of qualitative research, as well as quantitative research, I return to phenomenography again and again because I think the research enhances my understanding of people and how they see and operate in the world in a way no other research methodology does. This is why I am enthusiastic about promoting the potential of phenomenographic research to others, and why I am happy to call myself a 'phenomenographer'.

1. Introduction to phenomenography and the aims of this book

Why phenomenography?

Phenomenographic epistemology presents a theory of how we, as humans, become aware of and make sense of our world, through a relationship between the structure of our awareness of phenomena in the world and the meaning those phenomena hold for us.

If you are interested in how we, as humans, make sense of our world; if you want to enrich your own and others' understanding of important phenomena in the world, including particular skills and concepts in your discipline or profession, or social concepts in a particular community group or culture; if you want to investigate why and how people can understand the same phenomena in different ways, and how this can vary between different groups in society; if you are looking for new insights into what can interfere with student learning, individual development or professional expertise; if you want to pinpoint what is needed to help people learn and develop in particular ways; and if you see value in highlighting key features and patterns in human experience (in contrast to the detailed richness of individual experience), then you will be interested in phenomenography and the insights into phenomenography provided in this book.

Empirically, the phenomenographic interest in human experience is reflected in a unique research design that investigates variation and commonality in people's understanding, or awareness, of phenomena in the world. This is undertaken through an analysis of the 'structure of awareness' underlying the different understandings, or meanings, people experience for ostensibly the same phenomena in the world. From a phenomenographic perspective, the terms meaning, understanding, experience and awareness are often used interchangeably, because they are all seen as inherently interconnected in the act of ongoing sense-making in the world.

What makes phenomenography unique as an empirical research tool, is its focus on:

- simultaneously explicating variation and commonality amongst people in their ways of experiencing the same phenomena; and
- simultaneously explicating the meaning and structure associated with those ways of experiencing—where 'meaning' refers to our holistic understanding of a phenomenon, and 'structure' refers to the structure of our awareness of the phenomenon.

The purpose of this book

Whilst the intertwining of variation-commonality and meaning-structure has always been the focus of phenomenographic research, it has been expressed in different ways at different times in the evolution of the methodology. Phenomenography originated as a research approach some fifty years ago, led by Ference Marton and colleagues (Marton and Säljö, 1976; Marton, 1981a, 1986a). But phenomenographic research of the 1970s, 1980s and 1990s is not the same as phenomenographic research of the 2000s. Phenomenography changed irrevocably towards the turn of the century, following publication of Marton and Booth's (1997) book, *Learning and Awareness*. This text clarified the theoretical underpinnings of phenomenography and, as a consequence, introduced a more sophisticated approach to conducting phenomenographic research (Pang, 2003; Marton and Pong, 2005; Pang and Marton, 2005; Åkerlind, 2015; Kullberg and Ingerman, 2022).

This change in phenomenographic practice forms a key reason for writing this book. Too often, I see authors using phenomenography who justify their research methods by referring only to earlier works on phenomenography (e.g., Marton, 1981a, 1986a, 1994; Bowden and Walsh, 1994). But phenomenography did not commence as a fully developed research methodology in the 1970s, thoroughly thought out before ever being applied. No, it developed as an experimental method, an idea and approach that was further developed and refined over time. So, whilst the earlier works will always be of historical interest, they are not the basis on which current approaches to empirical analysis using phenomenography should be founded. I explain this further in Chapter 2, describing and illustrating key changes in phenomenographic research over time, and why Marton and Booth's (1997) book, *Learning and Awareness*, should be regarded as the foundational publication[1] for phenomenography in the 21st century, not Marton's first mainstream publication on phenomenography in 1981.

Another imperative for me in writing this book is that, as phenomenography has grown in popularity, those new to phenomenographic research have often found themselves in the position of trying to learn about phenomenography without someone experienced in the methodology to guide them. This is particularly unfortunate for doctoral researchers who may not have a supervisor experienced in phenomenography to consult. I have been contacted for help by many such students around the world, as well as seeing the typically unfortunate outcomes for students in this position when asked to examine their dissertations. I have previously argued that the currently limited publications on methodological aspects of phenomenography make it extremely difficult to truly understand the approach from reading the literature alone (Åkerlind, 2022, 2024a). So, one of my aims in writing this book is to help research students and others interested in undertaking phenomenographic research who do not have an experienced mentor to advise them. In Chapter 6 and Chapter 7, I present detailed guidelines for phenomenographic data gathering and analysis, with concrete examples from a variety of phenomenographic researchers. These two chapters should finally overcome previous barriers to understanding the methods from literature alone.

An unfortunate consequence of the growth over time in popularity of phenomenographic research is that misunderstandings and misapplications of the methodology have proliferated, and can act to mislead novice researchers about the nature of phenomenographic

---

1   By 'foundational', I do not mean that *Learning and Awareness* should be the first thing one reads on phenomenography, because it would form a rather complicated introduction to the methodology. Marton 1986 and 1994 would provide good preparatory reading before attempting Marton and Booth (1997).

methods (Åkerlind, 2022, 2024a). Furthermore, a lack of journal reviewers experienced in the methodology means that, just because a study describing itself as using phenomenographic methods has been published, that does not mean that the description of phenomenography in the paper can be relied on to accurately reflect appropriate methods. Not all published descriptions of phenomenography are equally reliable, but how can novices be expected to assess the quality of different studies? This is something I explicitly address in Chapter 3 of this book, on more and less sophisticated ways of understanding phenomenography amongst educational researchers.

But this book is not just for those new to phenomenography. Experienced phenomenographers will also find the book valuable—partially as a source of teaching materials for their research students, but also because I present new perspectives on phenomenography. In Chapter 3 and Chapter 4, I describe the results of an empirical study of collective awareness of 'phenomenography' and 'structural relationships' in phenomenography. Through investigating variation in understandings of phenomenography in this way, I uniquely apply phenomenographic methods to better understand phenomenography itself. Based on a survey of researchers familiar with the approach, I explore collective understanding of phenomenography and the key role played by the focus on 'structure' in phenomenographic research. This exploration will inevitably enrich everyone's understanding of the approach, novices and experts alike, by enabling each of us to see our own way of understanding phenomenography within the context of other ways of understanding it.

In addition, in Chapter 5, I present a unique integration of the different epistemological claims from *Learning and Awareness*, and their relationship to different analytic practices in phenomenographic research. As mentioned above, *Learning and Awareness* (Marton and Booth, 1997) forms the foundational text describing the epistemological assumptions underlying phenomenography. But the theoretical claims in the book are not as integrated as they could be. In Chapter 5, I explicitly clarify the relationship between different epistemological assumptions and associated analytic methods in phenomenography. This highlights different lenses to the notion of 'structure' in phenomenographic research, which is generally regarded as the most difficult aspect of phenomenography to understand. So, this is also a chapter that will be of interest to experienced phenomenographic researchers.

Phenomenography has always emphasised the search for key or 'critical' aspects in human awareness of phenomena, that is, those aspects that are critical for distinguishing one way of experiencing a phenomenon from a qualitatively different way of experiencing it. But following *Learning and Awareness*, the search for critical aspects of human experience has commonly taken the form of identifying independently-constituted 'dimensions of variation' in our awareness of phenomena. In Chapter 8, I describe an alternative approach to identifying critical aspects of human awareness, in the form of dimensions of variation that are structurally-related along 'themes of expanding awareness', and analyse the differences between the two analytic approaches.

This chapter is important in helping to dispel a confusion that is developing in the phenomenographic literature, with a growing number of researchers presenting critical aspects in the form of themes of expanding awareness, whilst misleadingly referring to them as dimensions of variation (e.g., Lupton, 2004; Gonzalez, 2011; Light and Calkins, 2015; Täks et al., 2016; Töytäri et al., 2016; Mimirinis, 2019; Mimirinis et al., 2023; Kettunen et al., 2020; Kettunen and Tynjälä, 2022; Wilson et al., 2021; Stoffels et al., 2021; Wardak et al., 2023; Brauer et al., 2023). Whilst both forms of analysis are legitimate, it is important for researchers to recognise that there are two analytic approaches to constituting dimensions of variation circulating in the literature, not just one, and to be clear about which approach they are using.

Implicit in the epistemological assumptions outlined in *Learning and Awareness* is a theory of learning, the 'variation theory of learning', which has become well developed over time. But there is also a concomitant 'variation theory of awareness' implicit in the book that has not been similarly developed (see Chapter 5). This is no doubt a consequence of phenomenography being most popular amongst researchers in the field of education, leading to a natural bias towards developing educational aspects of the methodology. In line with this, in Chapter 9, I describe the relationship between phenomenography and the variation theory of learning traditions, drawing out associated implications for education and pedagogy.

However, phenomenography also holds potential value for fields of research other than education, a potential that I feel has been neglected. So in Chapter 10, the final chapter of the book, I draw out the implications of phenomenography for investigating collective understanding within different socially, culturally and historically situated groups, which I hope will be of interest beyond the bounds of educational research.

In summary, the overall aim of this book is to clarify and extend phenomenographic research by integrating theory and practice, presenting detailed examples of empirical research-in-practice, addressing common misinterpretations of the approach, and looking beyond phenomenography's primary focus on empowering learning and teaching to highlight its simultaneous focus on unpacking collective awareness. Because the writing of this book led me to further discriminations and connections in my own understanding of phenomenography, I hope the same will be true for you, as readers. And just as re-reading early chapters after I had reflected on and written later chapters led to me wanting to introduce further discriminations in the earlier chapters, I hope that this is a book that will be re-read numerous times, with readers gaining something new (discerning additional critical aspects of phenomenography) on each reading.

My personal involvement in phenomenography

I have already stated that not all publications on phenomenography are equally reliable in accurately depicting the methodology. Consequently, I feel there may be value in describing my own experience with phenomenography, so that readers of this book are able to contextualise my comments within the different influences I have experienced. My story also provides an example of how and why someone may become involved in phenomenographic research.

My own involvement with phenomenography started in the mid-1980s, when I was working with David Watkins in an academic development unit at the Australian National University (academic development units in Australia include development of academics as teachers). David, who later moved to Hong Kong and became prolific in publishing phenomenographic studies, was interested in phenomenographic research into student learning and introduced me to a lot of the early literature. Others in the Australian academic development community were also becoming interested in phenomenographic research at the time, and I was fortunate to be invited to a symposium on phenomenographic research in 1986, *The Marysville Symposium*, where Ference Marton was the key guest. So, I met Ference for the first time in 1986, then many times thereafter.

The symposium was organised by John Bowden at the University of Melbourne, a close colleague of mine in academic development, who also went on to become a leading figure in phenomenography over the next twenty years, with a particular focus on clarifying phenomenographic methods (e.g., Bowden and Walsh 1994 [2000]; Bowden, 1996; Bowden and Green, 2005). Australia developed a very active community of researchers in higher education and academic development interested in phenomenography, and other close colleagues of mine who were active in phenomenography at the time included Keith Trigwell, Mike Prosser and Elaine Martin who, often with Paul Ramsden, formed a long-lasting and active team of researchers into student learning and university teaching viewed from a phenomenographic perspective (summarised in Prosser and Trigwell, 1999; Trigwell and Prosser, 2020).

So, from the early days of the development of phenomenography, I was fortunate to be part of an extended community of researchers in Australia interested in the implications of phenomenographic research for teaching and learning in higher education. And these researchers were in regular contact with Ference Marton and his colleagues. I should add, however, that despite the close contact with phenomenographic colleagues in Sweden (where phenomenography originated), researchers in Australia developed their own particular variation on data analysis methods, which has since been adopted by many researchers internationally, even though it is not the preferred method in Sweden. This is the analysis of phenomenographic interviews on a 'whole of transcript' basis, in contrast to the method preferred by Marton and colleagues of taking extracts from transcripts to form a decontextualised 'pool of meanings' for analysis (Åkerlind, 2005a [2012]). Both methods are now accepted practice, and I explain the similarities and differences between them in more detail later in the book (Chapter 7).

I started my doctoral work in 1996, with Mike Prosser and John Bowden as my supervisors. In 1997, I attended a two-week workshop on phenomenography run by Ference Marton in Sweden, with a particular focus on the role of variation, discernment and simultaneity in awareness of phenomena. And it was at this workshop that I first developed my career-long interest in helping others understand phenomenography, because the workshop was attended by numerous doctoral candidates, some of whom did not have a supervisor experienced in phenomenography. My own assessment of the field of phenomenographic research was that the available literature was inadequate for learning to do phenomenography without the help of an experienced guide. I felt privileged to have two experienced phenomenographers on my supervisory panel, and my heart went out to those who were not so fortunate.

This was an exciting time in the development of phenomenography, as Ference was now focusing on the more theoretical aspects of phenomenographic research, in terms of clarifying and developing the underpinning epistemological and ontological assumptions. This had new implications for conducting research, and it also established the beginnings of a new theory of learning, the variation theory of learning mentioned above (Marton and Booth, 1997; Bowden and Marton, 1998; Marton and Trigwell, 2000; Marton and Tsui, 2004; Marton, 2015).

A special interest group (SIG) on phenomenography had been created, attached to the European Association for Research into Learning and Instruction (EARLI). This became the main source of information on current developments in phenomenography for those living outside of Sweden. So, from 1997 onwards I regularly attended the SIG at EARLI conferences, in order to stay up-to-date with developments in the field of research. I subsequently co-convened the SIG with Airi Rovio-Johansson from 1999–2002, and am still a member. I went on to run national and international workshops and hosted conferences on phenomenography from 2002–2018, or was part of the organising committees helping others to do so.

The theoretical ideas presented in *Learning and Awareness* led to a series of doctoral dissertations exploring different ways of putting these ideas into practice. This cohort of dissertations in the late 1990s and early 2000s formed the first series of in-depth attempts to implement 'variation theory' and what I am now calling '21st-century phenomenography'. My dissertation, which I completed in 2003 (Åkerlind, 2003a [2011]), was one of these, and I was fortunate enough to have Ference Marton as an examiner. By the time I completed my dissertation, I was not just using phenomenography as the primary method for my research, I was also interested in phenomenography for itself, as a methodological field of research practice. Ever since reading a pre-print version of *Learning and Awareness* in 1996, I have been as interested in the epistemological aspects of phenomenography as the empirical aspects. As I describe in the preface to this book, for me, phenomenography is not just a research method, and not just a tool for improving teaching and learning, but also a way of thinking about the world and human interaction in the world.

Consequently, throughout my career, I not only used phenomenography as an empirical tool for my research, which I could then use to inform my teaching and academic development practice, but I also published methodological articles on phenomenography itself (Åkerlind, 2005a, 2005b, 2005c, 2005d, 2012, 2015, 2018, 2022, 2024a, 2024b; 2024c; Åkerlind et al., 2005; Åkerlind et al., 2014). So, readers can be assured that what I write in this book will be thoughtfully positioned within a sound knowledge of the phenomenographic tradition. But that does not mean that everything I write should be taken as gospel. There is accepted variation in practice in phenomenography and, despite numerous visits to Sweden, I am inevitably most influenced by the way the tradition has developed within Australia. But to continue developing, phenomenography also has to be open to new ideas and practices, and not simply replicate what any one scholar advocates. Of course, this does not mean that 'anything goes'; any suggested variations must also be well-located within a thorough knowledge of existing literature and practice.

Structure of the book

A unique feature of this book is that I do not describe phenomenography just once, but many times, from different angles and perspectives, focusing on different aspects of phenomenography in different chapters. This is an inherently phenomenographic way of approaching the description of phenomenography, acknowledging that there is no one way of experiencing any phenomenon, including phenomenography, and that variation in experience with a phenomenon increases your opportunities for discerning it in more complex ways. In addition, the context in which a phenomenon is embedded can be expected to highlight different aspects of the phenomenon. So, each chapter in the book provides a different context for looking at phenomenography, which will hopefully make different aspects of the methodology come to the fore in different chapters.

1. Introduction to phenomenography and the aims of this book

In this first chapter, in addition to introducing phenomenography and describing my purposes and perspectives in writing this book, I attempt to position myself within the methodological tradition and explain what attracts me to phenomenography at a personal level. I also highlight the extent to which phenomenography has changed over time, and how phenomenography of the 21st century is not the same as phenomenography of the 1970s–1990s.

2. Developments in phenomenography over time: From an 'approach' to a 'methodology'

In Chapter 2, I describe how phenomenography has changed and developed over time, grouping developments into four key stages: (1) commencement of phenomenography; (2) clarification of methods; (3) theoretical developments in phenomenography; and (4) phenomenographic practice in the 21st century. In order to make the implications of the changes more meaningful, I present concrete examples in the chapter of different kinds of research questions and outcomes expected at different stages. In introducing terms like 21st-century phenomenography, I want to be clear though that early approaches to phenomenographic research are still recognisably and acceptably phenomenographic; it is just that more sophisticated ways of conducting phenomenographic research are now encouraged.

3. Variation in understandings of phenomenography

In Chapter 3, I turn phenomenography on itself as a learning tool. Phenomenographic research initially developed with the aim of delineating qualitative variation in ways of understanding a phenomenon, with the intention of using that variation to identify what it is that learners need to become aware of about the phenomenon to develop a sophisticated understanding of it. So, conducting a phenomenographic study of variation in understandings of phenomenography, which can then be used to improve ways of learning about the methodology and the sophistication of our collective understanding of phenomenography, seems a logical thing to do. In this chapter, I describe five qualitatively different ways of understanding phenomenography, and the relationships between them, based on a survey of researchers that I conducted in 2018–2019.

4. Variation in understandings of structural relationships in phenomenography

The notion of 'structure' and 'structural relationships' in phenomenography is perhaps the most distinctive and educationally useful part of the methodology. But it is also the most difficult and commonly misunderstood part. In order to clarify what we need to notice about the phenomenographic notion of structure and structural relationships to develop a sophisticated understanding of it, the phenomenographic study of phenomenography initially described in Chapter 3 continues in this chapter. In Chapter 4, I describe five qualitatively different ways of understanding structural relationships in phenomenography, and discuss associated implications for phenomenographic research practice and outcomes.

5. Epistemological assumptions in phenomenography: Implications for methods

As described in Chapter 2, phenomenography developed from a research approach that was based on a common object of study in the 1980s, to a research approach with an accompanying set of accepted methods in the 1990s, to a research methodology with associated ontological and epistemological assumptions in the 2000s. This last development was initiated by the publication of Marton and Booth's (1997) book, *Learning and Awareness*, in particular. This means that, from the 2000s, anyone who attempts to undertake phenomenographic research simply by applying a set of accepted methods, without an accompanying understanding of the theoretical assumptions underpinning those methods, will be short-changing their research. Chapter 5 describes the key epistemological assumptions put forward in *Learning and Awareness*, and clarifies how they relate to the methods adopted in phenomenography.

6. Study design, data gathering and the phenomenographic interview

Interviews are the traditional source of empirical data for phenomenographic research. But the phenomenographic interview is quite distinctive in nature. Phenomenographic interviews have a particular focus on working from concrete examples of participants' interactions with the phenomenon under investigation, and seeking in-depth reflections from participants on why they interacted with the phenomenon in those particular ways. Participants are not expected to be able to describe their experience of a phenomenon directly, but to demonstrate that experience indirectly, through the ways in which they interact with the phenomenon. This chapter explains the design and conduct of interviews, illustrating the key principles with extended concrete examples from my own and others' research. Although the focus of the chapter is on interviews, key principles for other forms of phenomenographic data gathering are also clarified.

7. Analysing data and reporting research outcomes

Phenomenographic data analysis is complicated, involving multiple analytic goals and many iterations through the data. Plus, phenomenography in the 21st century is more complex and rigorous than earlier phenomenographic research, with additional research goals. To help readers understand the analytic process, I present a set of ten iterative steps to the process, illustrating each step with concrete research examples. The chapter concludes with a discussion of indicators of rigour in phenomenographic research, describing strategies that enhance the trustworthiness of the interpretive research process and the credibility of relationally constituted research outcomes.

8. Adding further structure to the outcome space: Structural relationships between dimensions of variation

A key indicator of phenomenography in the 21st century is the constitution of 'dimensions of variation' and associated 'critical aspects' in experience of phenomena. However, two ways of identifying and describing dimensions and critical aspects have emerged in the literature. In the traditional approach, dimensions of variation (and thus critical aspects) are constituted independently of each other. In the alternative approach, dimensions of variation (and thus critical aspects) are constituted in a structurally related way along common themes of meaning, called 'themes of expanding awareness'. This adds additional structural complexity to the constitution of critical aspects of phenomena. This chapter clarifies the difference between the two approaches, provides concrete illustrations of the research outcomes that result from the two approaches, and discusses the different insights that each approach provides to our understanding of critical aspects of human experience.

9. Phenomenography and variation theory: The development of complementary traditions

The epistemological assumptions outlined in *Learning and Awareness* also led to a theory of learning, called 'variation theory'. This has been of great value to educational research and development, and has led to its own strand of applied research and practice based on pedagogical applications of variation theory in the classroom and in teacher education and development. Whilst variation theory research is often not strictly phenomenographic, they may be usefully applied together and complement each other in numerous ways. This chapter describes how the variation theory tradition developed during the 2000s, and outlines its ongoing relationship with phenomenography.

10. Phenomenography and collective awareness: The potential of phenomenography to contribute to the broader social sciences

Phenomenography initially commenced as a distinctive research approach based on two primary goals: to improve our understanding of learning from the students' perspective; and to describe humanity's collective awareness of different phenomena in the world. To date, the majority of phenomenographic research has focused on the former, educational goal. This means that the potential of research based on the second goal, investigating collective understanding of socially significant phenomena, has been underdeveloped. This forms the focus of this final chapter in the book. I start by unpacking the ongoing interest in collective awareness throughout the history of phenomenography, with examples of where phenomenographic research has been used outside of education. To help envisage the ways in which phenomenographic research might integrate with other social science research, I also outline phenomenography's implicit position on the socially-mediated nature of human experience, and present a number of examples of studies that have integrated phenomenographic research with social and practice theories. The chapter is forward looking, with the aim of encouraging future research into collective awareness of phenomena within specific socially, culturally and historically situated groups, using phenomenographic methods.

Chapter summary

This chapter provides an introduction to phenomenographic research in terms of what is most distinctive about the methodology and why researchers may be interested in using it. I also summarise my personal experience as a phenomenographic researcher to help contextualise my descriptions of phenomenography in this book. The chapter closes with an overview of the organisation of the book, and a brief summary of each chapter.

In the next chapter, I describe how phenomenography has changed and developed over its fifty year history, and illustrate the changes with empirical examples from my own research.

2. Developments in phenomenography over time: From a research 'approach' to a 'methodology'

In this chapter, I outline the development of phenomenography over the last fifty years, so that those newly introduced to the methodology can contextualise the articles they read in terms of the time period in which they were written. I also provide empirical examples of changes in analytic practices that have occurred over time.

Phenomenography initially arose in the 1970s out of experimental research into student learning undertaken at the Department of Education at the University of Göteborg, Sweden (Marton and Säljö, 1976, 1984 [1997]; Marton 1986a, 1988; Svensson, 1997). This research was led by Ference Marton, with colleagues Lennart Svensson, Roger Säljö and Lars-Owe Dahlgren. The term, 'phenomenography' first appeared in the mainstream literature in 1981, in an article by Marton entitled, "Phenomenography—Describing Conceptions of the World around Us". According to Hasselgren and Beach (1997), the term is derived from the Greek *phainomenon*, meaning appearance, and *graphein*, meaning description—that is, a description of things as they appear.

It was in the 1981 article that Marton first proposed that the study of variation in ways of understanding phenomena be a research specialisation in its own right, called phenomenography, i.e., "research which aims at description, analysis, and understanding of experiences" (p. 180). This is why Marton's 1981 article is cited so frequently in publications on phenomenographic research. But even though this article was the first to suggest phenomenography as a distinctive research approach, the article does not provide a very good description of phenomenography, because the research approach was still being clarified at the time. Marton's 1986a article, "Phenomenography—A

Research Approach to Investigating Different Understandings of Reality", provides a better introduction to phenomenography and is the more useful resource.

The focus on human experience

In the beginning, the research design was exploratory, intended as more of a reaction against existing positivist research paradigms in educational psychology than the development of a new approach (Marton and Svensson, 1979; Marton, 1986a; Svensson, 1997). The underlying aim was to investigate learning and understanding from the perspective of students, with an emphasis on students' conceptions, meanings and understandings of disciplinary phenomena.

> This view of subjective knowledge as the object of research was developed in contrast to the positivistic and objectivistic views dominant in educational and psychological research (within the behaviouristic and human information processing traditions) and with inspiration from older traditions of psychology of thought and especially Gestalt psychology. (Svensson, 1997, p. 163)[1]

This interest in subjective experience[2] was in line with a broader paradigm shift that was occurring across the social sciences during the 1970s and 80s, with a growing trend away from quantitative research and towards qualitative research (Dall'Alba, 1996). To explain this paradigm shift, Marton coined the terms 'second-order' *vs* 'first-order' research perspectives. Phenomenographic research was described as taking a second-order perspective, with the aim of investigating the world as it is experienced, as opposed to a first-order perspective, with the aim of investigating the world as it is. Whilst the second-order perspective of phenomenography was made much of in early literature on the approach, it is less commonly emphasised in recent literature, presumably because the positivist research paradigm is no longer so

---

1 Though other traditions of thought have also come to influence phenomenography over time (see Chapter 5).
2 Though, from a phenomenographic perspective, it would be more accurate to describe human experience as 'relational' rather than subjective, i.e., experience as a relationship between subject-object or person-world (as described further in Chapter 5).

dominant in social science research and it is no longer unusual to focus on human experience.

As with all interpretive research into human experience, phenomenography owes a debt to phenomenology and the rise in popularity of this philosophy over the 20th century (Marton, 1981a; Sandberg, 2005). Whilst Marton explicitly states that "Phenomenography is *not* an offspring of phenomenology" (Marton, 1986a, p. 40, italics added), he also acknowledges that phenomenology offers a philosophical explanation for some aspects of phenomenography. In particular, phenomenography and phenomenology share the assumption of the 'intentionality' of human experience—that all experience is directed towards an object.[3] "We do not merely love, we love someone; we do not merely learn, we learn something; we do not merely think, we think about something" (Marton, 1986, p. 40). From this perspective, experience cannot be studied in isolation, but always as the experience of something. This underlies phenomenography's focus on investigating people's experience of a particular object or phenomenon.

> After all, human beings do not simply perceive and experience, they perceive and experience *things*. Therefore, descriptions of perceptions and experience have to be made in terms of their content. (Marton, 1986a, p. 33)

It is this focus on the 'content' of experience, in terms the meaning of the particular phenomenon being experienced, that underlies the frequent description of phenomenography as being 'content-oriented'.

But at this point, phenomenography and phenomenology diverge. While phenomenology focuses on the common essence of human experience of phenomena, phenomenography focuses on variation in

---

[3] The phenomenographic focus on 'how' and 'what' (or 'act' and 'content') aspects of experience has occasionally also been linked to the phenomenological notion of 'noema' and 'noesis', with the former referring to the 'what' and the latter to the 'how' aspects of a way of experiencing (e.g., Marton, 1984; Uljens, 1996; Marton, 1996). Personally, I see phenomenography's analytic separation of the how and what aspects of experience as arising in a logical way from the shared notion of intentionality, rather than the specific notions of noesis and noema in phenomenology. In support of this interpretation, in a detailed review of the development of the what/how 'framework' in phenomenography, Harris (2011) also describes the distinction as explained in terms of logic rather than theory.

human experience of phenomena. In addition, phenomenography owes as much to the influence of Piagetian psychology, with its focus on developmental stages in perceptions of the world, and Gestalt psychology, with its focus on part-whole structures, as it does to phenomenology (Marton, 1981a, 1984, 1988; Svensson, 1997). Nevertheless, interest in comparing phenomenography and phenomenology continues in the literature (e.g., Dahlin, 2007; Larsson and Holmström, 2007; Stolz, 2020; Moroz, 2021).

Phenomenography explicitly developed from an empirical, rather than philosophical or theoretical, base:

> In the early 1970s we began to develop an alternative research approach. ...we asked students to read excerpts from their textbooks... [and] tell us what they got from their reading. ...a striking fact appeared. Students understood the very same text materials in a number of qualitatively different ways. The fact that the same text, when considered as a whole, carried different meanings for different students was more interesting to us than the more usual [positivist-based] finding that students retained different quantities of information... Suffice it to say that in study after study, students reported quite different understandings of the same material and that their understandings could be classified into a few clearly definable categories. ... The fact that we repeatedly found sets of qualitatively different conceptions of text material... led our research in a new direction... [that] it was reasonable to expect that people in general hold qualitatively different conceptions of all kinds of phenomena. ... This is the basic idea of phenomenography, and it has been confirmed many times. (Marton, 1986, pp. 36–37)

In this way, phenomenography was initially defined in terms of the topic of research, "mapping the qualitatively different ways in which people experience, conceptualize, perceive, and understand various aspects of, and phenomena in, the world around them" (Marton, 1986, p. 31), rather than in terms of specific methods or epistemological assumptions. This may be why phenomenography traditionally refers to itself as a research 'approach', rather than a research method or methodology.

But the methodological expectations and epistemological assumptions of phenomenography were increasingly clarified throughout the 1990s (e.g., on *Methods*: Dahlgren and Fallsberg, 1991; Bowden and Walsh, 1994 [2000]; Marton, 1992, 1994a; Dall'Alba and Hasselgren, 1996; Sandberg, 1997; and on *Epistemology*: Marton, 1994b [2000], 1996, Marton and Booth, 1997, Marton and Trigwell, 2000). This continued in the 2000s, with a particular focus on clarification of appropriate approaches to ensuring rigour and trustworthiness in phenomenographic research (e.g., Ashworth and Lucas, 2000; Sandberg, 1997, 2005; Bowden and Green, 2005; Åkerlind, [2005a] 2012, 2022; Collier-Reed et al., 2009; Sin, 2010). So, phenomenography of the 21st century definitely meets the criteria for a methodology, with clear methodological expectations (see Chapter 6 and Chapter 7) built on an explicit theoretical framework (see Chapter 5). Consequently, I will be using the term, methodology, throughout this book.

Variation and structure in human experience

The search for different ways of experiencing the same phenomenon starts with a search for variation in the meanings expressed by research participants when describing or interacting with the phenomenon. These expressions of variation in meaning are then grouped and separated into categories based on qualitative similarities and differences in the expressed meaning.

> An effort is made to uncover all of the understandings people have of specific phenomena and to sort them into conceptual categories. (Marton, 1986, p. 32)

These 'conceptual categories' came to be called 'categories of description' in phenomenography. The term can be thought of as short for "categories for describing ways of perceiving the world around us" (Marton, 1981a, p. 195). Use of the term, categories of description, highlights the important distinction between the categories constituted during data analysis (which is an interpretation) and the way of experiencing that they represent (which is a human response). The term also helps to highlight that phenomenographic research cannot analyse people's experience or understanding directly, just their descriptions or expressions of their experience or understandings.

However, phenomenography does not simply investigate variation in ways of experiencing the same phenomena, but also 'structural relationships' that connect the different ways of experiencing. One of the most common misunderstandings of phenomenography is that it is simply about exploring variation in experience, without realising that organising that variation into a structure (typically a hierarchical structure of inclusively expanding complexity of awareness of the phenomenon) is just as important to the research (Åkerlind, 2024a). It is because of the focus on producing a structured set of categories, or research outcomes, that phenomenography uses the term 'outcome space' when referring to its research results. The term, outcome space, represents the notion of research outcomes (variation in ways of experiencing) organised as a structured 'space of variation'.

Although references to structure were backgrounded in Marton's first widely available paper on phenomengraphy (1981a), they can still be found in the paper in statements like, "We cannot separate the structure and the content of experience from one another" (p. 180). But the key role of structure in phenomenographic research is better highlighted in Marton's next major paper on phenomenography (1986):

> When we read and classify [participants'] different descriptions of a phenomenon, we are not merely sorting data; we are looking for the most distinctive characteristics that appear in those data; that is, we are looking for structurally significant differences that clarify how people define some specific portion of the world. ...each category is a potential part of a larger structure in which the category is related to other categories of descriptions. It is a goal of phenomenography to discover the structural framework within which various categories of descriptions exist. (Marton, 1986, p. 34)

However, these references to structure are easy to miss when reading these early articles, because they are mentioned only briefly in comparison to references to exploring variation. The importance of structure becomes more obvious in later works, where it is described in more detail (e.g., Marton, 1994). Nevertheless, phenomenography has always been interested in the structure of experience, in terms of structural relationships between different ways of experiencing, but also in terms of how particular ways of experiencing are themselves structured. This aspect of structure in phenomenography, in particular, became further developed and elaborated over time, but in the first instance was commonly expressed in terms of 'what' and 'how' aspects of experience.

Initial foci on the structure underlying each way of experiencing emphasised the analytic separation of the experience of learning into 'what' and 'how' aspects, sometimes also referred to as the 'content' and 'act' (Marton, 1986a) or 'outcome' and 'process' of learning:

> If there are qualitative differences in the outcome [or content] of learning it seems very likely that there are corresponding differences in the *process* [or act] of learning... (Marton and Säljö, 1976, p. 7)

This focus on the relationship between the outcome and process of learning in early phenomenographic research (i.e., that 'how' we go about learning and 'what' we learn are related) led to the development of a distinction now famous in higher education research between 'deep' and 'surface' approaches to learning.

> ...a distinction between a surface approach and a deep approach to learning is made. In the first case the student "directs his [sic] attention towards learning the text itself" ... and in the other case he [sic] is "directed towards comprehending what the author wants to say..." (Saljö, 1981, p. 49)

However, whilst the proposed relationship between process and content is easy to understand when the phenomenon we are discussing is 'learning', it becomes more confusing when applied to other types of phenomena, such as disciplinary concepts. As phenomenographic research expanded from studying the relationship between students' approach to learning and the outcomes of their learning, to studying variation in students' experience or ways of understanding particular disciplinary concepts, such as Newton's 3rd law in physics, the law of supply and demand in economics, the mole in chemistry, etc., the nature of the 'process', 'act' or 'how' aspect was less easy to understand. For example, one can easily imagine a process of learning, but what is a process of Newton's 3rd law?

This difficulty in translating the how aspect of experience to phenomena other than learning is apparent, for instance, in Johansson et al.'s (1985) research on students' ways of understanding Newtonian motion. In their research, they described the 'what' and 'how' aspects of students' different understandings as 'What is focused on [by students]' and 'How the explanation [of Newtonian motion] was given [by students]'. But in what way is 'How the explanation was given' equivalent to a 'process' or 'act', as described for learning?

What has become clear in developments in phenomenography over time is that, with all phenomena, there is an experiential 'act', which is an act of discernment, a process of constituting one's experience of the phenomenon in awareness. "A certain way of understanding...

springs from a corresponding act of understanding" (Marton, 1986, p. 205). With this added clarity, any way of experiencing can now be understandably described in terms of "*What* is experienced and *how* it is experienced" (Marton and Booth, 1997, p. 114), where 'how' refers to how the experience is structured in awareness.

Meanwhile, the terms 'structural' and 'referential' aspects of experience were also introduced into the literature and used in similar ways to the 'how' and 'what' aspects, with the referential aspect referring to the experienced meaning of the phenomenon, and the structural aspect to the way the experience is structured in awareness. This meant that, by the 1990s, a diversity of terms referring to largely equivalent notions were being used simultaneously across various studies:

1. the outcomes, content and what of *learning*, and the what aspect, meaning aspect and referential aspect of *experience*; plus
2. the process, act and how of *learning*, and the how aspect, organisational aspect and structural aspect of *experience*.

Harris (2011) also describes the diversity in use of how/what vs structural/referential 'frameworks' for phenomenographic analysis in different studies, and the confusion this created. But she does not comment on the link to whether the experience these terms are used to refer to is 'learning' or some other phenomenon. Whereas I argue that, over time, reference to what/how aspects have become the most common terms used in analyses of learning, in particular, and structural/referential aspects the most common terms used in analyses of phenomena other than learning (see Chapter 5).

Nevertheless, the terms what/how and structural/referential represent very similar notions, just applied to different phenomena, so they can and often are still used interchangeably. The common thread in these notions is that 'what' is experienced (or learned) corresponds to the content of the experience, or the meaning of the phenomenon being experienced, i.e., its 'referential aspect'. At the same time, 'how' the phenomenon is being experienced (or learned) corresponds to the act of experiencing, or how the experience of the phenomenon is structured or organised in awareness, i.e., its 'structural aspect'.

So, those who read phenomenographic research of the 1980s and 1990s can quite reasonably become confused about the approach being taken to analysing structure. But ongoing clarifications of method, conceptual distinctions and associated assumptions continued throughout the 1980s and 1990s, and culminated in the 1997 book, *Learning and Awareness* by Ference Marton and Shirley Booth. This book marked a turning point in the development of phenomenography. For the first time, epistemological and ontological assumptions underlying the methodology were specified in detail, and this also led to a more elaborated and consistent approach to empirical research.

In particular, a more rigorous approach to investigating structure in phenomenographic research outcomes developed in response to the book. This took the form of a search for 'critical aspects' in awareness that underlie different ways of experiencing phenomena (Pang, 2003; Marton and Pong, 2005; Åkerlind, 2015; Kullberg and Ingerman, 2022). This is another way in which 21st-century phenomenography differs from phenomenography of the 1970s–1990s. Not only are theory and methods now well-articulated, but a more elaborated approach to analysis has become common (see Table 2.1), as will be described further and illustrated below.

Table 2.1 Stages in the development of phenomenography

Key developments	Key publications	Research questions
Phenomenography commences	Marton 1981a, 1986a	a. What are the qualitatively different ways in which the same phenomenon can be understood? b. How are these different ways of understanding related in a structure of expanding complexity of awareness of the phenomenon?*

Clarification of methods	Bowden and Walsh 1994 [2000]	
	Sandberg 1997	
	Ashworth and Lucas 2000	
	Åkerlind 2005a [2012]	
Theoretical developments	Marton and Booth 1997	
	Bowden and Marton 1998	
21st-century phenomenography**	Pang 2003	a. What are the qualitatively different ways in which the same phenomenon can be understood?
	Marton and Pong 2005	
	Åkerlind 2015	
		b. What critical aspects of the phenomenon are discerned (and not discerned) within each way of understanding it?
		c. How are the different ways of understanding related in a structure of expanding awareness of an increasing number of critical aspects of the phenomenon?

*The second question is often left implicit in publications, but is apparent in the outcomes

**Methodological developments arising out of the theoretical developments

Research examples illustrating the shift from early to 21st-century phenomenography

Perhaps the best way to illustrate the key change to phenomenographic research that happened after the theoretical developments of the late 1990s is through a series of research examples illustrating the type of research processes and outcomes that result from the different stages of development. To do this, I will draw on a study I conducted with colleagues that looked at variation in first-year university students' understanding of 'legal reasoning' in law (Åkerlind et al., 2011, 2014).

In this study, four law lecturers from three different universities worked with three educational researchers/developers (including myself) to conduct a phenomenographic study of variation in students' understanding of 'legal reasoning'. This phenomenon was chosen by the lecturers as a disciplinary concept that their students commonly experienced particular difficulty in understanding, and was thus worthy of educational research effort. The underlying aim was to inform the design of pedagogical interventions to help improve students' understanding of the concept.

Following some training in phenomenographic methods, the lecturers (and in some cases their tutors) interviewed twenty-one first-year law students about their understanding of legal reasoning. During data analysis, the interviews were grouped into categories (which developed into 'categories of description') based on similarities in the ways in which the students experienced legal reasoning. Phenomenographic methods are not a focus of this chapter and will be described in detail in Chapter 6 and Chapter 7, so at this point I will simply jump to the outcomes of the study.

Example of research outcomes illustrating early phenomenography (1970s–1990s)

Three qualitatively different ways of understanding legal reasoning emerged from the analysis, ordered in a hierarchy of inclusively expanding complexity of awareness, from Category 1 (least complex awareness) to Category 3 (most complex awareness):

1. legal reasoning seen as a formulaic process of following a specific framework for predicting a legal outcome;
2. legal reasoning seen as an interpretive process of arguing for an outcome that benefits your client;
3. legal reasoning seen as a responsive and innovative process for developing the Law to reflect changing society.

These categories were also reconfirmed during a later written task with seventy-four additional law students, who were asked to write a description of legal reasoning as a class exercise.

To continue my illustration of phenomenographic research, I will now describe the categories in more detail and illustrate them with quotes from the study participants. It is standard practice when reporting phenomenographic outcomes to illustrate different ways of understanding a phenomenon with quotes from research participants. The quotes are intended to provide (a) a more concrete sense of how the meaning or understanding represented by each category is experienced by respondents; and (b) an opportunity for readers to gain a sense of the data from which the categories were constituted, and thus have some basis on which to gauge the validity of the researcher(s)' interpretations.

This example will also illustrate another distinctive feature of phenomenographic research, the 'stripped' or 'reduced' nature of phenomenographic descriptions of experience. That is, instead of a rich and detailed description of human experience, as would be found in case study or phenomenological research, for example, phenomenographic research describes human experience reduced to its key defining features. This is what enables participants' descriptions of experience to be grouped into categories. That is, although the participant responses allocated to each category are likely to differ in fine detail, they have key defining features in common.

Category 1: Legal reasoning seen as a formulaic process of following a specific framework for predicting a legal outcome

Participant responses allocated to Category 1 highlighted legal reasoning as a structured process for reaching a conclusion about the expected outcomes of a legal case. There was no reference to the possibility of developing varying arguments or reaching different conclusions for the same case, as was seen in later categories. To illustrate:

> Legal reasoning is important in deconstructing legal problems. In identifying the legal issues/rules which arise in the course of problem solving, legal reasoning provides a framework. This framework must be applied to the facts at hand sequentially and logically to reach a conclusion.

Category 2: Legal reasoning seen as an interpretive process of arguing for an outcome that benefits your client

Participant responses allocated to this category also highlighted the structured process of legal reasoning (as with Category 1), but in addition, emphasised the importance of using the legal reasoning process to make varying interpretations and arguments, identifying that different conclusions may be reached for the same case. To illustrate:

> The purpose of legal reasoning is to argue the facts of the case in different directions. There may be two or more similar cases with facts that have been decided and the issues/facts could be distinguished or have an analogy formed in relation to the outcome wanted. There may not be one particular right answer.

Category 3: Legal reasoning seen as a responsive and innovative process for developing the Law to reflect changing society

This category also highlighted the role of varying interpretations of the same legal case in legal reasoning, as with Category 2, but went beyond this to show awareness of wider issues that can impact the Law. To illustrate,

> The purpose of legal reasoning is to help comprehend, interpret and develop areas of Law. An understanding of legal reasoning is vital when determining possible outcomes and questions in Law, and also when predicting the development of specific areas of Law.

In Chapter 1, I said that phenomenography is distinguished by a simultaneous focus on 'variation and commonality' and on 'meaning and structure'. The three categories listed above describe variation in the experienced meaning, or understanding, of legal reasoning found in the sample group. This addresses the 'variation' and 'meaning' components of phenomenography's research focus, and answers the first research question from Table 2.1, 'What are the qualitatively different ways in which the same phenomenon (i.e., legal reasoning) can be understood?'.

But to address the second question, 'How are these different ways of understanding related in a structure of expanding complexity of awareness of the phenomenon?', we also need to describe 'commonality' and 'structure' in the outcomes. This involves (a) searching for relationships between the categories, in the form of overlapping commonalities in understanding; and (b) looking for the structure of those relationships, in the form of increasing complexity and inclusivity in awareness of the phenomenon. The final outcomes are presented as a structure of relationships across the categories, representing the 'outcome space'.

Returning now to the specific empirical example of legal reasoning, in terms of commonalities in meaning the three categories are not seen as exclusive, but as inclusive. That is, the understanding of legal reasoning represented by Category 2 includes awareness of key features of legal reasoning present in Category 1 (but adds more to the picture). And the understanding of legal reasoning represented by Category 3 includes awareness of key features of legal reasoning present in Category 2 (but again, also adds more to the picture).

In terms of structure, based on the simultaneously occurring variation and commonality in ways of understanding legal reasoning, the three categories can be organised into a hierarchical structure of inclusively expanding awareness of the phenomenon of legal reasoning. Category 3 represents the most complex way of experiencing legal reasoning, and Category 1 the least complex (and thus foundational) way of experiencing legal reasoning (see Figure 2.1).

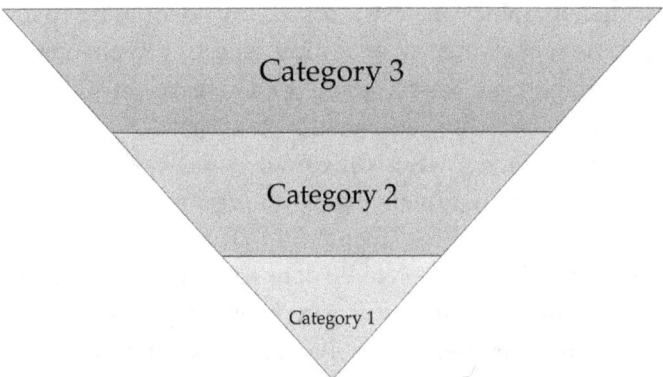

Fig. 2.1 Hierarchically inclusive structure of differential awareness of legal reasoning

This structure is often referred to in the broader literature as a 'phenomenographic hierarchy'. However, the hierarchy can be misunderstood as being based on value judgments of more and less expert ways of understanding the phenomenon (e.g., Webb, 1997). In fact, it is a hierarchy of inclusively expanding complexity of awareness of the phenomenon. But more complex ways of understanding inevitably constitute more sophisticated ways of understanding, which are often associated with expert understanding.

Example of research outcomes illustrating 21st-century phenomenography

In the research outcomes presented above, 'structure' is represented as the structure of 'collective understanding' of a phenomenon. That is, the structural relationships that emerge across the group of different ways of experiencing the phenomenon. As described above, this is a hierarchically inclusive structure. But it is also a part-whole structure, with each specific way of understanding legal reasoning forming an interconnected part of the whole collective of ways of understanding it.

Meanwhile, the theoretical developments in phenomenography described by Marton and Booth (1997) introduced an additional structure to phenomenographic outcomes, the structure of a 'specific understanding', i.e., the structure of awareness within each specific way of experiencing the phenomenon. This added an additional component to phenomenographic analysis, based on identifying patterns of awareness and non-awareness of 'critical aspects' of a phenomenon. (In phenomenography, an 'aspect' refers to a constituent part, feature or attribute of a phenomenon, and an aspect is regarded as 'critical' when awareness of that aspect acts to differentiate one way of understanding the phenomenon from a qualitatively different way of understanding it, as discussed further in Chapter 5.) This enables each way of understanding a phenomenon to be defined in terms of awareness and non-awareness of different critical aspects of the phenomenon.

Whilst phenomenography has always focused on 'key' or 'critical' aspects of experience (rather than detailed nuances of experience), it was not until the publication of *Learning and Awareness* that what constituted a 'critical aspect' was defined, and the identification of critical aspects of experience became an explicit part of phenomenographic analysis. So, a key difference between early approaches and 21st-century approaches to empirical analysis in phenomenography is the addition of analysis for awareness of constituent parts, or critical aspects, of phenomena that are discerned within each specific way of understanding the phenomena. As shown in Table 2.1, this is represented by the additional research question typical of 21st-century phenomenography: 'What critical aspects of the phenomenon are discerned (and not discerned) within each way of understanding it?'

At the same time, what is meant by 'expansion in awareness' has become more clearly defined, as discernment of an increasing number of critical aspects of the phenomenon. This definition adds extra rigour to the analytic process, with the outcome space now able to describe relationships between different categories with greater detail, clarity and empirical justification. Let me illustrate this through an extension of the analysis of the concept of legal reasoning (see Table 2.2).

Table 2.2 Critical aspects of legal reasoning discerned in the different ways of understanding it

	Ways of understanding legal reasoning		
	Category 1: *A formulaic process of predicting the Law*	*Category 2:* *An interpretive process of arguing the Law*	*Category 3:* *A responsive process of developing the Law*
Critical aspects discerned			

Re: the process of legal reasoning	Describing legal rules	Describing and interpreting legal rules	Describing, interpreting and changing legal rules
Re: ideal outcomes of legal reasoning	Predicting a legal outcome	Predicting and producing a legal outcome	Predicting and producing a legal outcome
Re: who benefits	Specific clients	Specific clients	Clients and society

Awareness of the different critical aspects of legal reasoning expands inclusively across the categories (or rows). For example, in the first row of Table 2.2, the understanding of legal reasoning represented by Category 1 is shown as underpinned by awareness of the critical aspect of describing legal rules. Then, the understanding of legal reasoning represented by Category 2 is underpinned by awareness of the critical aspects of describing and interpreting legal rules. And the understanding of legal reasoning represented by Category 3 is underpinned by awareness of the critical aspects of describing, interpreting and changing legal rules. And a similar expansion is seen across each row (although some categories may also have critical aspects in common, as with Category 2 and 3 in row 2, and Category 1 and 2 in row 3.)

Clearly, we have here another part-whole analysis, but focused at the level of each specific way of understanding legal reasoning, rather than across all ways of understanding it. Each column in Table 2.2 highlights awareness of critical aspects of the phenomenon of legal reasoning that are associated with each of the categories, and these critical aspects (or constituent parts) of the phenomenon combine to make up the holistic way of understanding the phenomenon represented by that category.

Based on this analysis of critical aspects of legal reasoning (as experienced by the students in the sample group), different ways of understanding legal reasoning can now be understood as underpinned by awareness, and lack of awareness, of different critical aspects of legal reasoning, as follows:

1. Category 1, an understanding of legal reasoning as 'a formulaic process of following a specific framework for predicting a legal outcome', is underpinned by student discernment of the possibility of describing legal rules and predicting the outcome for clients, and failure to discern the possibility of

interpreting and changing legal rules, and producing better outcomes for clients and society;

2. Category 2, an understanding of legal reasoning as 'an interpretive process of arguing for an outcome that benefits your client', is underpinned by student discernment of the possibility of interpreting legal rules and producing better outcomes for clients, but failure to discern the possibility of changing legal rules and producing better outcomes for society;

3. Category 3, an understanding of legal reasoning as 'a responsive and innovative process for developing the Law to reflect changing society', is underpinned by student discernment of the possibility of changing legal rules and producing better outcomes for society.

Phenomenography also explains the nature of 'discernment' and 'non-discernment' of aspects of phenomena in the world—but this is an epistemological issue that will be discussed later, in Chapter 5. For now, let us simply say that discernment indicates awareness, and failure to discern, non-awareness, of critical aspects of a phenomenon.

Meanwhile, the 20th-century analysis for discernment of critical aspects of phenomena was not simply added onto, but integrated with, the earlier form of phenomenographic analysis. So, identification of critical aspects of each way of understanding a phenomenon helps with the original search for variation in ways of understanding a phenomenon, and also the original search for hierarchically inclusive relationships between the different ways of understanding found. This is reflected in the modification of the original research question presented in Table 2.1:

From—How are the different ways of understanding related in a structure of expanding complexity of awareness?

To—How are the different ways of understanding related in a structure of expanding awareness of an increasing number of critical aspects of the phenomenon?

In publications of phenomenographic research, this extension to the original question is often left implicit, but I include it here for clarity.

Chapter summary

This chapter describes how phenomenography has developed over time, from (a) a research approach that was based on a common object of study in the 1980s; to (b) a research approach with an accompanying set of accepted methods in the 1990s; to (c) a research methodology with associated ontological and epistemological underpinnings in the 2000s. The more theoretical turn in phenomenography as it entered the 21st century was triggered by the landmark publication by Marton and Booth (1997), *Learning and Awareness,* and this book is essential reading for anyone wanting to understand phenomenographic epistemology.

Accompanying the theoretical developments in phenomenography, there has been an elaboration in the rigour and complexity of empirical research practice in the 2000s. The traditional research questions underpinning phenomenographic research are: (a) What are the qualitatively different ways in which the phenomenon of interest can be understood? and (b) How are these different ways of understanding related in a structure of expanding complexity of awareness of the phenomenon? In the 2000s, these have been complemented by an additional question: (c) What critical aspects of the phenomenon are discerned (and not discerned) within each way of understanding it? And this additional question has led to a more rigorous way of defining and describing different ways of understanding a phenomenon, and the expansion in awareness of the phenomenon that can be found in more complex ways of understanding it, with expansion now defined as awareness of an increasing number of critical aspects of the phenomenon.

In the next chapter, I move from this descriptive approach to explaining phenomenography, to a more experiential approach, presenting the outcomes of a study of different ways of understanding phenomenography itself amongst educational researchers.

3. Variation in understandings of phenomenography

In the previous chapter, I presented a developmental perspective on phenomenography, describing and illustrating changes over time. In this chapter, I present an experiential perspective on phenomenography, looking at how it is experienced by a sample group of educational researchers. In this way, this chapter uses phenomenographic principles to help inform our understanding of phenomenography itself, by undertaking a phenomenographic study of phenomenography.[1]

As illustrated in the previous chapter, this involves an empirical search for:

- the range of qualitatively different ways of understanding phenomenography present in the sample;
- the constituent parts, or critical aspects, of phenomenography that are discerned and not discerned within each way of understanding it; and
- hierarchically inclusive structural relationships between the different ways of understanding phenomenography.

The benefits of conducting a phenomenographic analysis into phenomenography is that it can be expected to highlight often hidden differences in understandings of phenomenography amongst researchers, and clarify critical aspects of phenomenography that researchers need to become aware of in order to attain a sophisticated understanding of it.

---

1   The first 'phenomenographic study of phenomenography' was by Trigwell (1994 [2000]). But it was only a mock study, in the form of an interview with himself.

Study methods

Although phenomenographic research is typically based on interview data, for this study I used written survey data. Whilst surveys do not represent ideal phenomenographic data, because with surveys you cannot explore participant responses in the way you can with interviews, the use of surveys has still been found to elicit enough detail and variation in responses to be acceptable for phenomenographic research (Marton and Booth, 1997). I chose to use surveys rather than interviews in order to provide greater anonymity to participants, given that a number of participants would have been known to me personally.

Survey design

At the commencement of the survey, participants were asked, "As background, could you first briefly summarise your experience with phenomenography". This was followed by three open-ended questions:

1. What interests you about phenomenography?
2. How do you use phenomenography?
3. Phenomenography is often described as focusing on structural relationships—what does that mean to you (if anything)?

However, the last question, with a specific focus on understandings of structural relationships in phenomenography, was analysed separately and is described in the next chapter (Chapter 4).

Sample recruitment

As the aim of a phenomenographic study is to investigate variation in the ways people can understand the same phenomenon, it is important to select a sample of participants that is likely to have had varied experiences of the phenomenon. So, I selected a varied sample of educational researchers familiar with phenomenography. Within this sample, the background characteristic that I regarded as most likely to have produced variation in participants' experience of phenomenography was the extent to which participants had used it in their own research and professional activities. Hence, the introductory question asking participants to provide a brief summary of their experience with phenomenography. Geographical location provided an additional source of variation in experience, with invitations sent to potential participants located in Australia, New Zealand, the United Kingdom, Sweden, Finland, the United States of America, Canada, Brazil and Hong Kong.

The sample was recruited in two ways: (1) by email invitations sent to scholars who were personally known to me; and (2) by email invitations to scholars not known to me but who had been listed on ResearchGate as having cited one of my papers on phenomenography, and whom I could thus assume had some interest in the approach. All participants were engaged in some form of educational research and were familiar with phenomenography, but did not necessarily engage in phenomenographic research themselves.

In total, forty researchers were invited to participate in the survey, and eighteen responses were received. Of these,

- six were classified as having *little experience* with phenomenography, i.e., scholars engaged in educational research who had read publications of phenomenographic research (and may have used the outcomes in their professional practice) but had never used phenomenography in their own research;
- five as having *some experience* with phenomenography, i.e., scholars engaged in educational research who had used phenomenography in their own research to some degree (e.g., recent doctoral graduates);
- seven as having *extensive experience* with phenomenography, i.e., scholars engaged in educational research who had used phenomenography extensively in their own research and were recognised as 'phenomenographers'.

Data analysis

The focus on this chapter is not on methods, which are described in Chapter 6 and Chapter 7, so I will simply give a brief overview of my analytic methods rather than describing them in detail:

1. *categorisation of responses into groups* representing qualitatively different ways of understanding the phenomenon (whole understandings);

2. *identification of different critical aspects* of the phenomenon discerned across the sample of responses as a whole (parts of understandings);

3. *mapping of the critical aspects* of the phenomenon that were discerned, and not discerned, within each category of qualitatively different understandings of the phenomenon (how parts combine into wholes);

4. *ordering of the different understandings* from step 1, into an inclusive hierarchy of expanding complexity of awareness of different critical aspects of the phenomenon from steps 2 and 3 (how different understandings combine into a collective whole).

As described in Chapter 2, steps 1 and 4 have always been part of phenomenographic analysis, but steps 2 and 3 are more recent expectations that arose out of new developments in phenomenography that were introduced in Marton and Booth's 1997 book, *Learning and Awareness*.

Outcomes—variation in ways of understanding phenomenography

Six qualitatively distinct ways of understanding phenomenography were identified, with phenomenography variously experienced as:

1. a part of the field of educational research;
2. a distinctive method in educational research;
3. a research method that elucidates variation in ways of understanding the same phenomena;
4. a research method that elucidates structural relationships amongst the variation in ways of understanding the same phenomena;
5. a powerful pedagogical tool for improving educational outcomes;
6. a way of thinking and operating in the world.[2]

---

2   These outcomes are also reported in Åkerlind (2024b).

As is usual in phenomenographic research, I will describe each category or way of understanding phenomenography in more detail below and illustrate each category with quotes from participants. As described in Chapter 2, it is standard in phenomenography to use quotes from research participants to illustrate the different ways of understanding a phenomenon identified in a study.

Category 1: Phenomenography experienced as a part of the field of educational research

In the first, least complex, way of understanding phenomenography (as a part of the field of educational research), it is experienced as just one of many types of research that constitute the broad educational research literature. There is no awareness of what is distinctive or, indeed, that there is anything distinctive about phenomenographic research, and thus no sense of any particular purpose for engaging in phenomenographic research in particular.

> I write about the field of pedagogy and curriculum in higher education and consider the contribution of phenomenography important and influential. (Response 4—little experience)

> I am not sure I would say I have a particular interest in it ... [but] I was constantly coming across it in the teaching-learning literature (Response 5—little experience)

Category 2: Phenomenography experienced as a distinctive research method in educational research

In the second way of understanding phenomenography (as a distinctive method in educational research), there is awareness of it as a research approach that is distinctive in some way—variously described as rigour, technical requirements, and/or its educational origins. This provides a purpose for engaging in phenomenographic research on phenomena of interest to the researcher, but not a very detailed purpose.

> I see phenomenography as being a qualitative methodology that has an underpinning methodological rigour that makes it more defensible, and therefore more valid, than the range of other qualitative methodologies .... This is of interest as, in educational research, it is a qualitative (rather

than a quantitative) approach that lets us answer the more interesting questions. (Response 1—little experience)

What interested me about phenomenography was that it is a research methodology conceived from educational contexts to elucidate educational phenomena, unlike other research methodologies that have been imported from other academic areas into education. (Response 7—some experience)

Category 3: Phenomenography experienced as a research method that elucidates variation in ways of understanding

In the third way of understanding phenomenography (as a research method that elucidates variation in ways of understanding the same phenomena), a key purpose of phenomenographic research is to gain a better sense of the range of ways in which a particular phenomenon of interest to the reader is understood by a particular group of students, teachers, stakeholders, etc.

To me it offers a conceptually rigorous way of understanding how phenomena are experienced/constructed by people; I like its focus on variation and difference. (Response 3—little experience)

I was attracted to phenomenography for its focus on people's experience, particularly on people's qualitatively different ways of experiencing the same phenomena around us. (Response 16—extensive experience)

Category 4: Phenomenography experienced as a research method that elucidates structural relationships amongst variation in ways of understanding

In the fourth way of understanding phenomenography (as a research method that elucidates structural relationships amongst the variation in ways of understanding the same phenomena), a key purpose of phenomenographic research is to gain a sense of the ways in which different understandings of a phenomenon of interest increase in complexity.

That it is an empirical process that enables a concept to be analysed in terms of structure and meaning. So it not only provides information on the different meanings used to explain a concept but also a set of structural relations between the different meanings. (Response 8—extensive experience)

> I think the focus on variation and the intention to produce a structured outcome space are very powerful. A major weakness of some approaches to qualitative data analysis are that they do not produce a structured sense of the data set as a whole, which any [interview] extract (quotation) can be related to. Phenomenography does this in a very helpful and effective manner. (Response 10—extensive experience)

Category 5: Phenomenography experienced as a powerful pedagogical tool for improving educational outcomes

In the fifth way of understanding phenomenography (as a powerful pedagogical tool for improving educational outcomes), a key purpose of phenomenographic research is seen as using it to gain information to help inform instructional design.

> From an educational/developmental perspective, it is useful to have taxonomies of more and less sophisticated understandings of a phenomenon. I am particularly interested in how these understandings can guide instructional/curricular design through systematically varying the focus of students' attention. (Response 6—little experience)

> What interests me the most is that [phenomenography is]… of crucial importance for expanding our understanding of the perspectives of … learners. And this has great practical implications to the design of teaching activities. (Response 9—extensive experience)

Category 6: Phenomenography experienced as a way of thinking and operating in the world

In the sixth and most complex way of understanding phenomenography (as a way of thinking and operating in the world), a reason emerges not just for engaging in phenomenographic research, but also for reading about phenomenographic theory and epistemology, because phenomenography is seen as providing a different way of thinking about the world and how people operate in the world.

> I realised that it is a way of thinking that I had embraced. I found that phenomenography fosters a generosity in outlook on life as I am able to listen for and capture various perspectives on the same topic or situation. The phenomenographic approach to these roles has assisted my ability to listen to others and tease out nuances in perspectives and outlooks. (Response 2—some experience)

It has a sound theoretical background, clearly different kind of purpose and a way of analysing the data than other qualitative analyses. ... Also, it is a way of thinking and listening. So, ... [even] without any data collection or data analysis, I use 'phenomenographic thinking' in teaching and in listening, hearing and understanding students' responses. (Response 14—extensive experience)

Structural relationships between the different ways of understanding phenomenography

Each way of understanding phenomenography is accompanied by awareness of different critical aspects of phenomenography. The different critical aspects discerned also provide evidence for the hierarchical ordering of the outcome space, and the inclusive nature of that hierarchy, as shown in Table 3.1.

Table 3.1 Critical aspects of phenomenography discerned in the different ways of understanding it

Critical aspects discerned	Understandings of phenomenography					
	Cat.* 1	Cat. 2	Cat. 3	Cat. 4	Cat. 5	Cat. 6
Contribution to literature	✓**	✓	✓	✓	✓	✓
Research methods used		✓	✓	✓	✓	✓
Research outcomes produced - variation			✓	✓	✓	✓
Research outcomes produced - relationships				✓	✓	✓
Pedagogical applications					✓	✓
Everyday applications						✓

* Cat. = Category

** A tick indicates awareness of the critical aspect

Analytical aside

Some readers may notice that Table 3.1, as a way of summarising the critical aspects discerned in different ways of experiencing phenomenography, uses a different structure or format to Table 2.2 in the previous chapter, even though Table 2.2 also summarises the critical aspects discerned in different ways of experiencing a phenomenon. It is important to realise that the presentation of phenomenographic outcomes does not need to follow the same format in all studies. Researchers make decisions about the clearest and most persuasive ways of presenting results, which can vary between different studies as well as between different researchers. In fact, I would argue that decisions about how best to present the outcomes of a study form part of the interpretive methods of the research, though I rarely see it talked about in this way. I discuss this further in Chapter 7.

I would also like to comment on what I see as some limitations of this study. Phenomenography most commonly uses in-depth interviews for data gathering, though other forms of data, such as surveys, are also accepted. Nevertheless, I regard the reduced detail provided by survey responses (as compared with interview responses) as a limitation of the study. Although the study was successful in clarifying more and less complex ways of understanding phenomenography, and identifying different critical aspects of phenomenography, more precise distinctions may have emerged with more detailed data. Greater detail in participant responses would have meant that each category of description of phenomenography could have been described in more detail. Additional critical aspects may also have emerged.

Another limitation of the study lies in the sample, which was composed of educational researchers. Other ways of understanding phenomenography may have emerged if researchers from outside education were included. Although most phenomenographic researchers are in the field of education, because this is where phenomenography is best known, they are not entirely limited to education. Phenomenography is of interest in a number of professional fields, for instance as a means of understanding the nature of professions and professional work (e.g., engineering—Sandberg, 2000; law—Reid et al., 2006; academic research—Åkerlind, 2008b; accounting—Sin et al., 2011; case management—Värk and Reino, 2018; health professions—Röing et al., 2018).

The short quotes provided for each category above were intended to illustrate what is distinctive about each way of understanding phenomenography. But to illustrate what the categories have in common, and how this can be used to organise the categories into a hierarchically inclusive structure, I need to present much longer quotes. This is something that I have never seen any other phenomenographic researcher do, and it is also difficult to fit into common journal word limits. Nevertheless, I personally do this consistently when reporting my own research because I think it is important to illustrate for readers of the research what I regard as empirical evidence of inclusivity of awareness.

So, the point of the quote below is to demonstrate how more complex ways of understanding include awareness of the critical aspects evident in less complex ways of understanding. To do this, I have selected a quote from one of the responses allocated to Category 6 (reflecting the most complex way of understanding phenomenography). The quote illustrates how all of the previous ways of understanding phenomenography are also reflected in the most complex way of understanding it, and thus illustrates what I regard as empirical evidence of inclusiveness of awareness.

> *Q. 1: What interests you about phenomenography?* Phenomenography has had a major influence on understandings of teaching and learning in higher education and so I believe it is important for me to have an understanding of the research in this area and to be able to position it with respect to other theoretical perspectives [Category 1—literature]. I tend to think of it as a research method [Category 2—method] for uncovering the range of beliefs/conceptions about phenomena [Category 3—variation] and categorising the ways in which those conceptions vary from each other [Category 4—relationships]. I find many of the studies I have read interesting for understanding how people perceive and conceptualise different phenomena and have also found that I understand my own ideas better when I compare them with other people's understandings [Category 6—thinking].
>
> *Q. 2: How do you use phenomenography?* I use phenomenography in my teaching as one approach with which to help academics to become more aware of their beliefs and theories of teaching and learning [Category 5—pedagogy]. Also many academics are familiar with deep and surface approaches to learning so it is helpful to discuss these concepts. I have also used a loose phenomenographic approach as one of the ways in which

I analyse qualitative data by looking at the 'what' and 'how' aspects of people's conceptions [Category 4—relationships]. The methods are well developed in the literature [Category 1 and 2] and I think that it is a useful thinking tool for data analysis and reporting on the differences in how people think about or understand a phenomenon. [Category 3—variation]. (Response 12—some experience)

Implications of the study for phenomenographic research

In this study, six qualitatively different ways of understanding phenomenography were identified and organised into an inclusive hierarchy:

1. phenomenography experienced as a part of the field of educational research;
2. phenomenography experienced as a distinctive method in educational research;
3. phenomenography experienced as a research method that elucidates variation in ways of understanding the same phenomena;
4. phenomenography experienced as a research method that elucidates structural relationships amongst the variation in ways of understanding the same phenomena;
5. phenomenography experienced as a powerful pedagogical tool for improving educational outcomes;
6. phenomenography experienced as a way of thinking and operating in the world.

The first two ways of understanding phenomenography (1—as a part of the educational research literature; and 2—as a distinctive research method in educational research) may be explained by phenomenography being best known within the field of education, including higher education and teacher education. This is also why my sample of researchers were all educational researchers. It seems that, for some people, all they are really aware of about phenomenography is that it is relevant to educational research and literature. Whilst this description of phenomenography is not *in*accurate, it is a very limited way of understanding phenomenography, because there is so much more to the methodology than this.

The next two ways of understanding phenomenography (3—as a research method that elucidates variation in understandings; and 4—as a research method that elucidates both variation and structural relationships amongst the variation), both show awareness of the particular types of research questions that phenomenography can be used to address. However, the third way of understanding only notices phenomenography's focus on variation and meaning, not its simultaneous focus on commonalities and structure (see Chapter 2). So again, whilst the third way of understanding is not wrong, as such, it is incomplete. It is only when we reach the fourth way of understanding phenomenography that we approach what could be classified as a 'good' understanding of the approach.

The last two ways of understanding phenomenography (5—as a powerful pedagogical tool, and 6—as a way of thinking and operating) are interesting in that they go beyond what is needed simply to undertake phenomenographic research and, in this way, extend the usefulness of the research. The fifth way of understanding highlights pedagogical applications of the research and theory, and the sixth way of understanding highlights how phenomenographic epistemology can change our everyday ways of thinking and operating.

Analytical aside

Let me use these outcomes to help explain a couple of phenomenography's more esoteric claims. First, from a phenomenographic perspective, less complex ways of understanding are not regarded so much as 'wrong', but as 'limited'. And different ways of understanding are sometimes described as being more or less 'complete', rather than more or less 'complex'. What is meant by this is that, in the way phenomenography undertakes its analysis, every way of understanding discerns some aspects of the phenomenon, but not other aspects. So, in this sense, every way of understanding discerns something important about the phenomenon, but not everything that is important about the phenomenon. (Theoretically, this even includes the most complex way of understanding identified in a study. Whilst it represents the most complete way of understanding identified in a particular sample group, and hopefully the associated population, other ways of understanding can be expected to arise in different populations and time periods.)

Second, whilst the most complex way of understanding a phenomenon is inherently also the most sophisticated way of understanding it, phenomenography acknowledges that this way of understanding may not be necessary (or even desirable) in all situations. For example, in certain contexts, such as when teaching phenomenography as a research method, the teacher may not be interested in alerting students to ways of subsequently using the research outcomes. This would make the fourth way of understanding phenomenography the desired understanding in those situations. However, when teaching phenomenography for pedagogical purposes, the fifth way of understanding becomes more desirable (though again, there may be little interest in those situations in alerting students to the sixth way of understanding, i.e., that they can also use phenomenography personally within their day-to-day life).

But at the same time, the most complex way of understanding in an outcome space can never be a barrier to operating in line with less complex ways of understanding (when it is deemed appropriate to do so), because more complex ways of understanding include the less complex ways. This means that the ways of operating in the world enabled by less complex ways of understanding will always also be available within more complex ways of understanding, making it possible to operate flexibly to suit the situation or context. In other words, the most complex way of understanding will always enable the most powerful and flexible ways of operating in the world, even if it is not required in any one particular situation.

It is also important to note that the less complex ways of understanding phenomenography were *not* limited to researchers with little experience with the methodology, or the more complex ways to those with extensive experience. As can be seen from the illustrative quotes above, people with extensive experience with phenomenography may demonstrate relatively unsophisticated ways of understanding it (e.g., Response 16, Category 3), while people with little experience with phenomenography may demonstrate relatively sophisticated ways of understanding it (e.g., Response 6, Category 5). This is not an unusual finding in phenomenographic research, which often shows extensive variation in understanding of a phenomenon amongst 'experts' as well as amongst novices. Indeed, inevitable variation in expert understanding of a phenomenon is predictable from phenomenographic epistemology, which assumes there will be variation in understanding of the same phenomenon within *any* group of people, due to the partial nature of all awareness (see Chapter 5).

Meanwhile, such variation between experts refutes the common expectation that complexity of understanding of phenomenography will be a simple outcome of the amount of experience one has with the methodology. Whilst extent of experience can reasonably be expected to make a difference to one's understanding of a phenomenon, complexity of understanding will always be derived from more than just duration of exposure to a phenomenon. Particular types of experiences are required to come to see a phenomenon in particular ways (as described in Chapter 9), and these may or may not occur during exposure to a phenomenon.

The hierarchical ordering of complexity of understandings in this study identifies different layers to phenomenography that researchers need to become aware of to derive the greatest value from using it. This is because different ways of understanding open up or close down different potential purposes or uses for phenomenography. For instance, the six different ways of understanding phenomenography are inherently associated with different perceptions of its usefulness for educational researchers:

- in Category 1, phenomenographic research is not necessarily seen as particularly useful;
- in Categories 2–4, phenomenography is seen as empirically useful, as a useful method for research.;
- in Category 5, phenomenography is seen as pedagogically useful, able to inform the design of teaching and learning activities;
- in Category 6, phenomenography is seen as useful for one's personal thinking, understanding and ways of operating in the world.

Chapter summary

This chapter highlighted different aspects of phenomenography that researchers need to notice or discern about the methodology in order to understand it in a complex and sophisticated way:

1. its development within and contribution to the field of education;
2. specifics of the methods used for gathering and analysing data;
3. its focus on investigating variation in experience and understanding;
4. its focus on investigating structural relationships within the variation;
5. its potential usefulness for informing teaching and learning; and
6. its potential usefulness for informing personal ways of thinking and operating in the world.

Awareness of the first four aspects is essential for being able to conduct phenomenographic research, while awareness of the latter two aspects act to increase the potential applications and usefulness of the research and epistemology.

In the next chapter, phenomenography's focus on investigating structural relationships underlying the variation in different ways of understanding phenomena is explored in more detail, through a continuation of this empirical study.

4. Variation in understandings of structural relationships in phenomenography

As described in previous chapters, a search for structural relationships that link different ways of understanding a phenomenon has always been an important part of phenomenographic research. Indeed, many researchers regard phenomenography's focus on structure as the most distinctive and powerful aspect of the research, because it is the structural relationships within and between categories that pinpoints what is needed to move from a less complex to a more complex way of understanding a phenomenon. And it is this that can most directly inform approaches to learning, development and pedagogy.

Unfortunately, the role of 'structure' is also the least well understood and most frequently misrepresented aspect of phenomenographic research. Indeed, the most common error seen in research claiming to be phenomenographic, but which doesn't actually meet the requirements of phenomenography, is to describe variation in understandings of a phenomenon without also describing structural relationships within the variation (Åkerlind, 2022, 2024a). In this sense, the most basic misunderstanding of structural relationships in phenomenography that I see in the literature is to not even realise that they are a part of phenomenographic research.

This particular misunderstanding of phenomenography was also apparent in the previous chapter, where one way of understanding phenomenography was as 'a research method that elucidates variation in ways of understanding the same phenomena' (Category 3), which showed no awareness that there is a simultaneous focus on elucidating 'structural relationships amongst the variation in ways of understanding' (Category 4). For this reason, I am again using phenomenographic research to illuminate itself, this time focusing on the perceived nature of structural relationships in phenomenography.

The aim of this chapter is to increase the depth of readers' understanding of the nature of structural relationships in phenomenography, by highlighting different components (critical aspects) of structural relationships that may otherwise go unnoticed, or undiscerned. This chapter also clarifies what supervisors of research students using phenomenography need to bring to their students' attention to help them achieve a sophisticated understanding of the nature of structural relationships in phenomenography.

Meanwhile, you may have noticed that sometimes I (and other phenomenographic researchers) refer to 'structure', and at other times to 'structural relationships'. What is the difference? Or are they the same thing? The term 'structure' can be used to refer to a number of slightly different but strongly related ideas, including structural relationships, as will be discussed further in the next chapter. But what all of these ideas about structure have in common is the notion of organisation, of structure as a description of the way experience is organised. Typically, this organisation is described in the form of a part-whole structure, i.e., part-whole relationships. So, the terms 'structure' and 'structural relationships' are used largely interchangeably in most situations.

In this particular chapter, however, I will stick to the term structural relationships rather than structure, because that is the term I used when gathering the data. Although this study definitely illuminates our understanding of structure as well as structural relationships (because they are inherently related ideas), I will stay with the term structural relationships as an act of precision, or research rigour, because I cannot be certain that participants would have given the same response if I had used the term structure instead of structural relationships. It is important to be as precise as possible about the phenomenon being investigated in phenomenographic research, and consequently what claims the researcher is justified in making as a result of a study.

Study methods

As described in the previous chapter, a varied sample of educational researchers interested in phenomenography was invited to participate in a short, open-ended survey on the ways in which they understood phenomenography. One of the questions in the survey focused particularly on structural relationships: "Phenomenography is often described as focusing on structural relationships—what does that mean to you (if anything)?". It is responses to this question that formed the data underlying the outcomes presented in this chapter.

Forty researchers were invited to participate. As described in Chapter 3, they varied in their geographic location and level of experience with phenomenographic research. Of those invited, eighteen chose to participate; however, three of the eighteen did not provide enough detail in their response to the question on structural relationships for the data to be interpretable, so were excluded from analysis. This produced a total of fifteen usable responses. Of these,

- four respondents were classified as having little experience with phenomenography;
- four as having some experience with phenomenography; and
- seven as having extensive experience with phenomenography.

As with the analysis described in Chapter 3, the survey data were analysed by cycling iteratively through four primary stages: (1) *categorisation* of responses into groups representing different ways of understanding structural relationships; (2) *identification* of different critical aspects of awareness of structural relationships present in the categories; (3) *mapping* of the critical aspects of structural relationships that were discerned, and not discerned, within each category; and (4) *ordering* of the different categories into an inclusive hierarchy of expanding awareness of different critical aspects of structural relationships.

Outcomes—variation in ways of understanding structural relationships

In presenting the outcomes, I will first focus on describing the different ways of understanding structural relationships in phenomenography identified in the sample, then describe the critical aspects in ways of experiencing the phenomenon that demarcate the different understandings.

Five qualitatively different ways of experiencing structural relationships in phenomenography were identified, with a varying focus on structural relationships as:

1. hierarchical relationships;
2. hierarchically-inclusive relationships;
3. meaning-structure relationships;
4. part-whole relationships; and
5. multi-faceted relationships.[1]

Category 1: Structural relationships as hierarchical relationships

In this category, structural relationships were understood as the organisation of different ways of understanding a phenomenon into a hierarchical structure. For example,

> [structural relationships are] the way in which experience is represented as encompassing increasingly more complex representations of the phenomenon under study. (Response 5—little experience)

> The identification of structural relationships and hierarchical structure are of the essence of phenomenography. (Response 14—extensive experience)

Although there is awareness in this category of a hierarchical structure to phenomenographic outcomes, the nature of the hierarchy is taken-for-granted, or not in focus. This means that the hierarchy could consist of a simple ordering of the different ways of experiencing, based on attributes like complexity or accuracy, rather than necessarily an ordering based on inclusivity. This may be contrasted with Category 2, where the nature of the hierarchy is explicitly highlighted as one of inclusivity.

---

1   These outcomes are also reported in Åkerlind (2024c), although the outcomes have been revised slightly for this chapter following additional reflection on the data.

Category 2: Structural relationships as hierarchically-inclusive relationships

Like Category 1, this category emphasises a hierarchical ordering to the different ways of understanding identified during phenomenographic analysis. However, in this category it is explicit that this is an ordering based on inclusivity, where ways of understanding higher in the hierarchy include those lower in the hierarchy, whilst also showing awareness of something new. In this sense, the ways of understanding are not seen as simply increasing in complexity as you go up the hierarchy, but increasing in complexity in an inclusive and evidence-based way. For example,

> The structural relationship attributed to the outcome space can be constructed when the categories are ready. ... The hierarchy is not one based on value judgements of better and worse ways of understanding, but on evidence of some categories being inclusive of others. (Response 13—little experience)

Category 3: Structural relationships as meaning-structure relationships

In this category, the inherent relationship between meaning and structure posited in phenomenography (and described in more detail in the next chapter) is emphasised as the basis of structural relationships. For example,

> The results of phenomenographic research are a limited number of categories of description where each one concentrates a particular meaning, and all these different meanings can be characterized according to some features. Precisely, it is because of their different features that these meanings are different: this is the meaning-structure relation, on which phenomenography is built. (Response 7—some experience)

Category 4: Structural relationships as part-whole relationships

In this category, the basis of structural relationships is seen as lying in the way in which different ways of experiencing a phenomenon form parts of the whole range of ways of experiencing the phenomenon. This focus on part-whole relationships might also be expressed as the way in which different critical aspects of a phenomenon form parts of each holistic way of experiencing the phenomenon. For example,

> A lot of this is about part/whole relationships — during analysis, developing a sense of what is the whole and which are the parts ... Too often researchers doing phenomenography get too focused on the individual categories of description — but they are far less important than the whole that is captured by the aspects of variation across the outcome space. It is the variation, rather than the individual categories, that offer us a richer understanding and can support us to do interesting things. (Response 10—extensive experience)

Category 5: Structural relationships as multi-faceted

This category highlights awareness of multiple analytical frameworks for exploring structural relationships in phenomenography, and that a researcher may select one or another (or more than one) for their analysis.

> There are different ways of handling structure. I tend to lean towards expanding awareness—theme, thematic field, etc. (Response 17—extensive experience)

The reference to 'theme' and 'thematic field' refers to aspects of the contextual situatedness of experience, which will be explained further in the next chapter. Meanwhile, the point of this quote is not to highlight this particular approach to analysis of structural relationships, but that there are multiple legitimate approaches. Thinking that there is only one 'right' way to conduct phenomenographic analysis of structural relationships acts as a limitation on the researcher. At the same time, analysis is not a situation of anything goes. Whichever form of analysis the researcher chooses needs to be firmly grounded within phenomenographic epistemology and an awareness of the range of practices used within the research community. This is explained further in the next chapter, which takes a deep dive into phenomenographic epistemology and the ways in which different analytic practices are justified by different epistemological assumptions.

Structural relationships between the different ways of understanding

As explained previously, each way of understanding a phenomenon, in this case structural relationships in phenomenography, is associated with discernment of different critical aspects of the phenomenon. Five critical aspects of structural relationships in phenomenography were identified in the study, in terms of discernment that:

1. ways of experiencing may be ordered, rather than equivalent;
2. ways of experiencing may be ordered based on inclusivity;
3. ways of experiencing involve a meaning-structure relationship;
4. ways of experiencing involve part-whole relationships; and
5. ways of experiencing involve multiple structural relationships.

Each critical aspect is associated with a different way of understanding structural relationships, with Category 1 focusing on the first critical aspect, Category 2 on the second, and so on. But later categories are inclusive of earlier ones, in that they do not just show awareness of new aspects of structural relationships, but also awareness of the aspects discerned in previous categories (see Table 4.1).

Table 4.1 Outcome space for 'structural relationships in phenomenography'

	Ways of experiencing structural relationships				
Critical aspects discerned	Category 1	Category 2	Category 3	Category 4	Category 5
Ordering of categories	✓*	✓	✓	✓	✓
Inclusive ordering of categories		✓	✓	✓	✓
Meaning-structure relationships			✓	✓	✓
Part-whole relationships				✓	✓
Multiple relationships					✓

*A tick indicates awareness of the relevant critical aspect

This claim of inclusivity will be more convincing, and understood in a more concrete way, if illustrated through further quotes from the survey. In the previous chapter, I did this by presenting one extended quote that illustrated that the most complex way of understanding the phenomenon showed awareness of every critical aspect of the phenomenon. This reflects my practice when writing journal articles, because there is rarely room to present more than one extended quote. But writing this book provides a unique opportunity to show what I regard as empirical evidence for inclusivity of awareness in more detail, by presenting extended quotes from all the categories. This better illustrates the accumulating expansion of awareness of critical aspects of the phenomenon that occurs across the categories constituted in a phenomenographic study. It also provides an opportunity for me to comment on my analytic process.

I use the same respondents for the quotes below as with the quotes above, but the previous quotes were short extracts from the larger response, selected to succinctly highlight what is distinctive about each category. In what follows, these same quotes are extended to show what is also common to the different categories.

Extended quote that illustrates the limited focus of Category 1. I start with an extended quote from Category 1 to provide a comparison point for the later quotes.

> THE thing in phenomenography is to reveal qualitative differences between the various ways of seeing something and it is what clearly differs it from other qualitative methods and approaches. The identification of structural relationships and *hierarchical structure* [my italics] are of the essence of phenomenography. Without such a focus and related practices I would not ever reach (1) the understanding needed to promote student learning; or (2) the kind of thinking that helps me to listen and observe my students. Only then, I am truly able to promote my pedagogical content knowledge. (Response 14—extensive experience)

Analytical aside

A lot of things are mentioned in this quote. So, out of all of the things that are mentioned, how is it that I have interpreted the reference to "hierarchical structure" as being critical, rather than for example, the reference to being different "from other qualitative methods", or to "the understanding needed to promote student learning", etc.?

What is critical in a participant's response only stands out in comparison with other responses; it is never obvious when looking at the response in isolation. As described in Chapter 2, the phenomenographic search is for variation in critical aspects of awareness, not in all aspects of awareness. An aspect is regarded as 'critical' when it acts to differentiate one way of understanding the phenomenon from a qualitatively different way of understanding it. This means that not every comment that a participant makes about a phenomenon will be of equal significance in determining a category.

What is critical cannot be determined in advance of the analysis, nor can it be determined by looking at one response in isolation from the others. It can only be determined by comparing one response to another, or to the set of responses. To form a category, you look for similarities in what participants say about a phenomenon *across responses*. And to form different categories, you also look for differences in what participants say about a phenomenon *across responses*. It is only in comparing each participant response to what other respondents have said that what is critical comes to the fore, and what is non-critical fades to the background. So, what is distinctive in this first quote (from Respondent 14) can only be interpreted when compared with the other quotes, below.

This comparative process illustrates one of the ways in which phenomenographic analysis focuses on collective rather than individual experience. Although the collective can only be accessed via individuals, the analysis does not focus on the experience of individuals per se, but on individual experience interpreted within the context of collective experience.

Another analytical aside

Another thing that stands out in this quote from Respondent 14, is that it clearly comes from someone with extensive experience with phenomenography. But you would not expect someone with so much experience to show such a limited understanding of structural relationships. So, how can we explain this? Is it possible that they were actually experiencing a more complex understanding, but simply did not express themselves clearly in their response?

> Yes, that provides one possible explanation. It will always be possible for a single case to be misinterpreted during the analysis due to limitations with the data gathered. But I want to point out that, even if this is what occurred, it does not change the overall outcomes. The outcomes show the range of possible ways of experiencing the phenomenon within a sample group, not the relative frequency of the different ways of experiencing. So, as long as at least one of the responses allocated to Category 1 has been accurately interpreted, this demonstrates the existence of that particular way of experiencing. In this sense, phenomenographic outcomes are quite robust, in that some errors in interpretation can potentially be made without affecting the overall outcomes. (Of course, that does not mean that we do not make every effort to interpret every response as rigorously as possible.)
>
> But there is another possible explanation for Response 14. Because our awareness of a phenomenon can broaden or narrow in different contexts, because context can act to foreground different aspects of the phenomenon (discussed further in Chapter 5), it is also possible for an experienced phenomenographer to experience a temporary narrowing of awareness, and for that period of time, to experience structural relations in a more limited way than they might at other times and in other contexts. For example, in Response 14, the respondent is contrasting phenomenography with other qualitative methods and approaches, and this context may have acted to foreground the ordering of categories into a hierarchy that happens in phenomenographic research because this is not seen in any other qualitative methodology. So, in the context comparing phenomenography to other methodologies, the respondent may have experienced structural relationships differently to the way they would in the context of analysing data for an empirical study, for instance.
>
> This highlights again the value of the phenomenographic focus on collective experience rather than individual experience. The collective set of ways of experiencing is more stable and transferable than individual experience (although collective variation can still occur between different sociocultural groups or historical time periods).

Extended quote that illustrates the inclusive foci of Category 2. The survey responses seen as representing Category 1 all discerned a hierarchical structure to phenomenographic outcomes, but without highlighting the basis on which that hierarchy is constituted. In contrast, responses seen as representing Category 2 highlighted both the hierarchical structure to phenomenographic outcomes and that this hierarchy is based on inclusivity of awareness. For example,

> ...categories are required to be hierarchically constructed [*Category 1 awareness*] with high-level categories becoming more comprehensive and inclusive [*Category 2 awareness*] (Martin et al., 2003). This implies that, although these categories are qualitatively different, they have some structural relationship. This relationship should be hierarchical rather than parallel, from simplicity at the lower level to complexity at the higher level [*Category 1 awareness*]. The basic principle for developing a hierarchy is inclusiveness rather than arbitrary and groundless value judgement [*Category 2 awareness*]. (Response 13—little experience)

Extended quote that illustrates the inclusive foci of Category 3. The survey responses seen as representing Category 3 discerned a hierarchical structure to phenomenographic outcomes (reflecting Category 1) based on inclusivity (reflecting Category 2), and in addition, highlighted that this structure is underpinned by an inherent relationship between meaning and structure. For example,

> The results of phenomenographic research are a limited number of categories of description where each one concentrates a particular meaning, and all these different meanings can be characterized according to some features. Precisely, it is because of their different features that these meanings are different: this is the meaning-structure relation, on which phenomenography is built. [*Category 3 awareness*] ...this serves to unveil the structure where the different categories of description are anchored in an hierarchical order [*Category 1 awareness*]. In this sense, there are understandings that we all share, and others that only some people have developed. But, these different understandings are related to each other. ... So, there is an inclusive organization of the categories of description. [*Category 2 awareness*] (Response 7—some experience)

Extended quote that illustrates the inclusive foci of Category 4. The survey responses seen as representing Category 4 discerned a hierarchical structure to phenomenographic outcomes (reflecting Category 1) based on inclusivity (reflecting Category 2), and an inherent relationship between meaning and structure (reflecting Category 3), and in addition, highlighted that this forms a part-whole structure. For example,

Phenomenography is about understanding the structures of variation in peoples' experiences of phenomena. Examining the structure of variation—the referential [meaning] and structural elements[2] [*Category 3 awareness*]—is what gives phenomenography its power. A lot of this is about part/whole relationships—during analysis, developing a sense of what is the whole and which are the parts [*Category 4 awareness*]. Often these can shift [during analysis], like the changing faces of a cube, and what you thought was a part becomes the whole or vice versa. ... Too often researchers doing phenomenography get too focused on the individual categories of description—but they are far less important than the whole that is captured by the aspects of variation across the outcome space [*Category 1 and 2 awareness*]. It is the variation, rather than the individual categories, that offer us a richer understanding and can support us to do interesting things. (Response 10—extensive experience)

Analytical aside

Evidence of Category 1 and 2 awareness is less explicit in this last quote than in previous ones, but it is present. Reference to "the whole that is captured by the aspects of variation across the outcome space" implies an inclusive hierarchy. This is because the outcome space (the set of outcomes) can only become a 'whole' rather than a series of parts through being hierarchically linked, so references to a 'whole' logically implies a hierarchical arrangement.

In addition, because we have shown previously in Category 3 that awareness of the relationship between meaning and structure includes awareness of inclusive hierarchical structures between different ways of experiencing in an outcome space (Categories 1 and 2), then it is reasonable to assume that references to the meaning-structure relationship in Category 4 also includes awareness of inclusive hierarchical structures (Categories 1 and 2).

Phenomenographic publications often refer to a 'logical' hierarchy of inclusivity. The reasoning I have described here provides one illustration of how logic plays a role in interpreting evidence for inclusivity. In my approach to analysis, I would not expect every response within a category to explicitly demonstrate inclusivity; sometimes it will be implicit. But I would expect at least some responses in every category to demonstrate

---

2   As described in Chapter 5, the relationship between 'referential and structural' aspects of a way of experiencing is equivalent to the relationship between 'meaning and structure' in ways of experiencing.

4. Variation in understandings of structural relationships in phenomenography 63

> inclusive awareness explicitly. So, analytically, I require evidence of inclusivity within a category (the totality of responses assigned to that categorical grouping), rather than within every individual response seen as representing that category (parts of the totality).

Extended quote that illustrates the inclusive foci of Category 5. The response illustrating Category 5 discerned a hierarchical structure to phenomenographic outcomes (reflecting Category 1) based on inclusivity (reflecting Category 2), an inherent relationship between meaning and structure (reflecting Category 3), that this forms a part-whole structure (Category 4) and in addition, highlighted that there are multiple structural relationships in phenomenography. For example,

> Meaning/reference and structure are simultaneous in phenomenography [*Category 3 awareness*] ... It comes back to what does it mean to do phenomenography. I see some 'phenomenographies' that appear to be effectively loose thematic analyses, that claim to be phenomenographies. [But have] No elements of attempts to unpack structure and connect the 'categories' via these structures [*Category 1–2 awareness*]. On the other side, some phenomenographers live and breathe structure, which seems to me to lose an essential aspect... we are looking for variation in experienced meaning after all. [*Category 3 awareness*] ... If we don't hold structure and reference, the whole experienced meaning together, we do lose something of the essence of phenomenography, which is about wholes, the whole, internal relation as well as the parts [*Category 4 awareness*]. The gestalt is important. There are different ways of handling structure [*Category 5 awareness*]. I tend to lean towards expanding awareness—theme, thematic field, etc. (Response 17—extensive experience)

Evidence of Category 1 and 2 awareness is less explicit in this last quote than in previous ones, but it is implied by the reference to 'structure that connects the categories', which is typically a hierarchical structure. As stated above, not all references to critical aspects of a phenomenon will be as explicit as others.

> **Analytical aside**
>
> I would like to note that Category 5 was represented by only one survey response. It is not unusual in phenomenographic research for the most complex way of experiencing a phenomenon to be represented by

only one or two participants in a sample. (This indicates that the most complex way of experiencing a phenomenon is often not a common way of experiencing it.) But the focus of phenomenography is not on frequency of different ways of experiencing, but on variation in different ways of experiencing. Focusing on variation highlights what is possible to experience, and the order in which different ways of experiencing the same phenomenon build on each other. In this sense, having only one or two representatives of a specific way of experiencing within a sample is not a concern for the validity of the existence of the associated category of description, especially as the category needs to also make logical sense within the context of the hierarchy of categories.

However, having only one or two representatives of a category does impact the reliability of the description of that category. In other words, whilst one response is enough to demonstrate that another way of understanding or thinking about the phenomenon exists (i.e., that another category exists), not having a number of responses to draw on is a limitation when deciding how best to describe the meaning of that way of thinking (i.e., the meaning that that category represents), because there are fewer sample descriptions to draw on.

The quote from Respondent 17 illustrates this, in that two new aspects of structural relationships are mentioned in the quote: (a) that there are different ways of handling structure; and (b) that the respondent considers contextual structure in their analyses (i.e., theme, thematic field). In my interpretation, I have highlighted the first aspect as being 'critical', but not the second aspect. I did this based on logical reasons, arguing to myself that a consideration of 'contextual structure' is a subset, or illustration, of 'different ways of handling structure', rather than an aspect in its own right. But what I cannot say, because there are no other responses to draw on, is whether the two foci go together. That is, whether discerning a contextual structure to awareness is part of discerning that there are multiple structures to awareness. This is discussed further in the implications section of the chapter.

Personally, I would argue that analysis focused on between-category relationships, within-category relationships and meaning-structure relationships also represent different frameworks for analysing structural relationships, and thus the multi-faceted nature of structure. But this view was not evident in the data. While different respondents mentioned different types of part-whole structures, no single respondent mentioned more than one type. So, no response in this sample explicitly

> contrasted different types of part-whole structures in the way that would be necessary to see structural relationships as multi-faceted rather than uniform in nature. Perhaps this is something that might be seen in a larger or more detailed data set.

Implications of the study for phenomenographic research

The implication of discerning a critical aspect of a phenomenon is that that aspect can then be taken into account when dealing with the phenomenon. And the implication of not discerning a critical aspect is that that aspect cannot be taken into account when dealing with the phenomenon. Applying this to conducting phenomenographic research, this means that if an aspect of structural relationships in phenomenography has not been discerned by a researcher, then they cannot take that aspect into consideration when constituting structural relationships during empirical analysis, nor when reading about structural relationships constituted and published by others. So, the critical aspects of structural relationships that are discerned by a researcher will impact both their own research practice and their ability to fully understand others' research practice and outcomes.

Five critical aspects of structural relationships were identified in the study:

1. the hierarchical ordering of categories;
2. the inclusive nature of that hierarchical ordering;
3. the dialectical relationship between meaning and structure;
4. the part-whole nature of structural relationships; and
5. that there are multiple types of structural relationships.

Discernment of the first two aspects is essential for being able to constitute structural relationships *between* different ways of experiencing a phenomenon (i.e., a hierarchical outcome space). But if this is all that is discerned about structural relationships, then research analysis and outcomes will be limited to relationships between, and not within, ways of experiencing. As described in previous chapters, this approach to research (looking only for relationships between ways of experiencing) represents early phenomenographic analysis from the 1970s–1990s.

Discernment of the next two aspects enables an analysis of structural relationships *within* each way of experiencing, because both aspects can be applied to the structure of awareness within ways of experiencing. As described in previous chapters, this approach represents 21st-century phenomenographic analysis from the 2000s onwards (i.e., analysis for patterns of critical aspects discerned within each way of experiencing).

But whilst awareness of meaning-structure relationships and part-whole relationships enables a 21st-century analysis, it does not ensure it. This is because both aspects are relevant to the analysis of structural relationships between categories as well as within categories, so it is possible to discern these critical aspects without necessarily applying them to the analysis of within-category relationships. That is, discernment of these aspects is a necessary but not sufficient condition for conducting analyses of within-category relationships.

Discernment of the last aspect enables flexible research practice using different types of structural analyses. The fifth and most complex understanding of structural relationships as multi-faceted, adds further epistemological and/or analytical depth to the collective understanding, and moves away from the assumption that there is only one right way of constituting structural relationships in phenomenography.

The five critical aspects of different ways of understanding structural relationships identified in this study highlight what supervisors of research students, and others new to phenomenography, need to bring to novice researchers' attention to help them achieve a sophisticated understanding of structural relationships in phenomenography. Students need to become aware of the distinction between:

1. research outcomes that are hierarchical *vs* non-hierarchical—one way of making this distinction apparent to students might be to compare examples of phenomenographic outcomes with examples of outcomes from other research approaches (e.g., from content analysis or thematic analysis);

2. hierarchies that are based on value judgments *vs* inclusive awareness—one way of making this distinction apparent to students might be to ask them to guess the ordering of

categories in advance of completing a structural analysis, and then later compare their guess with their final outcomes;

3. relationships between meaning and structure that are dialectical *vs* causal—one way of making this distinction apparent to students might be to ask them whether they can think of a time when they personally have noticed something new about a phenomenon, and how the phenomenon *instantaneously* looks different to them;

4. categories and critical aspects that are looked at as a list of components *vs* looked at as parts of a larger whole—one way of making this distinction apparent to students might be to encourage them to reflect deeply on what it means to investigate variation in collective experience rather than variation in individual experience; and

5. the different ways in which structural relationships may be constituted in different studies—one way of making this distinction apparent to students might be to encourage them to experience analysing the same data set from multiple frameworks, looking at what each framework adds to the outcomes.

A more subtle implication of the findings relates to the order in which the critical aspects of structural relationships were discerned. Because the least complex way of understanding structural relationships discerned 'the hierarchical ordering of categories', and this was also then discerned within every way of understanding structural relationships, this implies that that aspect of structural relationships in phenomenography is the 'easiest' aspect to discern, or notice, within current research contexts. Everyone in the sample discerned this aspect of structural relationships, so it must be a fairly salient aspect in current ways of conducting, talking about and publishing phenomenographic research. I would guess that is because the ordering of different ways of understanding into a hierarchy is part of what distinguishes phenomenography from other qualitative research methodologies, so it is one of the first things one notices about phenomenography.

Meanwhile, the most complex way of understanding structural relationships in phenomenography discerned 'multiple types of structural relationships', and this was not discerned within any other way of understanding it. This implies that this aspect of structural relationships is the 'hardest'[3] aspect to discern, or notice, within current research contexts. Only one person in the sample explicitly discerned this aspect, so it cannot be a very salient part of current ways of conducting, talking about and publishing phenomenographic research.

The person in the sample who did explicitly discern multiple types of structural relationships in phenomenography also described using contextual embeddedness as an analytical framework in their research. There is a certain logic to this because, whilst research using the structural framework of theme, thematic field and margin certainly exists (e.g., Jarrett, 2016), it is not a popular analytical approach in phenomenography. So, if one uses this analytic approach, it is logically impossible to not also discern that there is more than one way of analysing structural relationships in phenomenography.

But that does not mean that being aware of the contextual framework of theme, thematic field and margin is the only way to discern that there is more than one approach to analysing structural relationships. For example, I would personally argue that analysis focused on between-category relationships (hierarchical structures), within-category relationships (critical aspects) and referential-structure relationships also represent different frameworks for analysing structural relationships (see Chapter 5), and thus the multi-faceted nature of structural relationships. But this is just my personal argument and was not apparent in the data (though that might be an outcome of the limited data set — only fifteen respondents and survey rather than interview data). Other conduits to discerning multiple types of structural relationships might be seen in a larger or more detailed data set.

Meanwhile, the multi-faceted nature of structure and structural relationships in phenomenography may become more obvious to (i.e., easier to discern by) novice researchers if, as a research community, we

---

3   By 'easiest' and 'hardest' to discern, I do not mean in terms of the inherent nature of the aspect, but in terms of patterns of variation and invariance in aspects of structural relationships that researchers are most commonly within current research contexts and that researchers are then exposed as part of current ways of conducting, talking about and publishing phenomenographic research (see Chapter 9).

start to refer to multiple forms of analysis more often in our discussions and publications. This is something I have tried to do in Åkerlind (2024b), and in numerous places throughout this book, including the next chapter.

Chapter summary

This chapter highlighted five aspects of structural relationships in phenomenography that researchers need to discern in order to understand it in a complex and sophisticated way:

1. the hierarchical ordering of categories;
2. the inclusive nature of that hierarchical ordering;
3. the dialectical relationship between meaning and structure;
4. the part-whole nature of structural relationships; and
5. that there are multiple types of structural relationships.

Discernment of the first two aspects is a requirement for being able to constitute structural relationships between the different ways of experiencing a phenomenon identified during a phenomenographic study. Discernment of the next two aspects is a necessary, but not sufficient, condition for being able to constitute structural relationships within each specific way of experiencing the phenomenon. Discernment of the last aspect enables flexible research practice using different types of structural analyses.

The next chapter turns to a discussion of the epistemological assumptions underlying phenomenographic research, and the way these assumptions explain the approaches taken to phenomenographic analysis, including analysis of structural relationships. To do this I draw in particular on Marton and Booth's (1997) *Learning and Awareness*.

5. Epistemological assumptions in phenomenography: Implications for methods

In this chapter, I focus on phenomenographic theory, and how this relates to phenomenographic research methods. And for this, I draw on the key reference on phenomenographic epistemology, *Learning and Awareness*, by Ference Marton and Shirley Booth (1997). This book marked a significant turning point in phenomenographic research. It is the point in the development of phenomenography at which the ontological and epistemological assumptions underlying the methodology were explicitly articulated. It is also the point at which a phenomenographic theory of learning was first proposed, the 'variation theory of learning', based on the claim that in order to learn we need to experience variation in different aspects of the concept, skill, or capability being learned. I discuss this further in Chapter 9.

So, *Learning and Awareness* is a landmark text in the development of phenomenography and a 'must read' for all researchers. However, it is not an 'easy read', and can be somewhat difficult to decipher, which is why I have devoted this chapter to clarifying and discussing its claims. One of the sources of difficulty is the subject matter itself, which is complex. But another is that parts of *Learning and Awareness* are focused on learning, parts on experience in general, and parts on phenomenography—and it is not always clear which topics are being addressed at any one point in the book.

> **Historical aside:**
>
> **Confusion between two figures in *Learning and Awareness***
>
> Confusion arising from uncertainties about whether Marton and Booth (1997) are referring to learning specifically or human experience more broadly is most evident in the figures they present in their chapter 5, on "The Anatomy of Awareness". One figure (their Fig. 5.2 on p. 85)

presents the structure of 'learning'—based on an analytic separation into 'how and what' aspects, accompanied by a further level of separation into the 'act, indirect object and direct object' of learning. Then, just three pages later, another figure (their Fig. 5.3 on p. 88) presents the structure of 'experience'—based on an analytic separation into 'structural and referential' aspects, accompanied by a further level of separation into the 'external and internal horizons' of the experience. This is reminiscent of the varying use of what/how analytic structures and structural/referential analytic structures described in Chapter 2, and has caused confusion over which of the two analytic structures should be used in phenomenographic research (Harris, 2011). More importantly from my perspective, given that learning is also an experience, why should their analysis be structured differently?

Unfortunately, Marton and Booth do not explicitly answer this question, nor do they describe the relationship between the two figures. And this has led to confusion amongst some researchers as to which figure represents the basic analytic structure to be used in phenomenographic research. For example, in a detailed and scholarly review of the development and use of the what/how and structural/referential frameworks in phenomenographic research, Harris (2011) found considerable variation in the ways these frameworks were defined and used in different studies. She also found considerable variation in the described relationships between the two frameworks. All of which indicates a substantial degree of confusion in the literature.

Whilst the two frameworks are strongly related at the analytic level of distinguishing the 'what and how' aspects or 'referential and structural' aspects of experience (as described in Chapter 2 and further below), they markedly diverge at the next analytic level of distinguishing the 'act, indirect object and direct object' of learning and the 'external and internal horizons' of experience. But what Harris failed to highlight in her review is that the what/how framework is more commonly used to refer to learning in particular, whilst the referential/structural framework is more commonly used to refer to experience in general. Though this is by no means universal.

Nevertheless, because learning is also an experience, I would argue that both the how/what and the structural/referential frameworks are appropriate when the object of study is learning, with researchers justified in taking either approach depending on their research question.

> But when the object of study is experience of phenomena other than learning, then the structural/referential framework is the only relevant framework to use. And because this chapter is concerned with phenomenography's theoretical assumptions about the nature of human experience, this is the framework I build on in this chapter.

Another potential source of confusion when reading *Learning and Awareness* can come from readers' pre-existing assumptions about the contents of the book (as I initially experienced myself). With Ference Marton widely acknowledged as the founder of phenomenography, when you see a book with Ference as the lead author, it is easy to assume that the book will be about phenomenography (at least until the 2000s when he moved his primary research focus to variation theory—see Chapter 9). But, in fact, *Learning and Awareness* is not primarily about phenomenography, but about learning, and how phenomenographic research has illuminated the nature of learning. So, the book is much more comprehensible if, instead of approaching each chapter with the question, "What does this tell me about the nature of phenomenography?", you approach with the question, "What does this tell me about the nature of learning, as illuminated by phenomenographic research?".

Some chapters in *Learning and Awareness* are more directly relevant to phenomenography than others, with chapters 1 and 5–8 essential reading for anyone interested in phenomenography. In writing this chapter, I draw in particular on chapters 5 and 6, describing the following epistemological assumptions:

- the meaning of an experience and the structure of an experience are dialectically related;
- awareness is inevitably partial and contextually variable;
- partial and varying awareness creates a figure-ground structure to experience;
- awareness of parts combines to create a holistic experience; and
- human experience is non-dualistic, a relation between individual and world.

The dialectical relationship between meaning and structure in human experience

The most foundational claim in phenomenographic epistemology is that there is a dialectical[1] relationship between meaning and structure, in the sense that the meaning a phenomenon holds for us is intrinsically related to the structure of our awareness of the phenomenon. Or put another way, the way in which we experience a phenomenon is intrinsically related to the structure of our experience.

> Structure presupposes meaning, and at the same time meaning presupposes structure. The two aspects, meaning and structure, are dialectically intertwined and occur simultaneously when we experience something. (Marton and Booth, 1997, p. 87)

This claim goes back to the early days of phenomenography and its starting assumption, drawn from phenomenology, of the intentional nature of human experience (as outlined in Chapter 2). Intentionality is the claim that all experience is oriented towards an object, "Love is always the love of someone and learning is always learning of something" (Marton, 1984, p. 54). In other words, you cannot have an experience without something being experienced. As a consequence, the act of experiencing a phenomenon and the meaning of the phenomenon being experienced are inherently entwined.

However, for analytic purposes, human experience can be artificially separated into the act of experiencing (what phenomenography initially called the 'how' aspect of experience) and the meaning of the experience (what phenomenography initially called the 'what' aspect of experience. Over time, the act of experiencing became defined in phenomenography as an organisational act, in terms of the way the experience is structured in awareness. This is elaborated in *Learning and*

---

1 Phenomenographers typically use the term 'dialectical' when describing the relationship between meaning and structure. This is because it is the term used by Marton. But I have discovered that this can be confusing for some people, who may see the term as implying a tension or opposition. That is not how the relationship is seen in phenomenography. In phenomenography, by dialectical, we mean that meaning and structure simultaneously constitute each other; that one cannot occur without the other. So, a change in one is inevitably accompanied by a change in the other, not in a causal way, but in a co-constituting way.

Awareness and forms the basis for phenomenography's unique focus on studying human experience via scrutinising its structure. This is why the notion of 'structure' is so significant in phenomenographic research.

> A way of experiencing something can thus be described in terms of the structure or organization of awareness at a particular moment. Similarly, qualitatively *different* ways of experiencing something can be understood in terms of differences in the structure or organisation of awareness at a particular moment or moments. (Marton and Booth, 1997, p. 100)

As part of the assumption of a dialectical relationship between meaning and structure, phenomenography argues that human experience of any phenomenon can be thought of as composed of two inherently interconnected and mutually constituting parts or aspects: a 'referential aspect' and a 'structural aspect'. Together, they form the way a phenomenon is experienced, made sense of, or understood by humans, i.e., the meaning it holds for us.

> The two aspects, meaning and structure, are dialectically intertwined and occur simultaneously when we experience something. Thus we can state that an experience has a structural aspect and a referential (or meaning) aspect. (Marton and Booth, 1997, p. 87)

The referential aspect has a focus on the unique meaning attributed to the phenomenon experienced, specifically looking at what people experience or understand about the phenomenon, i.e., 'What meaning does the phenomenon hold for them?'. This is because, in order to know what we are experiencing, we need to be able to assign a meaning to it. Consequently, sometimes the referential aspect is also referred to as the meaning aspect or the 'what' aspect of the experience of a phenomenon.

The structural aspect, on the other hand, focuses on how the phenomenon is experienced and understood, i.e., 'How is that particular meaning organised or constituted in awareness?'. Consequently, sometimes the structural aspect is also referred to as the organisational aspect, or the 'how' aspect of the experience of a phenomenon. Together, the referential/meaning/what aspect and the structural/organisational/how aspect of human experience constitute the two basic component parts of phenomenographic analysis and outcomes (see Figure 5.1).

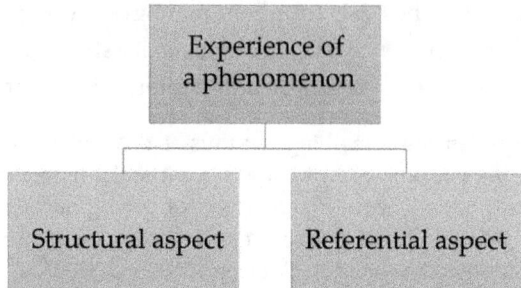

Fig. 5.1 Analytical constituents of experience—the referential and structural aspects of a way of experiencing (adapted from Marton and Booth, 1997, p. 88)

But it is important to distinguish between epistemological claims and analytic strategies. Whilst the proposed dialectical relationship between meaning and structure and the separation of ways of experiencing into referential and structural aspects are strongly related ideas, they are not exactly the same idea. The assumption of a dialectical relationship is an *epistemological claim* that explains the *analytic strategy* of separating ways of experiencing into referential and structural aspects. This distinction between epistemological claims and analytic strategies is one I will return to regularly throughout this chapter.

Awareness as inevitably partial and variable

Marton and Booth argue that, although human experience is potentially inexhaustible over time, at any one point in time and context, experience is inevitably partial. That is, it is impossible to experience all things at the same time. This means that only some aspects of what is available to be experienced will actually be experienced. So, at any one point in time, we will inevitably be aware of some aspects of the world, or phenomena in the world, but not aware of other aspects.

Consequently, we can expect that the meaning, or way of understanding, any phenomenon in the world will inevitably vary between people, because the partial nature of experience (combined with each person's unique experiential history), means that different individuals are likely to discern different aspects of the same phenomenon.² This is what justifies phenomenography's analytic strategy of looking at human experience through variation, and with a focus on the sum of collective experience, rather than on individual experience. It is only by looking at human experience from a collective perspective that the range of possible ways of understanding a phenomenon, and the range of parts or aspects of a phenomenon that are possible for us to discern, will become apparent.

There are, however, two types of variation in experience of the same phenomenon, one that we would call 'learning', where an aspect of a phenomenon is discerned for the first time, and one that we would call 'contextual', where different aspects of the same phenomenon are highlighted in different situations. Just as, at any one point in time and context, an individual will notice some aspects of a phenomenon but not others, so, at different times and contexts the same individual is likely to notice different aspects of the same phenomenon. For example, if you are observing a vanilla sponge cake when feeling hungry, then certain aspects of the cake are likely to come to mind (e.g., tasty, satiating, a treat, etc.). But if you observe the same cake whilst feeling full, then other aspects of the cake are likely to come to mind (e.g., sugary, fatty, not good for you, etc.). In other words, the meaning of the same phenomenon may be experienced differently by the same person when in different situations or contexts.

Although phenomenographic research does not traditionally explore the impact of different participant contexts on their ways of experiencing phenomena (aiming instead to abstract different ways of experiencing a phenomenon across contexts), from an epistemological perspective context is acknowledged as vitally important in any experience of a phenomenon.³

---

2   This will be true within a particular social group as well as between social groups. Although social learning can be expected to produce commonalities in experience, individual experience can be expected to produce variation within the commonalities. This is another reason why phenomenography searches for variation *and* commonalities in ways of experiencing.

3   Also see the discussion of context with respect to trustworthiness in phenomenographic research by Collier-Reed et al., 2009. They distinguish three types of context: the larger purpose of the research study; the collective context within which individual responses are considered; and the context (or thematic field) as experienced by individual participants (which may be contrasted with

> We cannot separate our understanding of the situation and our understanding of the phenomena that lend sense to the situation. ...we are aware of the phenomena from the point of view of the particular situation [in which they are embedded]. ... situation and phenomena are inextricably intertwined in experience. (Marton and Booth, p. 83)

This is why a research sample in phenomenography is always selected to maximise variation in contextual experience amongst participants, because this is seen as maximising the chances of as 'complete' a range of qualitatively different ways of experiencing a phenomenon as possible being present in the sample.[4] It also provides another reason for the phenomenographic focus on collective rather than individual experience. Phenomenographers expect an individual's experience of a phenomenon to change with changes in context, potentially even moment-to-moment changes. But the *range* of possible ways of experiencing the phenomenon within a particular group at a particular point in time is expected to be more stable, and thus more generalisable to different settings. In other words, collective experience is transferable to different contexts in a way that individual experience is not.

Meanwhile, Marton and Booth claim that not all aspects of any situation or context will be of equal relevance to a phenomenon—there is a 'relevance structure' to contextual awareness. They argue that it is useful to think of awareness as having a theme, thematic field and margin.[5] The theme refers to the focus of awareness, for example, this chapter. The thematic field refers to aspects of contextual awareness that are experienced as relevant to the theme, for example, other publications on phenomenography, other research methodologies, the design of a current research project, etc. (plus, there can be more than one thematic field). The margin refers to aspects of contextual awareness that are experienced as *not* relevant to the theme, for example, the time of day, weather, awareness of an upcoming appointment, and so on. Together the

---

the context as prepared by the researcher). It is the last type of context that I have been describing in this chapter.

4 By 'complete', we mean complete within the socio-historical constraints of the population from which the sample is selected. There is always room for other ways of experiencing to be present in a different population, with different socio-historical constraints and opportunities.

5 This notion of theme, thematic field and margin draws on the work of Gurwitsch (1964, cited in Marton and Booth, 1997, p. 98).

thematic field(s) and margin constitute the context in which the theme is embedded, forming "a single structure of relevance surrounding the theme" (p. 99).

Moving now from an epistemological to an analytical perspective, the focal theme and its context (thematic fields and margin) combine to produce two potential foci for analytical attention, what Marton and Booth have called the 'external horizon' of our experience of phenomena (how a phenomenon, as experienced, is distinguished from and related to its context) and the 'internal horizon' of our experience of phenomena[6] (how awareness of different aspects of a phenomenon combine to constitute a holistic meaning or experience).

> The structural aspect of a way of experiencing something is thus twofold: discernment of the whole from the context [external horizon] on the one hand and discernment of the parts and their relationship to the whole on the other [internal horizon]. (p. 87)[7]

This elaboration of structure in the experience of a phenomenon is shown in Figure 5.2.

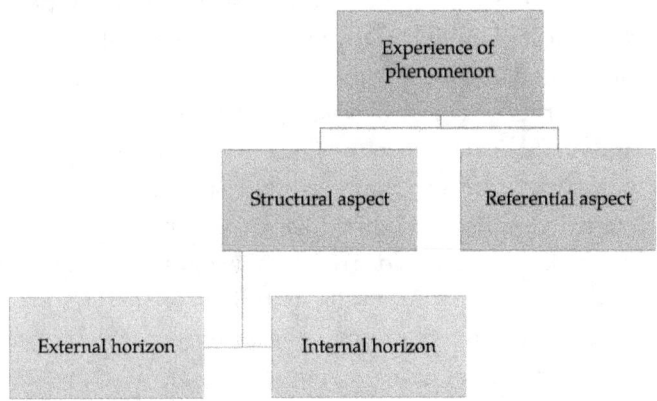

Fig. 5.2 Analytical constituents of experience—the internal and external horizons of awareness of a phenomenon (adapted from Marton and Booth, 1997, p. 88)

---

6   Marton and Booth borrow the terms, external and internal horizons from phenomenology (p. 87).
7   More precisely, this is just one of a number of structural aspects of a way of experiencing something.

Partial and varying awareness creates a figure-ground structure to experience

Given the simultaneously partial and variable nature of human experience, Marton and Booth argue for a figure-ground structure to awareness.

> Our awareness has a structure to it. At any instant certain things are to the fore—they are figural or thematized—whereas other things have receded to the ground—they are tacit or unthematized. (p. 98)

In other words, for any one individual at any one point in time, some aspects of a phenomenon or situation will be focal in awareness, whilst others will not. This is why any phenomenon will inevitably be experienced differently by different people—due to variation in their awareness of different parts or aspects of the phenomenon.

This enables each way of experiencing a phenomenon to be described in terms of which aspects of the phenomenon are figural (i.e., in focal awareness) and which aspects are ground (i.e., in the background or outside awareness). This figure-ground structure then provides a framework for describing qualitatively different ways of experiencing a phenomenon and distinguishing the different ways of experiencing from each other, in terms of which aspects of a phenomenon are discerned (figural) and not discerned (ground) in any one way of experiencing it.

In actual experience, the figure-ground structure would not be a simple dichotomy of discerned *vs* undiscerned aspects, but would have layers to it: "There are different degrees of how figural... things or aspects are in our awareness" (p. 98). In line with this, sometimes in *Learning and Awareness* aspects in the 'ground' of awareness are described as not having been discerned, while at other times they are described as having been discerned, but in the background, not foreground, of awareness. But whether regarded as outside awareness or in the background of awareness, such aspects are not in focal awareness, and this is the important issue. For analytical purposes, it is what is inside *vs* outside focal awareness that matters for creating the meaning of an experience, and precise distinctions between different types of non-focal awareness are not important in this regard. So, for the purposes of analysis and parsimony in representing research outcomes, it is useful to think in terms of a dichotomy: aspects of a phenomenon that have been discerned in focal awareness (figure) *vs* aspects that have not been discerned in focal awareness (ground).[8]

Although Marton and Booth did not explicitly add this figure-ground aspect of awareness to their figure representing human experience, I think it would be helpful to do so. So, I have built on their original figure (reproduced as Figure 5.2, above) to create an elaborated figure, Figure 5.3 below.

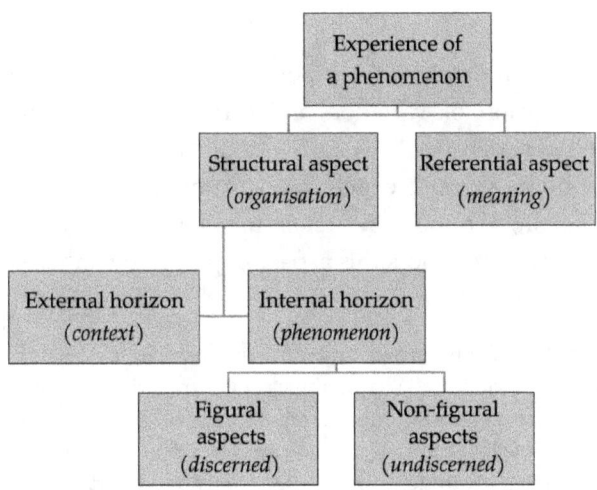

Fig. 5.3 Analytical constituents of experience—figural and non-figural aspects of the phenomenon (added to Marton and Booth's, 1997, figure, p. 88)

But what does it mean to be figurally aware of an aspect of a phenomenon? Marton and Booth argue that an aspect is brought into figural awareness, or 'discerned', through the experience of variation in that aspect. A common example used to illustrate this is colour. If everything in the world were green, then colour could not be experienced as an aspect of a phenomenon. Not even a sense of 'green' could be experienced, as one colour can only be experienced in contrast to another. It is only due to experiencing variation in colour that we discern, or become aware of, colour as an aspect of the world. So, for an aspect to be discerned and

---

8   What has *not* been discerned within one way of experiencing a phenomenon can only be identified by comparison with other ways of experiencing a phenomenon where these aspects *have* been discerned.

appropriately taken into account in handling a phenomenon, a current or previous experience of variation in that aspect is needed.

> Darkness can only be experienced in contrast to experienced (or imagined) light. You cannot experience greenness without the experience of other colours; without variation in colour, the very idea of colour cannot exist. If the level of happiness, or sorrow, never varied within individuals, nor differed between individuals, then happiness, and sorrow, would cease to exist. The fishes are the last one to discover water, it has been said; and if we always told the truth, then not only lies, but also even truth, would be extinct. (Marton and Trigwell, 2000, pp. 386–387)

Marton and Booth describe the experience of variation as the 'opening up of a dimension of variation' in awareness of the phenomenon. Without the experience of variation in that aspect or dimension of the phenomenon, the aspect is experienced as uniform in nature and either not noticed at all, or noticed in a taken-for-granted way, rather than in a way that focally experiences this aspect as part of the inherent meaning of the phenomenon.[9]

> An aspect that is discerned and held in focus is associated with a dimension of variation. 'What *is* the case is explicitly or implicitly seen against the background of what *could* be the case.' ... [whereas] When an aspect is not discerned .... we can say either that this aspect is absent altogether [from awareness] or is taken for granted and no alternatives are being explicitly considered. (Marton and Booth, 1997, p. 112)

These dimensions of variation in awareness of phenomena are described as representing 'critical aspects' in human experience of the phenomena.[10]

---

9   Just because variation in an aspect is available to be experienced, does not mean that it necessarily will be experienced at any one point in time and context. For pedagogical purposes, Marton et al., 2004, and Marton, 2015, go on to describe ways of increasing the likelihood of variation in an aspect being experienced, drawing on 'variation theory' (see Chapter 9).

10 So far in this book, 'critical aspects' in awareness of phenomena have been defined as those aspects that are critical for distinguishing one way of experiencing the phenomenon from a qualitatively different way of experiencing it. This definition was appropriate for early phenomenography, and is still accurate, but in 21st-century phenomenography can now be defined with more precision, with critical aspects also seen as representing a dimension of variation in awareness of the phenomenon.

How awareness of parts combine to create a holistic experience

> When we talk about structure... What we are discussing is how different parts are discerned... how they relate to each other.... and how they make up the whole. (Marton and Booth, 1997, p. 89)

From its earliest days, phenomenography has been influenced by Gestalt psychology, with its focus on the relationship between parts and wholes. This focus on how parts combine into wholes is evident in the approach taken in phenomenography to analysing the internal horizon of human experience of phenomena. This involves a part-whole analysis of how awareness of constituent parts, or critical aspects, of a phenomenon combine to constitute a holistic way of experiencing the phenomenon.

The previously described assumption of a figure-ground structure to awareness provides an underlying framework for this part-whole analysis, with different ways of experiencing a phenomenon able to be described, analytically, in terms of the aspects of the phenomenon that are discerned (i.e., that are figural in awareness) and not discerned (i.e., that are non-figural in awareness) in different ways of experiencing the phenomenon, as described above.

> The meaning of something for someone ... corresponds to the pattern of parts or aspects that are discerned and are simultaneously objects of focal awareness. (Marton and Booth, 1997, p. 112)

In concentrating on the internal horizon, we are focusing on part-whole structures and analyses at the level of *each specific* way of experiencing a phenomenon. As described in Chapter 2, this is a relatively new analytic strategy in phenomenographic research.

However, at the level of the *collective range* of ways of experiencing a phenomenon, part-whole structural analyses have been conducted since the very beginning of phenomenography, where each specific way of experiencing a phenomenon may be seen as a part of the whole collection of ways of experiencing the phenomenon. It is this part-whole structure that creates the structure of the collective outcome space, where a hierarchically inclusive structure is also a part-whole structure. So, in organising collective awareness into an interrelated outcome space, each specific way of experiencing a phenomenon forms the parts, and the combined ways of experiencing, the whole, of collective human experience of a phenomenon.

> ...there is a part-whole relationship between a *particular* way of experiencing a phenomenon and the *set* of different ways of experiencing the phenomenon identified. (Marton and Booth, 1997, p. 115, italics added)

So, part-whole analyses are undertaken in phenomenographic research at more than one level.

1. *Specific level*—each specific way of experiencing the phenomenon:
   a. *specific whole*—the holistic meaning associated with any one particular way of experiencing the phenomenon;
   b. *specific part*—the pattern of critical aspects discerned and not discerned in that particular way of experiencing the phenomenon.
2. *Collective level*—the collective range of ways of experiencing the phenomenon:
   a. *collective whole*—the full range of ways of experiencing the phenomenon found in a sample group;
   b. *collective parts*—each specific way of experiencing the phenomenon found in the sample.

Human experience of the world as non-dualistic

Phenomenography posits a non-dualistic or relational ontology to the human world, in which an individuals' way of experiencing a phenomenon is seen as a relationship between the individual and the phenomenon being experienced.

> There is not a real world 'out there' and a subjective world 'in here'. The world [as experienced] is not constructed by the learner, nor is it imposed upon her; it is constituted as an internal relation between them. (Marton and Booth, 1997, p. 13).

This is not to say that an external reality does not exist independently of human experience of it, but that it is a non-attainable object of study because the human world is an experienced world. And in experiencing the world, we form a relationship with it that simultaneously reflects both the world and the person experiencing the world.

> We cannot describe a world that is independent of our descriptions or of us as describers. We cannot separate out the describer from the description. Our world is a real world, but it is a described world, a world experienced by humans. (p. 113) ... Obviously, the world [in general] cannot be identical with the world experienced by a particular person, but the world experienced by a particular person and the world in general are not separate. The former is part of the latter. (Marton and Booth, 1997, p. 138)

As with the assumption of the dialectical relationship between meaning and structure, the assumption of non-dualism is also grounded in the assumption of the intentionality of human experience. If all experience is directed towards an object, then the experience and the object cannot be separated—they form a non-dualistic relationship.

The assumption of non-dualism then provides an epistemological justification for the analytic expectation that different ways of experiencing the same phenomenon will be related—related through the object being experienced. (Plus, in practical terms, how could people in a social group communicate with each other without shared aspects of awareness?) Analytically, this leads to a search for relationships between the different ways of experiencing the phenomenon that are constituted in a phenomenographic study. This search for relationships takes the form of a search for common areas of shared awareness of different aspects of a phenomenon.

However, the collective part-whole structure of an outcome space assumes not just a relationship, but a specific type of relationship between different ways of experiencing a phenomenon—that they will be *inclusively* related, through shared awareness of some of the same aspects of the phenomenon. During phenomenographic analysis, this assumption leads to a search for overlapping or shared aspects of awareness across different ways of experiencing a phenomenon, and typically produces an outcome space that is structured as an inclusively expanding hierarchy of increasing complexity of awareness of different aspects of the phenomenon.

> ...the qualitatively different ways of experiencing a particular phenomenon form, as a rule, a hierarchy. The hierarchical structure can be defined in terms of increasing complexity, where the different ways of experiencing the phenomenon in question can be defined as subsets of the component parts and relations within more inclusive (complex) ways of seeing the phenomenon (Marton and Booth, 1997, p. 183)

However, I know of no epistemological assumption that justifies the expectation that the relationship between different ways of experiencing will necessarily form a 'neat' hierarchy of expanding inclusivity. The expectation of a neat linear hierarchy seems to have arisen out of empirical experience, based on the outcomes of hundreds of studies. So, whilst theoretically, the relationship between different ways of experiencing the same phenomenon need not be strictly hierarchical, in empirical practice it is usually (though not always) found to be.[11] Consistently across studies, some ways of experiencing a phenomenon are found to be more complex than other ways, in that they include or build on the awareness shown in less complex ways of experiencing, whilst including additional aspects.

> ...certain ways of experiencing something are more complex or fuller than others. They spring from the simultaneous awareness of more parts or aspects of the whole. (Marton and Booth, 1997, p. 113)

Whilst this relational perspective, and the associated expectation of hierarchically inclusive structures to phenomenographic outcome spaces, dates back to the early days of phenomenography, following publication of *Learning and Awareness* the search for overlapping awareness relating the different ways of experiencing a phenomenon has become more precise. This is because each way of experiencing a phenomenon is now able to be defined in terms of the critical aspects of the phenomenon discerned, and not discerned, in that

---

[11] There must always be hierarchical elements to a phenomenographic outcome space, but the hierarchy need not always be simple and linear. In my own work, I have constituted some outcome spaces with categories of description that are not all inclusive (e.g., Åkerlind 2003b—also see Chapter 8, Table 8.3). Another example of a non-linear hierarchy can be found in Bowden et al (2005).

way of experiencing.[12] So, the relationships between different ways of experiencing are now able to be described in terms of shared awareness of some of the same critical aspects of the phenomenon, as described in Chapter 2 and Chapter 4. And this overlapping awareness can now be hierarchically ordered in terms of discernment of an increasing number of critical aspects.

> More advanced ways of experiencing something imply simultaneous experience or awareness of *more* aspects of the phenomenon, and less advanced ways of experiencing imply simultaneous experience of *fewer* aspects of the phenomenon. ...less advanced ways of experiencing it are partial in relation to more advanced ways of experiencing it. (Marton and Booth, 1997, p. 107)

In other words, more inclusive ways of experiencing a phenomenon inherently represent more complex and sophisticated[13] ways of experiencing the phenomenon, because they include awareness of some of the same critical aspects of the phenomenon found in less inclusive ways of experiencing, but also show awareness of additional aspects.

Summary of epistemological claims and associated analytic strategies

As was shown in Figure 5.3 above, phenomenography supports multiple ways of analysing the structure of human experience of phenomena—all underpinned by the fundamental assumption of a dialectical relationship between meaning and structure. Whilst no phenomenographic study includes every form of analysis of structure, every phenomenographic study must include *some* form of analysis of structure. The different structural analyses undertaken in phenomenographic research and the epistemological assumptions underlying them are summarised in Table 5.1.

---

12 In phenomenograpic research, what is not discerned in a way of experiencing a phenomenon is as important in creating meaning as what is discerned.
13 In phenomenography, this greater complexity of awareness is also described in terms of greater differentiation, that is, perceiving the phenomenon in more and more differentiated ways.

Table 5.1 Epistemological claims underlying different analytic strategies in phenomenographic research

Epistemological claims	Analytic strategies
A dialectical relationship between meaning and structure in awareness	Separation of human experience into referential and structural aspects
Awareness as inevitably partial and contextually variable	Search for different ways of experiencing the same phenomena as a collective group
Partial and variable awareness leads to figure-ground structures in experience	Search for figure-ground structures, including aspects discerned and not discerned in awareness
Awareness of parts combine to constitute a holistic experience	Part-whole analyses of specific and collective experience of phenomena
Human experience as non-dualistic, a relation between individual and world	Search for inclusive relationships between different ways of experiencing

It is interesting at this point to compare the different types of structural analyses described in this chapter (which were arrived at on a conceptual basis) with those described in the previous chapter (which were arrived at on an empirical-experiential basis). Chapter 4 described five different categories of ways of experiencing structural relationships in phenomenography, with structural relationships varyingly understood as:

1. hierarchical relationships;
2. hierarchically-inclusive relationships;
3. meaning-structure relationships;
4. part-whole relationships; and
5. multi-faceted relationships.

Category 1 is not a phenomenographic perspective, so won't be discussed further here. Category 2 is reflected in this chapter's emphasis on the 'search for inclusive relationships between different ways of experiencing', based on the epistemological assumption of human experience as non-dualistic. Category 3 is reflected in this chapter's emphasis on 'separation of human experience into referential and structural aspects' based on the epistemological assumption of a dialectical relationship between meaning and structure in awareness. Category 4 is reflected in this chapter's emphasis on 'part-whole analyses of specific and collective experience of phenomena' based on the epistemological assumption that awareness of parts combine to create a holistic experience. Category 5, with its emphasis on multi-faceted approaches to looking at structural relationships reflects the overall description presented in this chapter of different ways of analysing for structure in phenomenography. So, to a large extent, the two chapters support each other.

However, there is one analytic strategy that is highlighted in this chapter that has no explicit counterpart in the Chapter 4 empirical study. This is the 'search for figure-ground structures in awareness'. Whilst one respondent did refer to undertaking analyses based on theme and thematic field (which implies a figure-ground structure), this was not described in enough detail to form a clear category. It may well be that figure-ground structural relationships are missing from my Chapter 4 study outcomes due to sampling limitations. Figure-ground analyses are not common in phenomenographic research, and only a minority of phenomenographic researchers undertake such studies, so they may not have been well represented in my sample. It is certainly logically possible for a focus on figure-ground structures to be part of the collective awareness of phenomenographic researchers as a population, even though it was not an obvious part of the collective awareness of my particular sample.

Another interesting point is that, in Figure 5.3, I position the analytic breakdown of the internal horizon of awareness into discerned and undiscerned aspects of phenomena as involving a figure-ground analysis. This analysis is common in phenomenographic research, so why did a focus on figure-ground relationships not emerge in the Chapter 4 study on this basis? I think this is because the identification of critical aspects of phenomena can be experienced as a part-whole analysis rather than a figure-ground analysis. I would argue, however, that it is a part-whole *and* a figure-ground analysis, depending on the perspective you take. If you look at each specific way of experiencing in terms of the critical aspects discerned within that way of experiencing, then this forms a part-whole analysis. That is, an analysis of how awareness of particular critical aspects (parts) constitutes a specific way of experiencing (whole). Alternatively, if you look at each specific way of experiencing in terms of the critical aspects discerned, and not discerned, within that way of experiencing—where what is not discerned is seen as being as significant as what is discerned—then this forms a figure-ground analysis of how awareness of particular critical aspects (figure) and non-awareness of other aspects (ground) constitutes a particular way of experiencing.

Chapter summary

This chapter highlighted the relationship between epistemological assumptions in phenomenography and the analytic strategies employed in phenomenographic methods:

- the assumption of a dialectical relationship between meaning and structure in awareness is associated with the analytic separation of human experience into referential and structural aspects;
- the assumption that awareness is inevitably partial and contextually variable is associated with the analytic search for figure-ground structures in awareness;
- the assumption that awareness of different parts of a phenomenon combine to constitute a holistic experience (or meaning) of the phenomenon is associated with part-whole analyses of different ways of experiencing a phenomenon; and
- the assumption that human experience is non-dualistic is associated with the analytic search for inclusive relationships between different ways of experiencing a phenomenon.

Having described the basic assumptions underlying phenomenographic methods, the next two chapters turn to a detailed description of the methods themselves.

6. Study design, data gathering and the phenomenographic interview

As with any research design, conducting a phenomenographic research study involves:

- determining the object of study and research questions;
- designing methods for gathering data;
- selecting the sample;
- gathering the data;[1]
- analysing the data;
- presenting the outcomes; and
- maintaining research rigour throughout the whole process.

The choice to use phenomenographic methods should be made in conjunction with decisions as to the research project's object of study and the research questions the study is aiming to investigate. The object of study should be the starting point for any decision on which methodology (methods and epistemology) to draw on. Thus, in looking at phenomenographic methods, I will start by discussing how the phenomenon being investigated needs to be clarified and specified, and the type of research questions phenomenography is

---

1   I have chosen to use the term 'data gathering' rather than 'data collection' as part of the general move in interpretive research away from terms that convey an objectivist perspective. This is also why, for example, the term research 'outcomes' is favoured over 'findings' and research 'participants' over 'subjects' in most interpretive research. With phenomenographic research, in particular, data should not be seen as separate from and external to the researcher, but rather as 'constituted' or 'generated' in interaction between the researcher, research participants and the phenomenon being researched, as discussed further in Chapter 7.

designed to address. After that, I will discuss methods for designing interviews (though survey design will also be discussed), selecting a sample of research participants and gathering the data. Approaches to data analysis, reporting of results and ensuring research rigour will be discussed in Chapter 7.

Although very little has been written in the phenomenographic literature about data gathering and analysis at a practical, rather than in-principle level, there is a unique book edited by Bowden and Green (2005) focused on the practical 'doing' of phenomenographic research that I recommend to all readers, *Doing Developmental Phenomenography*. I will draw heavily on this book, plus my own work (some of it published in the book), when discussing methods for gathering data in this chapter, and data analysis in the next chapter.

Determining the object of study

An interest in using phenomenographic methods for a research study usually starts with interest in a particular phenomenon that the researcher wants to learn more about—and that they want to learn more about it from the perspective of how people experience it. But what is meant by a 'phenomenon' and by 'experience'? These are important questions that cannot simply be taken-for-granted, because a primary source of poor examples of phenomenographic research-in-action is a misunderstanding of what phenomenography means by a phenomenon and by experience (as will be discussed further below).

The phenomenon the researcher is interested in may be something that is not yet clearly understood, like being 'woke' or 'hip', or is just not clearly understood by certain groups of people, like students or novices. Alternatively, the phenomenon may have a clear formal definition, and there may be a taken-for-granted sense that 'everybody' knows what it means (at least amongst the specific community the researcher is interested in), but the researcher has a sense that there is actually unacknowledged variation in what the phenomenon of interest means to people in that community—how they experience it and how they understand it—and that this is worthy of investigation. For example, most university academics take for granted that they know what teaching means, what research means and what learning is, most engineers take for granted that they know what it means to be an engineer, or doctors a doctor, lawyers a lawyer, musicians a musician, etc. Yet, all have been objects of phenomenographic studies that showed substantial variation in the experienced meaning of these phenomena.

Having decided on a phenomenon of interest, the researcher then needs to clarify and specify the phenomenon with precision. For example, one of my research students, Lance Eaton, was interested in the experiences of scholars engaged in what is called 'academic piracy' (accessing academic literature from illegal sites). But over time, he clarified that the phenomenon of interest in his study was not the varied meanings of academic piracy per se, but of 'academic pirate networks', and more precisely, 'the use of academic pirate networks by scholars'. So, in the end, he was not investigating the different meanings of academic piracy for scholars, but the different meanings of using academic pirate networks for scholars.

This precision about the phenomenon under study is not usually made in advance of setting research questions and interview/survey questions, but in interaction with setting those questions. Research questions and interview/survey questions need to be constantly checked against the stated object of study while being designed, to make sure there have not been unintentional deviations from the phenomenon being studied, and if there have, then either the questions or the phenomenon being studied need to be reconsidered before gathering the data.

Another of my research students, Laura Killam, was interested in the experiences of students taking part in an educational innovation, the 'co-creation' of course materials by students and teachers. But because students can also co-create with each other, not just with their teachers, the phenomenon of 'co-creation' was more precisely specified as 'learner-educator co-creation'. Then, because she was exploring one specific example of this in one of her own courses (an assessment activity involving designing a simulated case study of the ability of socio-economically disadvantaged groups to access social services), the phenomenon was more precisely specified as 'learner-educator co-creation of a virtual simulation assessment item'.

Now, we would expect Laura's research outcomes to have implications for students' ways of experiencing co-creation in other settings and with other components of a course, just as we would expect Lance's research outcomes to have implications for scholars' ways of experiencing the broader concept of academic piracy, but such expectations become part of the discussion of the implications of their study outcomes, not part of the precise clarification of the phenomenon being studied.

The dangers of not clarifying a precise object of study or phenomenon when undertaking phenomenographic research may be illustrated through a study by Hajar (2020). This study was published as an example of phenomenographic research, but in fact, is not.[2] (Sadly, it is not uncommon for studies to be published claiming to be phenomenographic but which do not really meet the criteria for a phenomenographic study—see Åkerlind, 2022, 2024a). One reason that Hajar's study does not represent phenomenographic research is because he did not define a precise object of study. In his article, Hajar describes the phenomenon under study as participants' 'international academic experiences'. This could feasibly be a phenomenographic object of study, if participants were asked to describe and present personal examples of what they think constitutes an international academic experience. But Hajar investigated international academic experiences in terms of 'expectations, academic socialisation and strategy use' during one particular type of international experience, a ten-week English language course for international academics. Again, if Hajar had focused on the different ways in which participants experienced this same international experience, in terms of the experienced meaning and purpose of the course for participants as academics, this could still have constituted a phenomenographic study. But his decision to focus on 'expectations, academic socialisation and strategy-use', which clearly represent multiple phenomena, not a single phenomenon, precluded

---

[2] I do not mean to pick on Hajar in particular in illustrating my point. He is but one of many researchers who have misunderstood phenomenography, and I am used to seeing such misunderstandings in reports of empirical research. But empirical articles are most commonly read by people interested in the phenomenon being researched rather than the method being used. In contrast, Hajar went on to publish an article on phenomenography itself, Theoretical foundations of phenomenography (Hajar, 2021), likely to be read by research students and others interested in phenomenography as a methodology. I am concerned that this may then mislead those new to phenomenography, so feel that limitations in his approach need to be pointed out. Other methodological articles that concern me are by Straub and Maynes (2021) and Feldon and Tofel-Grehl (2018), but I will discuss these later in the book.

taking a phenomenographic approach to the research and meant that his research outcomes were not phenomenographic.

Furthermore, as explained in Chapter 5 and illustrated in Chapter 2 and Chapter 4, phenomenographic outcomes are supposed to represent qualitatively different ways of experiencing, understanding or ascribing meaning to the phenomenon being investigated. So, if the phenomenon in Hajar's study is 'international academic experiences', then the categories of description in the study outcomes should represent different ways of understanding, or different meanings for, what constitutes an international academic experience. However, the two categories of description he presented were: (1) impact of formal social actors; and (2) participants' expectations and altering learning goals. These categories do not represent a way of experiencing, as they do not describe what an international academic experience might mean to different participants. That is, it does not make sense to say that having an international academic experience was experienced as 'the impact of formal social actors' or as 'participants' expectations and altering learning goals'. In addition, these categories do not refer to different ways of understanding the same phenomenon, but to different phenomena, i.e., social actors and learning goals.

Another consideration in selecting an object of study is whether the researcher(s) have the appropriate knowledge base needed to observe and interpret nuances in the data. In short, if you are exploring a specialised phenomenon, then you will need specialised knowledge to bring to the analysis. For example, with the study presented in Chapter 4 on different ways of experiencing structural relationships in phenomenography, the data would have been difficult to interpret if I did not have an understanding of what was being referred to when participants mentioned inclusive hierarchies, part-whole structures, a dialectical relationship between meaning and structure, and the theme, thematic field and margin of awareness. In short, when conducting the analysis, you have to have enough knowledge of the phenomenon under study to be able to understand what the participants are talking about. At the same time, of course, it is vital to be sensitive to the ways in which your pre-existing understandings may impose expectations on the data and influence your interpretations in inappropriate ways—as discussed further in Chapter 7 on data analysis.

What is a phenomenon?

Marton (1981a) initially defined a phenomenon as an 'aspect of the world', i.e., as a component part of the world. Since then, the nature of a phenomenon has been largely taken-for-granted in the phenomenographic literature. But to provide a more precise description, I would say that a phenomenon is anything, conceptual or physical, that human beings are capable of experiencing as a bounded entity, that is, as something that is separate from something else and can be given its own label. What constitutes a phenomenon is socially agreed upon, and in a phenomenographic study it is socially agreed upon amongst the researchers and the study participants. This means that what is regarded as a phenomenon can change with context and social group. For example, when considering 'cars' as a phenomenon in the world, then in that context, the colour of a car is not a separate phenomenon but just a part or aspect of the phenomenon of cars. But when considering 'colour' as a concept then, in that context, colour becomes a phenomenon in its own right. (See Åkerlind, 2022, for further discussion of and illustrations of the nature of a phenomenon in phenomenographic research.)

As described in Chapter 5, from an experiential perspective, the phenomena we experience are not regarded as pre-existent in the world (at least, not in the way we experience them), but arise out of our interaction with the world. It is important to conceptually distinguish between the notion of 'phenomena' as representing entities out there in the world independent of human existence, and 'phenomena' as they are experienced by humans. The former is a dualistic perspective, with phenomena and human experience regarded as separate entities in the world. The latter is a non-dualistic perspective (also called a relational perspective), with phenomena and human experience regarded as inherently related, or interconnected, through the nature of experience. Any experience is an experience of something by someone. The something and the someone may be separate, but the experience itself is inevitably interconnected, a relationship between the two. So, from the perspective of human experience of the world, humans and world are interconnected, not separate.

Marton and Booth (1997) describe this non-dualistic, or relational, perspective as both an ontological (nature of existence) and an epistemological (nature of knowledge) assumption underlying phenomenography. However, my experience is that, whilst it is usually easy for researchers to understand non-dualism as an epistemological assumption, in terms of how humans develop knowledge of the world, some have more trouble understanding it from an ontological perspective. Indeed, the very language used by Marton and Booth (and in many other phenomenographic publications, including my own) often implies dualism—for example, references to 'human experience of the world' implies the existence of a world separate from human experience of it. Nevertheless, phenomenographic ontology is not focused on the nature of 'existence' independent of humans, but on the nature of 'human existence'. So, if you are struggling with the notion of non-dualism ontologically, you need to distinguish in your mind between 'the world' and 'the human world'. In phenomenographic philosophy, we are not discussing ontology in terms of the world per se, but in terms of the human world, because this is the only world we can ever know or experience.

> The world we deal with is the world as experienced by people … it is a world we experience, a world in which we live, a world that is ours. (Marton and Booth, 1997, p. 13)

What is meant by 'experience'?

Unfortunately, the term, experience, is ambiguous. For instance, think about the different meanings implied by the terms, 'experience', 'an experience' and 'a way of experiencing'.[3] This ambiguity in meaning has often led to misinterpretations of what phenomenography means by experience. In everyday usage, when we talk about how we experience something, we are commonly using the term synonymously with feelings, attitudes and perceptions of the phenomenon, e.g., "That was a most unpleasant experience!". But in phenomenography, we use experience synonymously with meaning, understanding and making sense of the phenomenon. What we are studying is not experience per se, but different 'ways of experiencing' the

---

3   Dahlin (2007) provides an example of how the ambiguity in the everyday meaning of the word, experience, can lead to misinterpretation of what phenomenographers are commonly referring to when they use the word (see p. 332).

same phenomena. As described by Marton (1988), whilst in everyday language a distinction is drawn between 'immediate experience' and 'conceptual thought', this is not the case in phenomenography.

> In our phenomenographic approach we do not use the distinction [between immediate experience and conceptual thought], at least not as a starting point. We are trying to describe relations between the individual and various aspects of the world, regardless of whether relations are manifested in the form of immediate experience, conceptual thought, or behavior. (Marton, 1988, p. 194)

In the early stages of the development of phenomenography, the most common term used to describe the object of study was different 'conceptions' of phenomena. But this term reduced in popularity over time due to the cognitive associations with the term, which are misleading in a phenomenographic context. Different 'ways of experiencing' a phenomenon then took over as the most common term for the object of study, but this also has misleading associations in terms of bringing to mind people's feelings, attitudes and beliefs about the phenomenon. So, there is no perfect term. I generally use the terms, 'ways of understanding' or 'ways of experiencing', but occasionally also 'conceptions', depending on the context. So, the term you use in your research can vary, but whatever term you choose when reporting a phenomenographic study, it is important to explain what you mean by it.

In explaining the ambiguous and varying terminology used to describe the object of study in phenomenography, Marton and Pong (2005) explain that,

> A conception, the basic unit of description in phenomenographic research, has been called various names, such as 'ways of conceptualizing', 'ways of experiencing', 'ways of seeing', 'ways of apprehending', 'ways of understanding', and so on. ... The reason for using so many different synonyms is that although none of them corresponds completely to what we have in mind, they all do to a certain extent. (Marton and Pong, 2005, p. 336)

I have put this a little differently:

> In phenomenography, a number of terms are used largely interchangeably to refer to the object of study. For instance, a 'way of experiencing' a phenomenon in the world is regarded as a way of making sense of the phenomenon or experiencing its meaning. This is on the basis that, in

order to know what we are experiencing, we need to be able to assign a meaning to it. Experience and meaning are seen as constituted on the basis of our awareness. So, a way of experiencing a phenomenon is also a way of being aware of it (or different aspects of it), which is also a way of understanding it, which is the meaning it holds for us. (Åkerlind, 2024b)

Given its stated focus on human experience, phenomenography has occasionally been criticised for its prevalent use of interview data, on the basis that interviews create an artificial context, rather than looking at human experience in a naturally occurring context (e.g., Mishler, 1980, cited in Marton 1988; Säljö, 1996, 1997).[4] Whilst agreeing that experience is always contextually situated, Marton (1988) clarifies that phenomenography is not studying the natural world of participants as such, but how people experience or think about particular phenomena in their world (see Chapter 2). Categories of description, as the expected outcomes of phenomenographic research, are intended to represent human experience of a phenomenon reduced to its key distinguishing characteristics, not the richness and naturalness of the human world.

Clarifying the research questions

As described in Chapter 2, the types of research questions addressed by 21st-century phenomenography are:

a. What are the qualitatively different ways in which the same phenomenon can be understood?

b. What critical aspects of the phenomenon are discerned (and not discerned) within each way of understanding it?

---

4   Säljö (1996, 1997) also argued that the use of interviews to access personal meaning ignores the socially-determined nature of discourse, and that the interview thus reflects social practice rather than personal meaning. It seems to me that interviews must reflect social practice *and* personal meaning, or at the least, the meaning participants ascribe to that social practice. This implies that meaning can still be accessed via interview, as long as it is an interrogative interview and not one that takes what participants say at face value. This further highlights the importance of the follow-up questions in phenomenographic interviews (see below), which ask participants to explain the meaning behind what they have said, and is thus disruptive of usual social discourse.

c. How are the different ways of understanding related in a structure of expanding awareness of an increasing number of critical aspects of the phenomenon?

But the kind of language used in this statement of phenomenographic research questions is rather esoteric and not likely to be meaningful to the kind of broad audience researchers attempt to reach in doctoral dissertations and publications. So, you may choose to phrase the research questions differently if you wish. For example, to reach a broader audience, Question (a) could be rephrased as, 'How do [the participant community] experience [the phenomenon]?' or 'What are the range of ways in which [the phenomenon] is understood/experienced?' or 'What do [participant community] mean by [phenomenon]?'. Question (b) could be rephrased as, 'What distinguishes the different meanings/ understandings?' or 'What do some [members of participant community] notice about [the phenomenon] that others do not?'. Question (c) is often rephrased as, 'What is the relationship between the different ways of experiencing?' or 'How are the different understandings related?' or 'What links the different meanings of [the phenomenon]?' Questions (b) and (c) can also be combined into one question, for example, 'What are the similarities and differences between the different ways of understanding [the phenomenon]?', 'How are these understandings distinguished from and related to each other?' or 'What links and separates the different meanings of [the phenomenon]?'

Irrespective of the phrasing of the research questions, to use phenomenographic methodology, you as a researcher must be interested in variation in how people see the world (what some people see about a situation or phenomenon that others do not). You must also be interested in relationships across the variation (what links and separates these different ways of seeing). In particular, you must be interested in 'structural relationships', that is, how the meaning of the phenomenon is constituted through a part-whole structure of awareness of different parts of the phenomenon (in terms of awareness of different critical aspects of the phenomenon). If you are not interested in these questions, then phenomenography is not the methodology for you.

Lastly, underlying any research question is not just what you want to know, but also why you want to know it, which relates to how you intend to use that knowledge or the ways in which you hope others will use it. Indeed, one of the suggested ways of evaluating the success of a phenomenographic research project is in terms of whether the research outcomes are useful for their intended purpose (Entwistle, 1997).

Research for educational purposes is the predominant purpose for most phenomenographic research, with a focus on investigating variation in understandings of teaching, learning and subject matter. But phenomenographic research has also been conducted with the aim of informing our understanding of the nature of professional work (for example, medical practice—Yu and Åkerlind, 2024; healthcare—Röing et al., 2018; employment counselling—Värk and Reino, 2018; accounting—Sin et al., 2011; nursing—Forbes, 2011; academic research—Åkerlind, 2008a; law—Reid et al., 2006; quality management—Hyrkäs et al., 2003; engine optimisation—Sandberg, 2001), as well as the nature of professional development in different professions (for example, physicians—Cuyvers et al., 2016; army medics—Andersson et al., 2013; and academia—Åkerlind, 2005e).

But phenomenographic research may also be undertaken for pure rather than applied research purposes, that is, an interest in simply informing our understanding of the ways in which humans collectively experience different phenomena. For example, in my own research, I have looked at academic freedom (Åkerlind and Kayrooz, 2003), with the sole aim of coming to understand why the concept may be spoken of so differently by different communities (for example, politicians *vs* academics). And I have investigated variation in university academics' understandings of the nature of research (Akerlind, 2008a), in an attempt to complement the numerous studies of academics' understandings of teaching and further our collective knowledge of the nature of academic work as a whole.

From the beginning, two primary purposes for phenomenographic research were proposed: improvement of teaching and learning, and insight into the 'collective mind' of humanity (Marton, 1981a), which we might also call collective awareness. Marton called research with the latter intention 'pure phenomenography' (Marton, 1986, 1988) and Bowden called research with the former intention 'developmental phenomenography' (Bowden, 1994 [2000]; 1996; Bowden and Green, 2010). The two terms are only rarely used nowadays, nevertheless the distinction they draw in the intended purpose of one's research can be useful. Phenomenography's potential to provide insight into teaching and learning is discussed in more detail in Chapter 9, and its potential to provide insight into collective awareness is discussed in more detail in Chapter 10.

> **Research aside:**
>
> **The special case of longitudinal research in phenomenography**
>
> There have been a number of longitudinal studies undertaken using phenomenographic methods. Such studies address a different type of research question to traditional phenomenographic research, intending to investigate potential change in individuals' ways of experiencing a phenomenon over time. But this raises the question of whether longitudinal studies can then be seen as in line with phenomenographic principles. My short answer, which I will explain in more detail below, is 'no'. Longitudinal research questions and data analysis inevitably deviate from the foci of phenomenography.
>
> But does this mean longitudinal studies using phenomenography should not be conducted? Of course not! Such studies have provided valuable insights into different objects of study (e.g., Marton et al., 1993; Ashwin et al., 2014; Ashwin et al., 2023; de Búrca, 2024). But I would describe such longitudinal studies as mixed methods research.[5] There is nothing wrong with combining other research methods with phenomenography (as illustrated in Chapter 10). However, longitudinal studies should ideally describe themselves as using mixed methods, rather than simply phenomenographic methods, and explain where the study deviates from traditional phenomenography (e.g., Ashwin et al., 2014).
>
> To help, I have identified three ways in which longitudinal studies commonly differ from phenomenographic methods:
>
> 1. *First-order vs second-order research questions*—In longitudinal studies the nature of the research question changes, or perhaps more accurately, an additional research question is asked. Typically, longitudinal data collection with the same set of participants is

---

5   An interesting article that discusses and illustrates phenomenography's potential to support mixed qualitative and quantitative methods is by Feldon and Tofel-Grehl (2018). However, whilst useful, the article needs to be read cautiously because the authors show some misunderstandings of phenomenography.

intended to address the question of whether change in ways of experiencing a phenomenon has occurred in response to a particular educational experience or intervention. This question involves a first-order, not a second-order, research perspective (even when based on the outcomes of second-order research).

2. *Focus on individual vs collective experience*—Answering a longitudinal question typically involves viewing each interview transcript as not only representative of a way of experiencing, but also representative of a particular individual and their particular way of experiencing (at that point in time and context). In this way, from a longitudinal perspective each interview transcript ceases to be viewed as just one element within a larger whole, and is considered as a whole in its own right.

3. *Quantitative vs qualitative analysis*—It is common (though not universal) for statistical analyses to be applied to longitudinal data to assess how frequently a change in ways of experiencing has been recorded, and sometimes also whether this frequency can be regarded as representing a reliable trend statistically. This moves the research from an interpretive to a quantitative focus.

For example, the first longitudinal study using phenomenographic research that I am aware of was by Marton et al. (1993). In this study, a sample of university students were interviewed annually about their view of 'learning' over a period of six years. A phenomenographic analysis was undertaken on the interview data, resulting in an outcome space of six inclusively related ways of experiencing 'learning'. The research then shifted from a phenomenographic focus to a focus on longitudinal change, with an accompanying shift in methods. As described by Marton et al., "Once the set of categories of description has been arrived at, they can be systematically applied to the same data from which they sprang (or to any other similar set of data for that matter). We can thereby classify the students, or rather classify the [students'] views that have been expressed in the interviews. As the same student may express different conceptions in the same interview, we must introduce a rule for handling this problem... namely, for each student, register the 'highest' conception expressed on each occasion" (pp. 294–295).

This approach was then seen as allowing for statistical analysis of the resulting data. On this basis, a developmental trend was identified, in that

> 'higher' (more complex) conceptions were found to be more common in later interviews than earlier interviews, indicating a development in the complexity of students' views of the nature of learning in response to time spent in study at the university.
>
> To illustrate variation in approaches to longitudinal studies, I would also like to present an unusual example from a recent doctoral thesis (de Búrca, 2024). De Búrca's approach to longitudinal analysis is more closely aligned with phenomenographic foci than is usual for such studies. Instead of investigating longitudinal change at the individual level, she investigated it at the collective level, by comparing the two outcome spaces that resulted from analysis of data gathered from the same sample before and after an educational intervention (see de Búrca's Figure 4, p. 196). Her outcomes showed that the least complex way of understanding the phenomenon seen in the sample before the intervention was no longer evident after the intervention. At the same time, a new and more complex way of understanding emerged in the post-intervention outcome space that had not been seen in the pre-intervention outcome space. These outcomes indicate a collective development (rather than the usual focus on individual development) in the complexity of students' ways of experiencing after the intervention.

Gathering data

The traditional and most common type of data gathered for phenomenographic research are semi-structured, in-depth interviews. But phenomenographic research is not limited to this form of data. Open-ended survey questions are not unusual (as illustrated in Chapter 3 and Chapter 4), and other written forms of data are also used, e.g., mock letters to a friend (Hella, 2008) or document analysis (Kettunen, 2024). More innovative forms of data and data combinations also occur, for example, combining interviews with use of photographs (Carlsson, 1999; Collier-Reed, 2006), concept maps (Yu, 2019) and gestures (Herbert and Pierce, 2013, as cited in Tight, 2016). But this chapter will focus on interview design and analysis, as this is the traditional and most common approach to gathering data in phenomenography. Nevertheless, the same principles can be carried across to other forms of data.

Phenomenographic interviews are usually undertaken with individual participants and then combined into collective or group data for analysis (as discussed in the next chapter). This raises the question of whether interviews could be conducted at the group level to begin with, for example, in the form of focus group interviews. However, this is not normally an option for phenomenographic research because, when participants respond to questions as a group they normally influence each other in their responses, even when there is debate. This conflicts with the phenomenographic aim of sampling as much variation in views as possible (as described below). The aim is to gather maximal variation in views, not reach consensus on a view.

Selecting participants

Phenomenographic interviews commonly aim for a sample of 10–30 participants (Trigwell, 2000 [1994]; Bowden, 2005; Collier-Reed et al., 2013; Kullberg and Ingerman, 2022). Small sample sizes are necessary because phenomenographic interviews typically generate a lot of data. With my doctoral research for instance, I had 28 participants, which may seem like a small sample size to some, but the interviews typically took 60–90 minutes and resulted in transcripts of 25–35 pages each, resulting in over 800 pages of text to analyse.[6]

Research participants are selected from a particular community or 'population'. In this sense, phenomenographic research is not looking just at variation in understanding of a particular phenomenon, but variation in understanding of a particular phenomenon within a particular community. Are they experts, students, the general public,

---

6   Whilst a target sample size is usually specified in advance of gathering data, there are also phenomenographic researchers who claim not to specify sample size in advance but to make the decision on the basis of the data gathered. In these cases, researchers describe continuing to gather interview data until 'saturation' of variation has been reached, or until no new variation is seen in the data, indicated by new participants starting to repeat the same understandings already expressed by previous participants. Whilst this sounds possible in principle, I have trouble seeing how issues of saturation can be determined during the data gathering phase, because it is only during analysis that what represents critical and non-critical variation, and what represents different ways of understanding the phenomenon can be determined. So, my own practice is to set a target sample size in advance.

a particular cultural or socio-economic group, etc.? Sometimes, for convenience, the sample is chosen from a subset of the larger community you are actually interested in. For example, you may be interested in all students, but select from just fourth-grade students, science students, or students from one particular institution, because this is the group you can most easily access. This will then have implications for the potential relevance, applicability or 'transferability', of your research outcomes to other communities and subsets of communities, which you should reflect on when reporting your outcomes (discussed further in Chapter 7).

Within the boundaries of the community (or subset) you have chosen, you must then aim for as great a heterogeneity of prior experience with the phenomenon as possible, because variation in exposure to a phenomenon is likely to lead to discernment of different aspects of the phenomenon (and thus variation in ways of experiencing it), and the aim of phenomenographic data gathering is to capture variation. As described in Chapter 5, the different contexts in which a phenomenon is experienced are likely to foreground and background different aspects of the phenomenon, leading to different aspects being discerned in different contexts. So, consider what sort of demographics and contextual situations you think are likely to lead to variation in experience with the phenomenon, and try to select participants to represent that range of demographic and contextual variation. Returning to my own doctoral research as an example, I was interviewing university academics, and participants in my sample were selected to represent varied disciplines, cultural backgrounds and gender, plus varying levels of work experience as an academic and varying conditions of appointment. These were all demographic factors that I anticipated would have led to varying experience, or exposure, to different aspects of the phenomenon I was studying (academic work and academic development).

If you are not in a position to actively select participants for demographic variation, for example if you are dependent on volunteers, then you should still record the demographic variation that eventuates within your sample and include this in your report of the research. Reporting the variation present within the sample is important for readers of the research, so that they can consider the similarity of your sample to the communities and settings that they are interested in. So, the ways in which you will document demographic variation also needs to be considered as part of your methods.

> **Analytic aside**
>
> I am using the word *experience* in two different (though related) ways here, to refer to potential variation in experience based on external criteria (i.e., demographic criteria) and to refer to potential variation in experience based on relational criteria (i.e., participant descriptions). On this basis, it might be better to think of variation in experience based on external criteria as 'exposure to variation' in the phenomenon, and variation in experience based on relational criteria as 'discernment of variation' in the phenomenon—because it is possible to be exposed to variation without necessarily discerning that variation. So, for any one participant, whether demographically based exposure to variation in experience with the phenomenon is matched by actual discernment of that variation is unknown, but across a group of participants, we can expect that such discernment will have occurred. This is another reason for the phenomenographic focus on collective rather than individual experience. To the extent that the variation within the sample reflects the variation within the selected community, it is expected that the range of understandings within the sample will be representative of the range of understandings within the community.

It is important to be clear here about what phenomenography means by the 'representativeness' of a sample, because it is different to common usage. A sample of participants is always selected to represent the community from which it was drawn, and the extent of representativeness then has implications for the potential transferability of the research outcomes to the larger community. But the standard criteria for judging the representativeness of a sample comes from quantitative research and aims for representativeness in terms of matching the frequency of different demographic characteristics in the sample with that in the community (e.g., if women represent 50% of the community, they should also represent 50% of the sample). But this form of representativeness is not appropriate for phenomenography. Instead, phenomenography aims for representativeness in terms of variation, not frequency. In other words, is the range of ways of experiencing that you can expect to find in the community represented in the sample? On this basis, we select for variation in exposure to the phenomenon as our best proxy for variation in ways of experiencing the phenomenon.

Furthermore, the point of selecting a heterogeneous sample in phenomenographic research is to be able to describe and relate the variation in understanding, not to attempt to explain the variation through demographic factors. Phenomenography does not draw causal relationships between demographic factors and variation in understanding, but constitutive relationships, i.e., how our understanding of phenomena is constituted on the basis of our experience or awareness of different aspects of phenomena.

Designing interview questions

Semi-structured interviews consist of a mix of pre-determined (structured) questions and follow-up (unstructured) questions that arise in response to participants' replies to the structured questions. But in phenomenography, whilst the pre-determined questions provide an overall structure to the interview, it is the unstructured follow-up questions that elicit the more important data—as I will describe further below.

Pre-determined questions generally fall into three types: (1) 'introductory' scene setting or background questions; (2) 'open' questions about participants' understanding of the phenomenon; and (3) questions seeking 'concrete examples' of participants' own interactions with the phenomenon.[7] This is followed by unstructured follow-up questions exploring participants' experience of the phenomenon based on their responses during the concrete examples.

> This type of interview should not have too many questions made up in advance, and nor should there be too many details determined in advance. Most questions follow from what the [participant] says. The point is to establish the phenomenon as experienced and to explore its different aspects jointly and as fully as possible. The starting question may aim directly at the general phenomenon such as, for instance,

---

7   Elsewhere, I have also called these 'contextual' questions, 'open' questions and 'situated examples' (Åkerlind, 2005c).

when asking the [participant] after some general discussion, "What do you mean by learning, by the way?". Alternatively, it is possible to ask the [participant] to come up with instances of the general phenomenon, asking for example, "Can you tell me something you have learned?". Most often, however, a concrete case makes up the point of departure: a text to be read, a well-known situation to be discussed, or a problem to be solved. The [interviewer] then tries to encourage the [participants] to reflect on the text, the situation or the problem, and often also on their way of dealing with it. (Marton, 1994, pp. 4427–4428)

The use of real examples that participants have actually experienced is vital. Concrete examples may be generated within the interview by asking participants to complete a task in relation to the phenomenon or reflect on a previously experienced event or action involving the phenomenon and using this as the basis for discussion. The event may be specified by the interviewer (as long as participants have actually experienced it) or participants may be asked to come up with their own examples of a previously experienced event.

Participant reflection on the way they engaged with the phenomenon during one or more concrete examples then becomes the focus of the rest of the interview, because the most informative data is elicited from actual instances of participants interacting with the phenomenon. As described by Bowden (2005),

> When 'what is X' questions are asked in such phenomenographic interviews, the outcomes tend to be less varied and more or less reflect the standard, espoused theories available in the literature. On the other hand, when people are asked to describe their own direct experiences, their immersion in that detail often reveals a much greater variation across the interviews in ways of seeing. ... [In addition] It is easier to get people to describe something they've experienced than to get them to philosophise about an issue to which they might not have given much thought before. So you get a much deeper insight into how the interviewees actually see the [phenomenon] in practice as well as have an opportunity to explore and probe in a comfortable and non-threatening way—given that you are asking for more information about their actual experiences rather than appearing to be 'testing' their theoretical knowledge. (pp. 17–18)

Introductory questions

Introductory questions may be designed to gather demographic information, start the process of encouraging the participant to reflect on their experience of the phenomenon being investigated, or put the interviewee at ease and make the transition into the interview proper seem more natural and conversation-like. For example, in my doctoral interviews on academic work and academic development, the introductory question was, "First, by way of context, can you tell me what your current appointment is and a little about your history as an academic". Similarly, in the survey of different ways of understanding phenomenography described in Chapter 3, the introductory question was, "As background, could you first briefly summarise your experience with phenomenography?". (This background information was then also used to help determine which demographic categories participants fell into.)

Open questions

Open questions are intended to give participants the opportunity to focus on whichever aspects of the phenomenon initially appear most significant to them. Such questions often take the form of, "What does [the phenomenon] mean to you?". For example, in my doctoral interviews, immediately after the introductory question, I asked, "Based on your experiences so far, what does it mean to you to be an academic?". Similarly, in the survey of different ways of understanding phenomenography described in Chapter 3, I first asked, "What interests you about phenomenography?"

Whilst open questions like these are encouraged by some researchers (e.g., Bowden, 2005), on the basis that they allow the direction of the interview to be guided by participants rather than researchers, they are discouraged by other researchers. For example, although for a long time supportive of 'What does [the phenomenon] mean to you' questions (Marton, 1994), Marton moved over time to discouraging such questions (Marton, 2015), on the basis that they do not demarcate the phenomenon of study as precisely as discussing a common task or event—for example, setting a common problem or task for participants to complete, and designing the interview around discussion of how they went about solving the problem or approaching the task.

As I have said before, there is accepted variation in phenomenographic practice. And whilst I agree that having a common task or scenario encourages participants to focus on the same phenomenon in a more precise way, it is also clear to me that there have been many successful phenomenographic studies with useful outcomes that allow participants to select varied tasks or events involving the phenomenon for discussion during the interview. And with regard to 'What does [the phenomenon] mean to you' questions, I think the issue is not so much that such questions need to be avoided, as that they cannot stand on their own and must be accompanied by questions based on one or more situated examples of the phenomenon.

Further, as described in Chapter 5, phenomenography anticipates variation in experience of a phenomenon to be associated with variation in the context in which it is experienced. So, although the attempt to provide as common a context for discussion of the phenomenon as possible ensures a more precise object of study, it also reduces the range of contexts in which understandings of that phenomenon are considered. So, I would say that whether the researcher sets a common concrete example for exploring the phenomenon with participants, or allows participants to set their own and varied concrete examples, depends on the nature of the research question and the anticipated situations in which the research outcomes are expected to be used.

Having said that, where I think all phenomenographers would be in agreement is that individuals' ways of experiencing the phenomenon are best illuminated through exploring real instances of the ways in which they relate to the phenomenon. So, whether or not one starts an interview or survey with open questions, it is then important to proceed to concrete examples of participants acting in relation to the phenomenon.

Concrete examples

Although I am someone who often uses open questions in my research, I would never make these a sole focus of analysis. The primary focus of analysis always lies in concrete examples of participants' personal actions or interactions with the phenomenon, and the explanations they provide for these actions/interactions in response to follow-up questions during the interview. For example, in my doctoral interviews, the open question was immediately followed by, "Can you give me a concrete example of something you do as an academic?". And after the response to that question had been explored, "Can you give me another example?". Similarly, in the survey on understandings of phenomenography described in Chapter 3, after my introductory and opening questions, I asked "How do you use phenomenography?" as an attempt to draw out concrete examples.

There are multiple reasons for the focus on concrete examples. More generic descriptions of what participants think about a phenomenon (such as those often provided in response to open questions) run the danger of reflecting what respondents think most people would say about the phenomenon or what they think the interviewer wants to hear, rather than the participant's personal understanding of the phenomenon. In addition, there is no reason to think that respondents are consciously aware of or able to clearly articulate their own understanding of a phenomenon. Using follow-up questions to work through concrete examples provides a way of accessing this understanding for both the researcher and the participant. It is not unusual for participants to say during an interview that they had not previously thought about a question the interviewer has just asked, and to say at the end of an interview that they now have a much clearer view of their own understanding of the phenomenon than they did before the interview.

Follow-up questions

Whilst concrete examples are essential to the interview, the majority of the interview will be taken up by unstructured questions designed to follow up on the concrete examples. Indeed, the most revealing parts of the whole interview are participants' responses to the unstructured follow-up questions, because this is where the detail of their ways of experiencing and thinking about the phenomenon becomes evident.

The back-and-forth nature of participant responses and interviewer follow-up questions is why phenomenographic interviews are often described as a 'dialogue' between interviewer and interviewee.

> The interview has to be carried out as a dialogue. It should facilitate the thematization of aspects of the [participant's] experience ... These experiences and understandings are neither there prior to the interview ready to be 'read off', nor are they only situational constructions. They are aspects of the [participant's] awareness that change from being unreflected to being reflected. (Marton, 1994, p. 4427)

It is through the follow-up questions that it becomes *im*possible for participants to simply give a generic description of what they think about the phenomenon based on social conventions, or what they think most people would say, or what they think the interviewer may want to hear. It is also through responses to the follow-up questions that participants' understandings of the phenomenon most clearly emerges. And the greatest limitation of survey *vs* interview data is that surveys do not enable follow-up questions.

However, this process of encouraging participants to reflect on the phenomenon through follow-up questions is often misunderstood. As I have discussed in a paper on common misunderstandings of phenomenography (Åkerlind, 2024a), this process has often been described as bringing interviewees into a state of 'meta-awareness' with respect to the phenomenon. The term meta-awareness can create the false impression that phenomenographic researchers think interview participants can become so reflectively aware of their way of thinking about a phenomenon that they become able to simply articulate it for the researcher. This is far from the case.[8] Interviewees are not expected to be able to explicitly articulate their understanding. Nor is what they

---

8   Occasional reference to phenomenographic interviews as having a 'therapeutic' element (Svensson and Theman, 1983; Marton and Booth, 1997) can also create a misleading impression, and has led to criticism on ethical grounds if the interviews are indeed intended to create a psychotherapeutic experience for participants (Richardson, 1999). But phenomenographic interviews are not intended to be therapeutic in any clinical sense. All that is meant by the analogy with therapy is that the intense focus on follow-up questions in phenomenographic interviews may sometimes make participants uncomfortable, and that through the course of reflecting on those questions, participants may realise things about the phenomenon that they had not noticed before.

are able to say about their understanding taken at face value. It is well accepted in phenomenography that the same words or phrases can be used to express different meanings, while different words and phrases can be used to express the same meaning. Consequently, a major role of the interviewer is to continually check for the meaning underlying the language used by the interviewee, through follow-up questions such as, "What do you mean by that?".

Even when interviewers think that what participants mean by a statement is obvious, as a point of rigour the meaning should be double-checked as much as possible within the time limits of the interview. However, it can feel socially uncomfortable at times to double-check meaning when you (and the interviewee) think the meaning is obvious. Green (2005) described overcoming this discomfort by 'playing naïve' (see below). Alternatively, I often simply say to the participant that I think I know what they mean, but it is important to hear it in their own words, so could they please explain what they mean by 'X'. (I can also testify that, at times, I have found that my confidence that I had understood what participants meant by something they said was misplaced, and this only became apparent after I asked them to explain what they meant.)

The idea that any one participant can simply describe their way of understanding to the interviewer also goes against the methodological assumptions of phenomenography, in particular the assumption that what one person says about a phenomenon can only be understood (from a collective perspective) in comparison with what other people say about it. So, the understanding of a phenomenon expressed within an individual interview can never be understood in isolation.

In the design of follow-up questions, it is important that they be phrased in a neutral or 'open' manner, with the intention of exploring participants' responses without leading them in any particular direction. For example, common follow-up questions that I use include:

- Why did you do that?
- Why did you do it that way?
- What would happen if you didn't do that?
- What were you hoping to achieve?

- Why is that important to you?
- Tell me more about that.

But there are also acceptable ways of following up on something the participant has said that are more leading, for example:

- When you say 'X', what do you mean by that?
- How does 'X' relate to what you said earlier about 'Y'?

While such questions could be considered leading in the sense that the interviewer has picked up on one particular thing the participant has said and decided to follow that up (which implies other things that are not followed up), at the same time, such questions are *not* leading in the sense that no new topics are being introduced into the interview that have not already been raised by the participant. As I have described previously,

> In one sense, the interviewer plays an active and leading role in phenomenographic interviews in that she/he defines the phenomenon being discussed and also the focus taken to that discussion, that is, the elicitation of underlying meanings and intentional attitudes towards the phenomenon. However, within these parameters, the interviewer takes as non-leading a role as possible, following only those ideas raised by the interviewees, and developing a repertoire of follow up prompts that invite the interviewee to expand on what they have said without leading them to expand in any particular direction. (Åkerlind, 2011, p. 79)

Other researchers' descriptions of possible follow-up questions include Bowden (2005), who groups follow-up questions into the following three categories:

1. neutral questions aimed at getting the interviewee to say more (example: 'Can you tell me more about that?', 'Could you explain that again using different words?', 'Why did you say that?');
2. specific questions that ask for more information about issues raised by the interviewee earlier in the interview (example: 'You have talked about X and also about Y, but what do X and Y mean?', 'Why did you talk about Y in that way?'); and

3. specific questions that invite reflection by the interviewee about things they have said (example: 'You said A and then you said B; how do those two perspectives relate to each other?') (adapted from p. 18).

Another example of follow-up questions comes from Green (2005), including:

- Seeking clarification—e.g., 'Tell me more about that?'; 'Describe that to me from start to end'; 'Tell me how you felt about that?'.
- Playing naïve—e.g., 'What do you mean? I am not clear...'; 'You used the term X, can you define it for me?'
- Exploring contradictions—e.g., 'It is interesting to me that earlier you noted that X was significant, but later you talked about Y. These seem to contradict each other. Can you tell me about that?'
- Resisting being asked to give your own opinion—e.g., 'I want your perceptions here; I'm happy to talk with you later about my views, but I would really rather focus on your views now'.
- Getting interview back on track—e.g., 'I don't mean to interrupt you, but I would really like to hear more about...'; 'I don't want an institutional (or textbook) view here, I want your view'; 'I'm not interested in what most people would say, only in your own view'.
- Recapping—e.g., 'Could you just summarise that for me?'.
- Check for gaps—e.g., 'Thank you for describing/explaining that. Is there any more you would like to add?'; 'Are there any other points you would like to raise?' (adapted from pp. 37–39).

Whilst the emphasis on follow-up probing is vital in phenomenographic interviewing, it can also be potentially uncomfortable for the interviewee, in that the questions invite them to reflect deeply on issues they have often not reflected on before. Sometimes this can be exciting for the interviewee, and I have certainly had participants comment that they found the interview process a valuable and energising opportunity to clarify their thoughts on the topic. On the other hand, sometimes interviewees find the experience of being asked to reflect at deeper and deeper levels during the interview an uncomfortable one. Being asked to explain why they thought something was important or why they did things in a certain way may require self-reflection at a level that is potentially effortful and tiring. Furthermore, sometimes interviewees cannot express an explanation of 'why' at a level that they feel satisfied with, which may also feel uncomfortable for them.

The idea that phenomenographic interviews may be uncomfortable for the interviewee is well accepted (Svensson and Theman, 1983; Trigwell, 1994; Marton and Booth, 1997). Nevertheless, I regard it as part of my ethical obligation to make the interview as pleasant as possible for the interviewee. In addition to trying to create a pleasant, conversational atmosphere for the interview, I employ a number of strategies for reducing any potential discomfort on the part of the interviewees in response to repeated probing. If they appear to be becoming uncomfortable or frustrated, I might:

- reassure them that it is common to have difficulty with such questions, because I am asking them to reflect on issues they have probably never been asked to reflect on before;
- try to rephrase the question in a different way that the interviewee may find easier to respond to; and
- let the question remain unanswered at the time, but return to it later in the interview in the hopes that the interviewee will feel more refreshed by then.

The ways in which the unstructured follow-up questions act to illuminate the nature of participants' thinking about the phenomenon will become more meaningful in the next section of this chapter, where I present concrete illustrations of phenomenographic interviews in progress.

Conducting interviews

Phenomenographic interviewing is, I believe, unique. And thus also commonly misunderstood due to people's greater familiarity with other forms of semi-structured interviewing. In Åkerlind (2005b)

I describe my own initial experience of difficulties with the nature of phenomenographic interviews, based on my previous experience of conducting semi-structured interviews within the framework of educational psychology. In particular, I highlight the important shift from focusing on 'what' questions in my previous interviews to focusing on 'why' questions in phenomenographic interviews. That means shifting from a focus on 'What did you do?' and 'What did you do next?' questions to 'Why did you do that?' and 'Why did you do it that way?' questions.[9] This highlights the importance of conducting pilot interviews, ideally with feedback from experienced phenomenographic interviewers, to ensure that the approach you are taking to follow-up questioning is effective (Bowden, 2005; Green, 2005; Åkerlind, 2005b, 2005c).

It is difficult to find extended interview excerpts in the literature that can be used to illustrate the technique of phenomenographic interviewing, but I present three examples below, by three different interviewers. The first is from Svensson and Theman (1983), based on Theman's doctoral work. In the interview, Theman is investigating different understandings of political power amongst citizens in the community of Göteborg, based on a contentious political decision that occurred in the community—so all participants are asked to discuss a common event in which they experienced 'political power'. The excerpt below starts in the middle of the interview, where the interviewer is trying to elucidate the meaning underlying certain words or phrases used by the interviewee, in particular 'having the last word', 'being in power' and 'the majority'. Much persistence is needed on the part of the interviewer before the participant finally clarifies what they mean by these phrases and how the phrases relate to each other. As an interviewer, you often have to persist through periods of confusion about what a participant means by what they have said before some sort of clarity is reached.

---

9   My emphasis on using 'why' rather than 'what' questions in interviews may be confusing in the context of advice from other phenomenographers who describe 'why' questions as being inappropriate in phenomenographic interviews (e.g., Sandberg, 1994; Uljens, 1996; Collier-Reed and Ingerman, 2013). However, they are referring to using 'why' questions to seek causal explanations of participants' ways of experiencing, rather than using 'why' questions to encourage participant reflection on their ways of experiencing, as I have suggested.

Interview excerpt 1

(from Svensson and Theman, 1983, pp. 20–23)

Before the excerpt starts, the respondent has been talking about "having the last word" and "being in power". So, the excerpt begins with the interviewer asking the respondent to elaborate on the relationship between these two statements.

I: The last word. Is that what power is?

[Interviewer encourages respondent to elaborate on the intended meaning of the phrase the respondent has used.]

R: Hm

I: Can you say more about it?

[Interviewer encourages respondent to elaborate, without contributing any content to the interview himself.]

R: Yes. ... I have to go to the one who is at the top to get that decision. ...

I: Hm. What do you do then, when you go to the one at the top, you said, what does that mean?

[Interviewer highlights a key phrase used by the respondent (go to the one at the top) and tries to clarify its meaning for the respondent.]

R: Well, I suppose I'd have to first go to the man who is director of the [relevant] company here in town.

I: Ye-es

R: And then I'd say it, and he'd say yes, hm, and thanks, that's good. If he says no, then it's often something else. ...

I: But power in this sense, what does it mean then — the last word, you said?

[Interviewer highlights a key term used by the respondent in the past (the last word) and tries to clarify how the respondent experiences its relevance to the phenomenon (power)].

R: Yes, they have said how things are going to be, doing as they wish. ... well, it is the majority that must decide.

I: Hm

R: So that things can't be like everybody wants them to be. Naturally one has to look to the majority.

I: Hm, why does one have to do that?

[Interviewer tries to get respondent to clarify.]

R: Because nothing would get done if there had been, if everybody had to take into account—or that is take into account everybody's opinion, then nothing would get done. Then one wouldn't have been able to decide on either one or the other [outcome], then 25% there would have wanted to have things [one way], and 30% would have wanted things to be sort of one way, you see, so they have to follow majority decisions, that's how it is with everything.

I: But in that case, otherwise nothing would happen if one didn't have this principle???

[Interviewer checks that he has understood the respondent's intended meaning.]

R: No-o, exactly.

I: Because it is a principle, I suppose. That's how I feel you're expressing it.

[Interviewer checks that they have understood the respondent's intended meaning.]

R: Ye-es, yes, I suppose that's the case with everything, it's not only in...

I: So, the one who is the highest, he's in a majority over you?

[Interviewer checks that they have understood the respondent's intended meaning.]

R: Hm.

I: How does he get to be that?

[Interviewer tries to get respondent to clarify.]

R: Yes, because I myself don't take those decisions which I...

I: But how does he become a majority over you? ...

[Interviewer tries to get respondent to clarify the intended meaning of the words the respondent has used.]

R: Hm, hm

I: Yes

R: Well, how he becomes the majority, of course, he's, of course, he's the one who has the power, like.

I: Does that make him the majority?

[Interviewer tries to get respondent to clarify the intended meaning.]

R: Well, yes.

I: In what way, then?

[Interviewer tries to get respondent to clarify the intended meaning.]

R: Because he's the one who makes the final decision about everything, you see.

I: Hm

R: And that's because he is the power when he becomes the majority.

I: But he then becomes the majority over you?

[Interviewer raises something said by respondent earlier in the interview to see how it fits in with what they are saying now.]

R: I don't know about majority—yes, but—no, he becomes the power, you see. Majority doesn't mean the same as power in this case.

I: No, exactly, because I thought you said that power comes via the majority, it's the majority that decides. But still we had talked earlier about this business that 'he has the last word', you said, or 'he has the power' you started by saying and then you said it was the last word, and so I'd like to hear how you fit this business about it being the majority providing the power. In that case, he has a majority over you in some sense—and what does it look like?

[Interviewer re-introduces terms used by the respondent earlier ('the last word' and 'being in power') and asks how they relate to the terms the respondent is using now ('the majority').]

R: I don't think I can make that comparison just in this case, you see, but in the case of local politics I think one can put it that way.

[Respondent shows how the meaning of a phenomenon can vary with context.]

I: Yes, but in this case, what sort of power is it? What sort of, what is the power? Clearly, it's not the majority. Is it something else?

[Interviewer brings the respondent back to the current context and tries to get respondent to clarify meaning.]

R: Ye-es. People listen to him [the company director], he's the one who knows everyone, as it were, and he's the one who knows, sort of, how many there are and what happens if one takes that kind of decision, as it were, and so on. Very often he thinks for people, as it were, because he's still very often the one who knows what different things lead to.

I: Hm

R: It's just that it's a pity there is [only] one. There should be more. There must be a certain, not everybody can sit there and say that they should do this and that. There must be someone who sees the direction in which everything is going, you see, like some people or someone who knows about things. Not everybody is as familiar with things.

I: Hm

R: And the one who is made director, who started—at least reached—started at the bottom, he knows an immense, from experience, the one who has the experience, the most experience, I suppose one can say, has a majority or power.

I: Hm

R: One could say so, I suppose.

I: So, he has the experience—it can, as it were, be a sort of majority related to your experience???

[Interviewer checks that they have understood the respondent's intended meaning.]

R: Hm [Non-verbal agreement].

[The interviewer now feels that the respondent's meaning has been clarified enough to be able to move onto another topic in the interview.]

In the next interview example, Johansson, Marton and Svensson are investigating different understandings of phenomena in physics amongst university students enrolled in a course on mechanics. The excerpt starts at the beginning of the interview, where Johansson presents respondents with a common opening scenario for the interview, a car being driven at a constant speed on a highway. He repeatedly checks whether he has understood what the interviewee means by the terms they have used.

Interview excerpt 2

(from Johansson et al., 1985, pp. 237–238)

I: A car is driven at a high, constant speed straight forward on a highway. Can you draw the forces acting on the car?

R: A car?

I: Hm

R: Viewed from above, then?

I: Hm

R: On a motorway?

I: Hm. Ye-es.

R: Well, we have gravity drawn straight down there... [Respondent draws a simple diagram.]

I: OK.

[Interviewer encourages respondent to elaborate without contributing any content to the interview himself.]

R: In a point.

I: Hm

R: And then, there's air resistance, right.

I: Hmm

R: Then friction against the road surface, where there is also some resistance. Then there's...

I: Now, let's see. I'll call the air resistance '1' and the friction against the road surface—you write that there, yes, an arrow—I shall call [friction] '2'.

[Interviewer highlights two key terms used by the respondent (air resistance and friction) and tries to clarify the meaning of each for the respondent. The interviewer has not yet checked on the significance of 'gravity', which was also a key term mentioned by the respondent, but as you will see, gravity is subsequently re-raised at a later point in the interview.]

R: I'd draw it like that, too.

I: Yes.

R: It'll be the same here against the wheels.

I: All of them are '2', yes?

[Interviewer checks that he is understanding the respondent's meaning as intended.]

R: It'll be the same here against the wheels.

I: All of them are '2', yes?

[Interviewer continues to check that he is understanding the respondent's meaning as intended.]

R: Hmm. Then the car is moved forward by the engine.

I: Hmm.

> R: And then a force that is directed forward that has to be greater than those there. Number '3' [3 for force added to the diagram] thus has to be larger than number '1' and number '2'; otherwise it wouldn't move forward.
>
> I: So that the car's, the force that moves the car forward is larger than those in the wheels, as you said, and this together...???
>
> [Interviewer checks that he is understanding the respondent's meaning as intended.]
>
> R: Yes, they have to be.
>
> I: And then you had a force directed downward, that was gravity???
>
> [At this point the interviewer returns to a key term mentioned by the respondent earlier in the interview (gravity) and checks its meaning for the respondent.]
>
> R: Yes.
>
> I: Yes. Have you got anything more?
>
> R: Hm. Well then, it could be windy, there could be a wind too, if you drive across large open fields and the wind's blowing.
>
> I: Ye-es, exactly.
>
> R: I guess it's a good idea to put them all down, in any case.

In the third and final example of phenomenographic interviewing, I draw on my own work, using an excerpt from my doctoral thesis, as published in a chapter in Bowden and Green's book on *Doing Developmental Phenomenography* (Åkerlind, 2005c). In this section of the interview, I am investigating different understandings of being an academic amongst a sample of academics. In this excerpt, unlike the previous two examples of interviews, rather than respondents being presented with a common example of the phenomenon to discuss during the interview, I ask respondents to provide their own example of the phenomenon. Multiple key words and phrases are introduced by the participant at the same time and, as the interviewer, I have to make choices about how and when to follow-up on the words and phrases they use. I usually take notes during interviews in which I write down key words and phrases used by participants that I would like to follow up on later in the interview, when I cannot do so right away.

Interview excerpt 3

(from Åkerlind, 2005c, pp. 109–113)

I: Would you like to give me a concrete example of what you do that you feel exemplifies what being an academic means to you, and then we can explore that.

R: I think it is reading and writing lectures actually.

I: Okay, so what are your aims when you are doing that. What are you trying to achieve?

[Interviewer encourages respondent to elaborate, without contributing any content to the interview herself.]

R: I guess I try and see my job as teaching, I have a strong interest in teaching. I read quite broadly across, I guess my recreational reading crosses over to my professional reading quite a lot.

I: Are you talking about reading in psychology?

[Interviewer checks that she has understood what the respondent is referring to. Their discipline is psychology.]

R: [Non-verbal agreement.] Reading for me is, I find reading quite enjoyable and I like the challenge to try and understand things. And I guess transplanting that into exposition things for the students that will, I guess, likely stimulate them and excite them about the excitement I feel about intellectual pursuits.

I: I am happy to follow that train of thought through. How do you go about exciting students and why do you want to excite them?

[Interviewer encourages respondent to elaborate on the meaning of a particular word they have used (excite). Alternative words to follow-up could have been 'stimulate' or 'intellectual pursuits', but only one word can be chosen at a time.]

R: I guess because it is a personal history thing. I grew up in a working class family and I hadn't read a book by the time I had left school. There were no books in my home. I did really badly at school and I left school early and I did a number of terrible jobs and realised I was kind of stuck unless I did something about it. So, I went back and did my Higher School Certificate at Tech College. I had been told all the time at school I was very bright, but I think I doubted that. I did very well at the HSC [Higher School Certificate] and got into university. There were then a couple of years when I did other things before I went to university. It was a bit hard for me to believe that I was going to go to university, and when

I got there I think I was intellectually fascinated. I worked and I was curious and I just found it an enjoyable experience to go to lectures, and if the lecturer was good, I just found it fascinating and enjoyed it. I thought about that a bit when I started to prepare lectures. I find myself going back to what they did. I think they were passionate about what they were doing. I am actually teaching some lectures on Freud next term. I was taught by Freudians and that was greatly interesting to me then, although in the broader perspective there is much more. I am kind of thinking about how to present his work in a way that would show them how interesting it is as a set of ideas.

[Respondent introduces not just one, but a number of meaning-laden terms here that are all worthy of follow-up—'intellectually fascinated', 'curious', 'enjoyable', 'passionate', 'interesting'—but the interviewer can only follow up on one at a time and continues to explore 'exciting'.]

I: Let me take you back to another question, if that helps. What would happen if a student is excited?

[Interviewer now moves to encouraging respondent to elaborate on the intended meaning of another key term they have used, 'excited', and its relationship to the term 'interested'.]

R: When they are excited they will be enthusiastic about the course. They will be interested to read the textbooks, to go and figure out the extra reading, maybe discuss it with their peers. They will think about it more broadly; think about themselves, who they are. Coming to university, especially for the younger students and for the older students—it certainly was for me—is part of a developmental thing. In a way, you go in at one end and when you come out at the other end you have changed in some way. If they are more curious about the topic that I am teaching, at a first level, if they are not interested they will not engage in the topic, so if they are bored they will not do any reading. So, at a very pragmatic level, if it is presented in a way that can ignite their interest, they will be engaged in the topic. An example is that the [topic] course was taught last year by a visiting fellow and it was the only course that was evaluated. And it was the course that they complained about because the person who taught it turned it into more experimental; apparently achieved making what is an interesting topic into something else.

I: That gives me a better feeling for it, thank you. Now, can you give me another example of…

6. Study design, data gathering and the phenomenographic interview 127

[In the process of exploring the meaning underlying the respondent's use of the words, 'exciting' and 'excited', the meaning of other words they have used ('intellectually fascinated', 'curious', 'enjoyable', 'passionate') also becomes clear, so that each word does not have to be followed up individually. Consequently, the interviewer is ready to explore another meaning-laden word.]

I: So, you are trying to interest students, and the example you gave is your lectures and you try to interest them???

[Interviewer checks that they have understood the respondent's intended meaning.]

R: [Non-verbal agreement.]

I: Why?

R: Well, it is getting them engaged.

I: Yes—why? I am trying to get you to home in more clearly on why you want to interest them.

[Interviewer encourages respondent to elaborate on the intended meaning of the term 'interested'.]

R: It is getting them engaged. I guess, if you think of it as an educational thing, if you are getting them engaged then they will educate themselves by attending and reading more. I guess it is a very personal thing about what I enjoy and what I would like to think. I have certain educational objectives to get across a certain amount of material, but I guess I would like them to take something more away with them, maybe raise a few questions, get them to think, get them interested in the life of the mind of knowledge.

I: What would happen to students if they were interested? What would happen if they weren't? I am trying to get an idea of why you want to interest them.

[Interviewer continues to encourage respondent to elaborate on the intended meaning of 'interested'.]

R: I have not thought deeply about that; I haven't had the time.

I: No, why should you?

[Interviewer trying to reduce any possible discomfort for the respondent about not having a ready answer.]

R: I have just taught a course to the Masters students, a small group of students, a combination of lecture and workshops, and that went really well. I did not want to [formally] evaluate my first course, so I just gave out the [evaluation] forms myself. But then it was independently evaluated by the course coordinator, and there was an even better response. So, it went really well. But that is a really good group of students. They are highly motivated. They all have [Honours] Class 2 or 1 or better, and they are doing jobs that they want to do. To say that they were interested; I was teaching them a course on [course topic]. And I think that psychologists have tended to ignore it because it is too difficult, and I wanted to get them interested and show that they could treat these disorders, so they are as successful or unsuccessful with these as they are with anything else. So, I wanted to get them interested in that topic, I guess for pragmatic purposes—for it is a belief I have, me and a lot of other people in the [course topic] area, that psychologists should be more involved [in the topic].

That is kind of different to undergraduate lectures. I am a kind of wandering lecturer. I haven't done a lot of undergraduate lecturing so far. I gave a series of five lectures on [course topic], I am teaching a first-year series next semester, and I will be doing more the semester after that.

I: Do you have the same aim of interesting students at the undergraduate level?

[Interviewer encourages respondent to elaborate on an issue they have raised relevant to issue of student 'interest' (the difference between graduate and undergraduate students, i.e. context).]

R: I think of what my aim is for the course. There are certain departmental objectives that have to be met. And I am teaching a course in [course topic], so there are certain topics that have to be covered and [course topic] has not been taught in this department for a while in any extensive form. That seems to be how I am going to translate my job into something. I have opted to take on this course. And so, I guess my aim in the course is to give them a proper overview of what [course topic] is, as it is understood in this particular time in history.

But I would have to say that many students study psychology for reasons that are thwarted quite quickly. They are interested in people's character so that they can understand themselves, or they are inquisitive about human nature—most people. And most of the course is to actively tell them that that is not what psychology is about. It is about science, and statistics, and perception and stuff like that. And everyone in the

> department is aware of this, and the [topic] course is thought to be very important because it is like what they expected. So, I am looking forward to teaching it. And it is in that sense that I don't think that psychology has to be about experimental procedures. I mean, I am pretty much committed to a research paradigm, but I think that interesting the students, I don't know, getting them excited must implicitly believe that I think it is important for people to be intellectually curious.

These three extracts illustrate how the type of unstructured follow-up questions described in the previous section are used during interviews and the key role that they play in eliciting and clarifying the underlying meaning of comments made by participants. The extracts also illustrate what sort of comments are followed-up with further questions from the interviewer (i.e., words and phrases the respondent has used that seem particularly 'meaning-laden'), as well as the sort of comments that are not explored further. I would normally say that it is impossible to describe what makes a word, phrase or comment seem particularly laden with meaning, and that it can only be illustrated, as I do in the interview extracts. However, Sjöström and Dahlgren (2002) propose three indicators of significance in meaning: frequency of mention, position within the interview and 'pregnancy' of the comment.

> In practice, some indicators may be used for assessing the significance of elements in an answer [to an interview question]. Some of these are frequency, for example, how often a meaningful statement is articulated; position—very often the most significant elements are to be found in the introductory parts of an answer, and finally pregnancy, for example, when the subject explicitly emphasizes that certain aspects are more important than others. (p. 341)

Lastly, the interview extracts above illustrate the point at which an interviewer decides to stop seeking further clarification of a particular term or comment. I usually stop probing for the underlying meaning of a particular comment when I come to feel reasonably confident that the interviewee has now more clearly expressed their meaning, and this is illustrated in the interview excerpts above. But other reasons to stop probing include if participants start repeating themselves in their answers, or start having difficulty answering requests for further elaboration—both of which indicate that participants have reached the end of their current reflective capacities. However, if I think the word or phrase they have used is particularly significant, but its meaning is still not clear, I may stop probing at the time, but then reintroduce the issue at a later point in the interview in the hope that the participant might feel more able to reflect on it then. From an entirely practical perspective, another reason I may stop probing is if I run out of time in an interview, or think that spending too much time exploring this particular comment may not allow me enough time to explore another one that also feels significant.

Another issue sometimes raised about interviewing is whether it is essential that all interviews be conducted by the same person. The option of multiple interviewers can arise during collaborative research and also during funded research with employment of research assistants. Normally, all interviews are undertaken by one person, in order to maintain as much similarity across interviewees in the context of the interview questions as possible. Nevertheless, I personally do not think having multiple interviewers is unduly problematic. There is so much natural variability within phenomenographic data, in terms of each participant's specific context and interpretation of the questions asked, that variability in the person asking the questions is just one more source. Phenomenographic interview questions are in no way standardised, so standardisation of the interviewer should also not be essential.

Transcription of interviews

We have spent a lot of time talking about gathering data through interviews, but it should be noted that it is not the interviews per se that are analysed, but transcriptions of the interviews. So, the analysis is actually undertaken on written text. Whilst this distinction is not a common topic of discussion in the phenomenographic literature, Svensson and Theman (1983), Dortins (2002), Sandberg (2005), Bowden (2005) and Bowden and Green (2010) for example, draw out some of the implications of working from transcripts, not from interviews per se.

Some researchers conduct, transcribe and analyse the interviews all themselves. But it is also common to have the interviews conducted by a research assistant and transcribed by a professional service. In this case, some researchers (e.g., Bowden and Green, 2010) suggest that whoever conducts the analysis should listen to the interview recording with the transcription in front of them, partially to become more familiar with the interviews as such, and partially so they can check and correct any possible errors in the transcription. But this is a very time-consuming process and I, personally, am not convinced that it is vital.

Chapter summary

This chapter described the design and conduct of phenomenographic interviews, with a focus on determining the object of study, designing methods for the gathering of data, selecting the sample and gathering the data. The chapter starts with a discussion of the nature of a 'phenomenon', an 'experience' and a 'way of experiencing' from a phenomenographic perspective, and the type of research questions phenomenography can address. The importance of clarifying the community the sample is selected to represent, what the representativeness of the sample means from a phenomenographic perspective, and the need to maximise demographic variation within the sample are discussed. The importance of basing the interview on discussion of concrete examples of participants interacting with the phenomenon, and spending most of the interview time exploring those examples using unstructured follow-up questions is explained. Lastly, three concrete examples of a phenomenographic interview in progress were presented to illustrate how participant meanings are elicited and clarified during the interview.

The next chapter moves on to describe and illustrate the process of analysing the data, presenting the research outcomes and ensuring rigour throughout the research process.

7. Analysing data and reporting research outcomes

In Chapter 5, I referred to five analytic strategies that arise from phenomenographic epistemology:

- separation of human experience into referential and structural aspects;
- search for different ways of experiencing the same phenomena as a collective group;
- search for critical aspects that are discerned and not discerned in different ways of experiencing phenomena;
- part-whole analyses of (a) specific ways of experiencing the same phenomena and (b) collective ways of experiencing the same phenomena; and
- search for inclusive relationships between different ways of experiencing the same phenomena.

But these foci are in the form of analytic directions rather than concrete strategies. They help explain why phenomenography approaches data analysis in the way it does, but do not tell us how to actually go about the analysis in practical terms. Similarly, although general principles in phenomenographic analysis have been described in numerous publications, it is rarely at the level of concrete guidelines. And although there are many published studies using phenomenography with associated descriptions of methods, the methods sections in journal articles are normally not detailed enough to provide any sort of concrete sense of what is involved in phenomenographic data analysis. So, what is needed to help those new to phenomenography is a clear set of guidelines and some concrete illustrations of analytic practice—which is what I provide in this chapter.

A ten-step guideline for the analytic process

The most useful set of analytic guidelines that I have found come from a lesser-known article by Dahlgren and Fallsberg (1991).[1] In the article, they propose seven steps to phenomenographic analysis: Familiarisation; Condensation; Comparison; Grouping; Articulating; Contrasting; and Labelling. But this was before the developments in phenomenography that occurred during the 1990s (described in Chapter 2). So, in this chapter I build on their steps to create a ten-step set of guidelines that better represents 21st-century phenomenography: Familiarising; Condensing; Comparing; Grouping; Delimiting; Discerning; Articulating; Checking; Relating; and Labelling (where Delimiting is a re-naming of Contrasting, Discerning is a new step in 21st-century analysis, and Checking and Relating are steps that were always undertaken during phenomenographic analysis, but were not explicitly acknowledged in Dahlgren and Fallsberg's guidelines). After describing each step, below, I then illustrate them with examples from research practice.

It is important to note, however, that the sequence of steps should not be followed in a simple linear order; there is a constant back-and-forth iteration and interplay between the various steps, with some steps cycled through numerous times before the researcher will feel confident in interpreting the outcomes.

> The different steps in the phenomenographic analysis have to be taken interactively. As each consecutive step has implications not only for the steps that follow but also for the steps that precede it, the analysis has to go through several runs in which the different steps are considered to some extent simultaneously. (Marton, 1994, p. 4428)

The ten steps are:

1. **Familiarising** oneself with the data: The researcher(s) read through all of the transcripts numerous times, to become acquainted with them as a set.

---

[1] The analytic steps were subsequently revised in Sjöström and Dahlgren (2002) but I prefer the original steps.

2. **Condensing** the data: The most significant and meaning-laden statements found within each transcript are highlighted or extracted to give a shorter, but representative, version of the meaning(s) expressed across the transcripts. (Some researchers also write summaries of key points from the transcripts.)
3. **Comparing** the data: The condensed data are compared, to identify variation and similarity across the collective pool of meanings.
4. **Grouping** the data into categories: Transcripts or condensed data that appear to be similar in meaning are grouped together to form preliminary categories of description.
5. **Delimiting** different categories: The different groupings (preliminary categories) are compared to clarify what distinguishes each grouping, as well as what they have in common. Cycles of Grouping and Delimiting work together to alternately focus analytic attention on similarities and differences within the data, with the aim of maximising similarity within groupings and differences between groupings.
6. **Discerning** critical aspects: Particular aspects of the phenomenon that are referred to in some groupings but not in others are highlighted. This focuses analytic attention on critical aspects (i.e., different parts) of the phenomenon that are discerned within each grouping (i.e., holistic meaning).
7. **Articulating** the parts and whole of each category: Descriptions of each category are developed in terms of the overall meaning of the phenomenon represented by that grouping (whole) and the awareness of critical aspects of the phenomenon that underlie that meaning (parts).
8. **Checking** interpretations: Preliminary interpretations based on Comparison, Grouping, Delimiting, Discerning and Articulating are regularly checked back against the original data and the condensed data to confirm or challenge the interpretations.

9. **Relating** the categories in an outcome space: Structural relationships between categories are established based on inclusive discernment of the different critical aspects of the phenomenon. An outcome space is constituted by relating the categories in a hierarchical structure of increasing complexity of meaning, based on the critical aspects of the phenomenon discerned.

10. **Labelling** the categories and critical aspects: A suitable short title is created to succinctly label each category and the critical aspects that demarcate each category. This is distinct from the larger description of each category and critical aspect that occurs in Articulating.

Before trying to describe these steps in more detail, I want to mention a key point of variation in phenomenographic analytic practice, which is whether the boundaries between individual transcripts are maintained or collapsed during data analysis (Åkerlind, 2012 [2005]). Whilst the ten-step guidelines apply to both approaches to analysis, many of the steps will be undertaken a little differently depending on which approach is employed. This will become evident in the concrete descriptions of practice provided below. Meanwhile, to give some sense of the difference behind the two approaches, let me quote from two researchers:

Collapsing boundaries:

The first step in the process... is to populate the pool of meaning with the collection of fragments from all the interviews... This is achieved by carefully reading the transcripts and looking for *meaning units* in the text that relate to this phenomenon... The key here is that the [respondent] should be focusing on a single aspect of the phenomenon for the duration of the meaning unit. Once the individual meaning units have been identified across all the interviews, the interviews are deconstructed and only the individual meaning units retained. (Collier-Reed and Ingerman, 2013, p. 249)

Maintaining boundaries:

All the time I am reading a transcript, I have in the back of my mind the question 'What does this tell me about the way the [participant] understands [the phenomenon under study]?'. In other words, what must [the phenomenon] mean to the [participant] if he or she is saying this or that? ... [This] can only be discovered by holding all the ideas in mind at one time and trying to draw a picture that explains the underlying meaning... (Bowden, 2000, pp. 56–57). I look for the key elements of the phenomenon as seen by the interviewees, and the way they see those elements relating to each other and to their underlying meaning of [the phenomenon]. (p. 53)

It is important to be aware when reading this chapter that I was trained in the tradition of maintaining boundaries between transcripts, and this is the approach I have typically used. So, this creates a limitation in my ability to describe the analytic approach of collapsing boundaries. For this reason, I draw on a range of phenomenographers' descriptions of their practice in the section below, rather than just describing my own practice.

Analytical aside:

Maintaining or collapsing boundaries between transcripts

The traditional approach to phenomenographic analysis is to collapse the boundaries between transcripts. This was first introduced by Marton (1986) and has been advocated since the inception of phenomenography. The aim is to create a 'pool of meanings' for analysis based on significant statements drawn from the transcripts, but then 'decontextualised' from the specific transcripts in which they were found. Before extracting significant statements from the transcripts, the meaning of each statement is first carefully interpreted within the context of the larger transcript, but all such statements are subsequently separated, or decontextualised, from the transcripts for comparison with each other. Proponents of decontextualising statements from individual transcripts see this approach as a more rigorous way of ensuring an analytic focus on collective rather than individual meaning.

The alternative approach is to maintain boundaries between transcripts. This has been a widespread practice since the 1990s (e.g., Bowden, 1994a, 1994b; Dall'Alba, 1994; Prosser, 1994) and has been argued for by Bowden in particular (Bowden, 1994b [2000b]; 2005; Green and Bowden, 2009; Bowden and Green, 2010). The main intention of this approach is to ensure that key statements in the transcript are always analysed for meaning within their broader interview context. But as a consequence, the pool of meanings created tends to be based on whole transcripts (and summaries of transcripts), considered as a contextualised whole. Significant statements may still be extracted from (and/or highlighted within) the transcripts, but all statements from the one transcript are considered together, as representing a part of the meaning conveyed across the transcript as a whole. Proponents of keeping all statements contextualised within the larger transcript see this approach as a more rigorous way of interpreting the intended meaning of each statement.

The point of agreement between these two approaches to analysis is that the interview data are regarded as representing a 'pool of meanings', in the sense of a collection of different ways of experiencing the phenomenon. Where the boundaries between transcripts are maintained, each transcript is then usually treated as representing one particular meaning for the phenomenon. So, each transcript (or summary of a transcript) is treated as a unit of meaning within the larger pool. But where the boundaries between transcripts are collapsed, meanings are seen as best represented by significant statements made by respondents during the interview, not by the interview as a whole. So, each significant statement is treated as a unit of meaning within the larger pool.

In practical terms, the difference between the two approaches leads, in particular, to different ways of 'condensing' the data (step 2 in the guidelines). Where the boundaries between transcripts are maintained, condensation occurs on a transcript-by-transcript basis—significant statements are drawn from or highlighted within transcripts, and then grouped together to represent a single unit of meaning. But where the boundaries between transcripts are collapsed, condensation occurs on a meaning-by-meaning basis, irrespective of whether these different meanings are seen to occur within or between transcripts. So, significant statements are extracted from transcripts, with each statement seen as representing a unit of meaning in its own right.

One concern with categorising the meaning of a phenomenon based on whole transcripts is the possibility that an interview participant may experience different meanings at different points during the interview. As described in Chapter 5, human experience has the potential to vary on a moment-by-moment basis, based on changes in the perceived context. So, different interview questions and different recollections on the part of the participant can bring up different contexts in which the phenomenon is being experienced. Researchers who maintain transcript boundaries typically address this by categorising the transcript according to the most complex meaning expressed in the transcript. At the same time, less complex meanings expressed within the transcript can still be compared with similar meanings in other transcripts during the analysis process.

> In my personal approach to analysis, an added benefit of considering the transcript as a whole is that I am then able to interpret the expression of more and less complex ways of experiencing within any one transcript as indicative of the inclusive nature of the more complex meanings, as described in the sections on 'Research rigour' and 'Credibility of research outcomes', below. This means that the hierarchy of complexity and inclusivity of categories of description in my outcome spaces are more strongly based on empirical evidence of inclusivity shown within transcripts, than on the primary use of logic in ordering the categories advocated by Marton. However, it is possible that this particular use of variation in expressions of meaning within each transcript may currently be unique to me (and my research students).

Concrete descriptions of practice

In 2005, I published an article in which I noted the dearth of concrete descriptions of practice in the phenomenographic literature (with the notable exceptions of Bowden and Walsh, 1994 [2000] and Bowden and Green, 2005) and then attempted to draw together a small set of such descriptions based on the literature available at the time (Åkerlind 2005 [2012]). Sadly, almost twenty years later, this dearth of concrete descriptions in the literature has not changed. So, in trying to provide a practical description of the nature of phenomenographic analysis, I will draw in particular on the Bowden and Walsh and Bowden and Green publications to source concrete examples of each analytic step in the guidelines.

Familiarising

The primary purpose of the familiarisation stage is to gain a sense of the dataset as a whole. This is what allows elements of variation within the data to become apparent, as variation in meaning can only become apparent when looking at varied meanings, i.e., when looking across a group of transcripts or meaning units, not when focusing on an individual transcript or meaning unit.[2] So, Familiarising yourself with

---

2   Whilst this statement forms a good general principle, I should acknowledge that it is not completely accurate, as there may also be variation within individual responses.

the whole dataset is necessary before it is possible to attempt the next steps of Condensing and Grouping.

> **Concrete examples of Familiarising**
>
> Phenomenographic analysis relies on the processes of reading and re-reading [transcripts]. For some, this prospect might seem daunting and indeed it is at the beginning when the data seem quite unfamiliar (even when one has done all of the interviewing!). The reading becomes more manageable as familiarity increases, but then the pressure on the researcher(s) to be even more diligent in their analysis grows further. It is essential that the researcher read and re-read (and re-read and so on) from the full set of data—from start to finish. ... This is not a rapid process. In fact, it proved to be a very time consuming but fascinating activity. (Green, 2005, p. 41)
>
> I initially read the preliminary set of 17 transcripts as a whole. My focus was on the similarities and differences between transcripts, so the sense of what was significant within each transcript would emerge out of the context of what was present in the set of transcripts as a whole. On the first reading, I simply read with a sense of openness towards what the set of transcripts might contain. On the second reading, I started to home in on the questions relating to the phenomenon of interest, and marked [as not relevant] any passages that addressed unrelated phenomena, to reduce future reading time. On the third reading, I started to make notes on each transcript, summarising key issues and themes that were emerging within it, based on my preliminary sense of the whole set [Condensing]. These notes were written on separate sheets of paper, not on the transcripts themselves. The use of notes was an attempt to come to terms with the amount of data in the transcript set, and represented an interim stage of the analysis. At a later stage, I returned to reading the transcripts only, without the use of notes. However, during the interim stage, I alternated between reading the transcripts as a set and reading my notes on the transcripts as a set, with a focus on similarities and differences running through them. (Åkerlind, 2005c, pp. 120–121)

Condensing

Due to the size of most interview transcripts and resulting datasets, some form of summarising or condensing of the data is needed to make the data more manageable.[3] The condensed form of data is then able to be used for initial analyses and interpretations. However, all such interpretations must be regularly re-checked against the original data for confirmation, to ensure that nothing significant has been lost in the condensation process.

A key process of Condensing is to downplay less relevant statements and highlight particularly significant statements in the transcript. Inevitably, not every statement made by participants during an interview will be of equal pertinence and provide equal insight into the object of study. Some statements will inevitably be more relevant to the phenomenon than others. In addition, some statements will be more 'meaning-laden' than others, i.e., will tell us more about the meaning of the phenomenon for the participant.

> [In] an unstructured interview many statements are only partly expressed or contain hidden references to something having been mentioned earlier. Every reply is a reply to a question and almost every question emerges from the previous reply. Everything is connected to something else. Still, in reading the [transcript] one finds that there are different parts dealing with different questions and that some statements seem to address the theme involved more directly than others. This identification of parts and more significant statements is the first step in the analysis and it is deepened and revised through further analysis and interpretation. (Svensson and Theman, 1983, p. 10)

But how are such 'more significant' or particularly 'meaning-laden' statements recognised? To illustrate the process, let us return to the interview extract from Svensson and Theman (1983) presented in the previous chapter, that explored the meaning of 'political power'. At one point in the interview the respondent says,

---

3   An additional strategy used by some researchers to make the data more manageable is to conduct preliminary analyses on a subset of the data (commonly 10-15 transcripts) before moving on to include the whole data set (Åkerlind, 2012 [2005]).

> I have to go to the one who is at the top to get that decision... I'd have to first go to the man who is director of the [relevant] company here in town. And then I'd say it, and he'd say yes, hm, and thanks, that's good. If he says no, then it's often something else.

Then at a later point, after further exploration, the respondent explains why they "have to go to the one who is at the top",

> Because he's the one who makes the final decision about everything, you see. And that's because he is the power...

I would argue that the second statement is much more significant in revealing the meaning of political power for the respondent than the first statement, i.e., more 'meaning-laden'. This is because the first statement merely describes what the respondent would do (go to the man at the top to get a decision), but it does not reveal why the respondent would do that (what their intention is in doing that) or what that action reflects about their way of experiencing power. In contrast, the second statement clarifies why they would go to the man at the top (because he is the one who makes the final decision) and how that reflects the respondent's way of experiencing power (being able to make the final decision is an indicator of power). So, in analytical terms, it would be important to highlight the second statement as part of the pool of meanings, but not the first statement, because the first statement tells us very little about the meaning of power for the respondent.

> **Concrete examples of Condensing**
>
> **A: While collapsing boundaries between transcripts**
>
> The first phase of the analysis is a kind of selection procedure based on criteria of relevance. Utterances found to be of interest for the question [phenomenon] being investigated ... are selected and marked. The meaning of an utterance occasionally lies in the utterance itself, but in general the interpretation must be made in relation to the context from which the utterance was taken ... The phenomenon in question is narrowed down to and interpreted in terms of selected quotes from all the interviews. The selected quotes make up the data pool which forms the basis for the next and crucial step in the analysis.
>
> The researcher's attention has now shifted from the individual (i.e., from the interviews from which the quotes were abstracted) to

the meaning embedded in the quotes themselves. The boundaries separating individuals are abandoned and interest is focused on the 'pool of meanings' discovered in the data. Thus, each quote has two contexts in relation to which it has been interpreted: first, the interview from which it was taken [individual meaning], and second, the 'pool of meanings' to which it belongs [collective meaning]. The interpretation is an interactive procedure which reverberates between these two contexts. (Marton, 1986, pp. 42–43)

The first step in the process towards constituting an outcome space is to populate the pool of meanings with the collection of fragments from all the interviews that refer to an experience of the phenomenon in question (assuming a Martonian constitution of the pool of meaning). This is achieved by carefully reading the transcripts and looking for meaning units in the text that relate to this phenomenon. These sections of text could be a single answer to a question or part of a larger conversation. The key here is that the [participant] should be focusing on a single aspect of the phenomenon for the duration of the meaning unit. Once the individual meaning units have been identified across all the interviews, the interviews are deconstructed and only the individual meaning units retained. This is achieved by literally taking out the appropriate sections of text and discarding the irrelevant text. These meaning units are then 'placed' in the pool of meaning that then contains all of the possible relationships with the phenomenon in question. The individuals interviewed have thus provided fragments of the ways of relating to [i.e., experiencing] the phenomenon in this pool, and the assumption is that, at a collective level, this would represent the variation in ways in which the phenomenon is related [i.e., ways of experiencing the phenomenon]. (Collier-Reed and Ingerman, 2013, p. 249)

B: While maintaining boundaries between transcripts

I followed the model more common in Australia of analysing the transcripts as a whole initially, and then in large chunks incorporating all responses to the specific questions about the phenomenon I was investigating. Responses to contextual questions and questions relating to other phenomena were not focused on after the first one or two readings, but every other

> part of the transcript was read as a whole whenever the transcript was consulted. Inevitably, some comments within the transcripts seemed more meaning-laden than others, and I would often underline these statements in the transcript. Nevertheless, the designated sections of the transcript were always read as a whole, so that these underlined sections were never read out of context or focused on to the exclusion of other parts of the transcript. (Åkerlind, 2005c, p. 117)
>
> As a general rule, I read transcripts with the following thoughts in mind. If the interviewee is saying this about X or Y, what must the phenomenon mean to them? If they are now saying Z as well, does this change my interpretation of how they are seeing the phenomenon? ... I prefer to read key statements and then move backwards a few pages and read forward, going several pages beyond what was regarded as the key statement. I then ask myself about the significance of the key statement with respect to both the focus of the study and the meaning you can ascribe to the statement given the context in which it was provided. (Bowden, 2005, p. 28)

Comparing, Grouping and Delimiting

The steps of Comparing, Grouping and Delimiting will be illustrated together because they mutually reinforce each other, and commonly occur together as iterative cycles of analysis. Comparing the statements or transcripts that make up the pool of meanings is intended to highlight similarities and differences in the way the phenomenon is experienced within the sample group. Comparison thus enables both Grouping of similar meanings and Delimiting of different meanings to occur. But whilst Grouping is initially achieved through comparison of the statements and transcripts, Delimitating the different groups involves comparison at the level of groupings.

> **Concrete examples of Comparing, Grouping and Delimiting**
>
> As a result of the interpretive work, utterances are brought together into categories on the basis of their similarities [Grouping]. Categories are differentiated from one another in terms of their

differences [Delimiting]. In concrete terms, the process looks like this: quotes are sorted into piles [Grouping on the basis of Comparing], borderline cases are examined, and eventually the criterion attributes for each group are made explicit [Delimiting]. In this way, the groups of quotes are arranged and rearranged, are narrowed into categories, and finally are defined. (Marton, 1986, p. 43)

[The research assistant] was asked to read through the whole set of transcripts ... several times until she felt she was reasonably familiar with them [Familiarising]. She was then to try to construct a set of categories which she felt encompassed her perceptions of what the [participants] were trying to say [Grouping on the basis of Comparing]. She then went back over the transcripts, adjusted the categories, and cycled between the categories and the transcripts until she felt she had a reasonably stable set of categories [Iteration between Comparing, Grouping and Checking]. When she had completed this task, we met to discuss the set ... My task at this stage was to read through the categories, decide whether I felt they reasonably represented the conceptions reflected in the transcripts [Checking] and to adjust the categories in a way to construct a more logically related set [Delimiting and Relating]... The research assistant took this set, again cycled between the categories and the transcripts, adjusted the categories and produced a third set. We then cycled through the whole process, until we felt we had developed a reasonably stable set of categories. [Iteration between Comparing, Grouping, Delimiting, Checking and Relating] (Prosser, 2000, p. 38)

At this point I started literally to place the transcripts (and/or summary notes on the transcripts) in piles on the floor, placing those that seemed more similar closer together and those that seemed less similar further apart [Grouping on the basis of Comparing]. The initial placement was based on a fairly unarticulated and imprecise sense of the similarities and differences in meaning conveyed within each transcript. Consequently, this preliminary grouping was in no way tidy, nor was it intended to be. Transcripts that seemed most similar were placed on top of each other, ones that seemed less similar but not to belong to another pile were placed nearby, ones that

> seemed to fall between two piles were placed between them, and transcripts that did not seem to fit into any pile were placed to one side [Grouping]. I then re-read the transcripts in these piles, focusing on similarities and differences within and between piles [Delimiting], leading to a rearrangement of the group of transcripts. Then began a lengthy process of regular re-reading and re-grouping which continued over some months... [Iterative Grouping and Delimiting] (Åkerlind, 2005c, p. 121)
>
> For the next round of analysis, the transcripts and transcript summaries were again grouped according to the latest categories of description. With each regrouping of the data, I was able to pick up finer discriminations in my ongoing search for:
>
> - any transcripts which did not align with the proposed categories, which would indicate that there were aspects of the data that had not been accounted for by the proposed outcomes [Checking];
>
> - within group similarities and differences, which might support my proposal that a group of transcripts reflects the same way of experiencing or, alternatively, clarify differences which might suggest a group be divided into separate categories [Comparing and Grouping]; and
>
> - between group similarities and differences, which might support or challenge my proposed categories, as well as indicating the presence or absence of inclusive relationships between categories. [Comparing and Delimiting] (Åkerlind, 2005d, p. 175)

All of the examples given above appear to describe analysis based on hard copies of transcripts, but software packages, especially NVivo, are also often used in phenomenographic analysis. Ozkan (2004) provides a useful overview of how to use the features of NVivo for qualitative analysis, but I have not been able to find any phenomenographic-specific descriptions of using NVivo to aid analysis, beyond the simple claim that NVivo was used. So, I will illustrate the possible use of NVivo in phenomenographic analysis by drawing on the dissertation of one of my doctoral students, Suet Voon Yu (Yu, 2019). In her dissertation, Suet Voon describes the ways in which she used NVivo to assist with her analysis. She created a 'case node' in NVivo for each transcript, as part of the process of Familiarising and Condensing. Then, she grouped excerpts that expressed similar meaning across transcripts by coding them to 'free nodes'. In this way, the free node function was used to gather all data related to tentative groupings, which was particularly helpful in developing categories and identifying critical aspects. At the same time, reflections and insights about the significance of different nodes and their relationship to emerging categories and critical aspects were recorded by jotting down notes as 'memos' in NVivo.

Her early development of free nodes is shown below with respect to the phenomenon of 'Being a Doctor' (see Table 7.1). However, you are not expected to understand Table 7.1 in any detail; the aim of presenting the example here is just to give you a feeling for the way NVivo can be used for phenomenographic analysis. The right-hand columns show the number of 'sources' (i.e., transcripts) coded at each node, and the number of 'references' in the transcript text (i.e., excerpts from transcripts) selected for each node.

Table 7.1 Example of using the 'free node' feature in NVivo to assist with Grouping and Discerning of data on 'Being a Doctor' (adapted from Yu, 2019, p. 184)

Nodes	Name	Sources	References
●	Continuing professional development	8	23
●	Curious, intellectual satisfaction	2	3
●	Development over time	30	505
●	Equal	1	1
●	Ethics	13	39
●	Experience	8	44
●	Feedback	1	1
●	Focus	1	2
●	Help	3	3
●	Honest	1	3
●	Humility – diagnostic, therapeutic	1	3
●	Issues – time. isolation	20	54
●	Knowledge	27	321
●	Listening	7	46
●	Looking after doctor self	7	21

●	Privilege	10	48
●	Purpose	21	69
●	Reflection, self-awareness, feedback	12	40
●	Relationship, interaction with patient	9	23
●	Research	30	187
●	Respect	10	50
●	Responsibility, obligations	9	54
●	Status	1	1
●	Teaching	30	238

Suet Voon also used word frequency queries and searches for transcript excerpts that mentioned a particular word as ways to facilitate Comparison and Grouping—bearing in mind that participants can use the same word to mean different things and different words to mean the same thing.

> **Analytic aside:**
>
> **The case of a grouping based on a single transcript**
>
> Before leaving the topic of Grouping and Discerning, I think it is important to mention the possibility of forming a grouping based on the data contained in just one transcript (as illustrated in Chapter 4). This can occur due to the relatively small sample sizes in phenomenographic research, but it is not a problem in the sense that phenomenography is concerned with possible ways of experiencing a phenomenon, not frequency of ways of experiencing it. Nevertheless, it may be nerve-wracking for the researcher because it appears on the surface as if a category is being constituted based on just one individual. But this is never the case. Any category proposed must form a logical structural relationship with all the other categories, as well as providing evidence of discernment of a critical aspect of the phenomenon that has not been discerned in other categories. So, decisions on groupings are always being decided at a collective level, and any category is being constituted as much on the basis of all the other categories as on the basis of the transcript(s) that represent it. I discuss this further below, in the section on rigour in phenomenographic research.

Discerning

Discerning involves identifying aspects of the phenomenon that are referred to in some groupings (or categories) but not in others. This is achieved through another process of comparison, but comparison of the different groupings, not the individual statements or transcripts. This sounds similar to Delimiting, but the difference is that Delimiting aims at distinguishing and demarcating different holistic meanings (categories of description) of the phenomenon, whilst Discerning aims at distinguishing and demarcating different constituent parts (critical aspects or dimensions) of the different meanings of the phenomenon.

The focus on Discerning critical aspects of the variation between categories raises the issue of how critical aspects are distinguished from non-critical aspects of variation. Whilst what is critical and non-critical is unclear during the early stages of analysis, as the groupings more clearly develop, what is critical in distinguishing the different groupings also becomes clearer. I described this in more detail in Chapter 4, as part of one of my 'analytical asides', which I repeat here:

> What is critical in a participant's response only stands out in comparison with other responses; it is never obvious when looking at the response in isolation. As described in Chapter 2, the phenomenographic search is for variation in critical aspects of awareness, not in all aspects of awareness. An aspect is regarded as 'critical' when it acts to differentiate one way of understanding the phenomenon from a qualitatively different way of understanding it. This means that not every comment that a participant makes about a phenomenon will be of equal significance in determining a category.
>
> What is critical cannot be determined in advance of the analysis, nor can it be determined by looking at one response in isolation from the others. It can only be determined by comparing one response to another, or to the set of responses. To form a category, you look for similarities in what participants say about a phenomenon *across responses*. And to form different categories, you look for differences in what participants say about a phenomenon *across responses*. It is only in comparing each participant response to what other respondents have said that what is critical comes to the fore, and what is non-critical fades to the background.

The process of comparing groupings enables you to identify characteristics or attributes of the phenomenon that are referred to in one grouping, but not in another. In this way, aspects of the phenomenon that critically distinguish one grouping from another become apparent. As always, in practice, this step builds on and integrates with other steps.

> **Concrete examples of Discerning**
>
> After the relevant quotes [excerpts from interviews] have been grouped, the focus of attention is shifted from the relations between the quotes (expressions) to the relations between the groups. It is necessary to establish what are the critical attributes of each group and what are the distinguishing features between the groups. In this way the set of 'categories of description' are developed in relation to a given criterion... they represent different capabilities for seeing the phenomenon in question. (Marton, 1994, p. 4428)
>
> My initial search for dimensions of variation [critical aspects] in awareness focused on identifying different aspects of the phenomenon that were referred to in some transcripts but not in others. In this way, I started to tentatively identify dimensions that appeared critical in distinguishing between transcripts and between emerging categories of description. ... [This] involved *systematically* looking through each transcript and preliminary groupings of transcripts for themes and dimensions I had tentatively identified on earlier readings, as well as for the different forms or levels that variation along these themes may take. For instance, ... it was apparent from early on that at least one transcript in the data set [on being a university researcher] represented research activity in terms of external outcomes, and another in terms of internal outcomes. However, whether this variation would emerge as critical, what the various manifestations or levels of the variation would be, whether it would remain as a single dimension or split into a number of themes, and whether the [labels] I was using was the best way of describing the variation was not clear until later on in the analysis. (Åkerlind, 2005c, pp. 122–123)
>
> This is achieved by applying the principle of focusing on one aspect of the object and seeking its dimensions of variation while holding other aspects frozen. One particular aspect of the phenomenon can be selected and inspected across all of the [extracted statements], and then another aspect, that to be followed, maybe, by the study of whole interviews to see

> where these two aspects lie in the pool [of meanings] relative to the other aspects and the background. In a study that involves [presenting participants with] a number of problems for solution, for instance, the analysis might start by considering just one of the problems as tackled and discussed by all the [participants], and then a selection of whole transcripts that include particularly interesting ways of handling the problem. This process repeated will lead to vaguely spied structure through and across the data that our researcher/learner can develop, sharpen, and return to again and again from first one perspective and then another until there is clarity. (Marton and Booth, 1997, p. 133)

Articulating

The transition from Comparing, Grouping, Delimiting and Discerning to Articulating the distinctive meaning and critical aspects of each way of experiencing the phenomenon is not a clear cut one. Nor should it be, because all of the analytic steps are interrelated. It is the process of Comparing, Grouping, Delimiting and Discerning that enables the researcher to clarify what demarcates each category, or way of experiencing, and distinguishes it from the other categories. Each iteration of Comparing, Grouping, Delimiting and Discerning thus enables the distinguishing characteristics of each category to be more and more clearly defined and able to be 'articulated'. So, again, each stage of the process informs the others and there is constant iteration between the different stages.

> **Concrete examples of Articulating**
>
> At each stage of our discussions about what characterized each conception we read the transcripts again, each time from a slightly different perspective as our initial understanding of them developed ... We sought to formulate progressively more complete and refined descriptions of the six conceptions [Articulating]. As we did this, we continually sought evidence within the transcripts that either was consistent with our draft categories or conflicted with them [Checking]... In addition, we looked for commonality from one transcript to another within

> the same category [Grouping]. Through this process we jointly drafted categories of description based on the evidence in the transcripts. In refining those categories we engaged in a process of discussion that involved formulating or justifying each aspect of a category, referring back to the relevant transcripts as we did so [Articulating]. (Prosser, 2000, p. 38)
>
> [We] independently assigned the transcripts to particular draft categories [Grouping] ... In discussing the categorisation of those transcripts, our focus was on determining the qualitatively different ways in which these [participants] understood [the phenomenon]. This process occurred at two levels of analysis. First, we attempted to identify the conception of [the phenomenon] that was evident in each transcript [Articulating] and second, we sought to clarify the features [critical aspects] of each conception by comparing and contrasting it with the other conceptions that were emerging [Discerning] ... When we had agreed on the categorisation of many of the transcripts, we attempted to describe the most characteristic features of each conception, with constant reference to the transcripts [Articulating]. (Dall'Alba, 2000, p. 90)

Checking

As should be apparent from the quotes above, checking preliminary interpretations against the original transcript data is also not a once-only activity, but a part of the ongoing iteration between different stages of analysis. Although the process of Checking was not explicitly mentioned in Fallsberg and Dahlgren's original guidelines, it has always been an important part of phenomenographic analysis. An outcome of the continual checking of interpretations against the data is that researchers can expect to move through a number of preliminary sets of categories of description as their analysis proceeds. In a unique 'behind the scenes' look at different stages in the development of categories of description and identification of associated critical aspects, the appendices to Bowden and Green's (2005) book illustrate the development of interim stages in the interpretive process. One study described developing eight interim sets of preliminary categorisations before the final outcome was reached, and the other study, five interim sets.

Checking also involves a strong element of 'interpretive awareness', further explained later in the chapter in the section on research rigour, and the willingness to take a 'devil's advocacy' role towards one's own interpretations (also explained further in the section on research rigour, and in the examples below).

> **Concrete examples of Checking**
>
> ...categories are tested against the data, adjusted, retested, and adjusted again. There is, however, a decreasing rate of change and eventually the whole system of meanings is stabilized. (Marton, 1986, p. 42)
>
> The next stage was to return to the individual transcripts and analyse them in terms of the categories we constructed. We [the team of researchers] did this independently ... we examined the categorisations, and where there seemed to be mismatches [in our interpretations], we returned to the transcripts, and either adjusted our categories, adjusted our categorisations or left the mismatch remaining, depending on our interpretation of the transcripts. This we repeated several times over a number of meetings [until agreement was reached and all mismatches resolved]. (Prosser, 2000, p. 38)
>
> In previous places (Bowden, 2000, for example), I have argued strongly for team analysis and the importance of the devil's advocacy role. ... The way we worked was this. One person prepared the next set of categories of description [of success as a researcher]. ... [In subsequent team discussion of the categories] Often there was a focus on, say, just one category that was puzzling us at the time. The person responsible went back and re-read the transcripts and produced the new version. At the next meeting, the rest of us had the role of questioning the reformulation of the category. ... What the devil's advocates—the rest of us—do is to ask the originator the basis for their particular way of writing the category of description. [For example] Why did you focus attention on success being related to outcomes satisfying to the researcher? Why did you choose those particular words? Where in the transcripts can we see evidence that this is the best way to describe this particular category? (Bowden, 2005, pp. 23–24)
>
> ...going through five, ten, or fifteen versions of the categories of description is necessary. I don't believe you could read the

> transcripts once and then write the final categories of description. ...you read the transcripts again with different eyes. The draft categories guide your reading, but you are looking for evidence to undermine that draft representation—to test the coherence of a category description or to question the difference between two different draft categories. Aspects of the transcripts that were not seen as significant before become significant now. You see them afresh. Despite having read the transcripts many times, it seems like you are seeing that aspect for the first time. Every new reading of the transcripts is a fresh experience. Perhaps when it ceases to be like that is when you've reached the last version. (Bowden, 2005, p. 29)

Relating

Although the search for potential relationships between categories occurs throughout the analytic process, whenever similarities and differences between categories are being considered, it is most obvious towards the end of the process when the final outcome space is constituted. Explicitly drawing out inclusive relationships that organise the different categories of description into a hierarchical structure of increasing complexity of awareness is essential to meet the phenomenographic aim of exploring collective experience (rather than individual experience). It is only through connecting the different categories into a structured and interrelated 'outcome space' that a holistic view of collective experience is made possible. Without this, the categories would represent just an unrelated series of different meanings (i.e., a series of unrelated parts), not an integrated description of collective meaning, in which the parts are related in a holistic structure.

Although Relating categories of description has always been an important part of phenomenographic analysis, there is a new component to this step in the 21st century, which is that identification of critical aspects of awareness of phenomena is now an expected part of the step (as described in Chapter 2 and Chapter 5). Before the 21st century, inclusive relationships between different categories were primarily argued on logical grounds, that one holistic way of experiencing logically implied or required simultaneous awareness of the critical elements of another holistic way of experiencing. In 21st-century phenomenography, however, it is expanding awareness of different critical aspects of a phenomenon that provides the basis for structuring the outcome space. This is often presented in the form of a table, for example, Table 3.1 and Table 4.1 in Chapters 3 and 4, or Table 7.2 below, from Marton and Pong (2005).

Table 7.2 An example of structural (part-whole) relationships between different categories in an outcome space, based on a study of the different ways in which students can experience 'price' (adapted from Marton and Pong, 2005, p. 342)

Categories	Ways of experiencing 'price'	Critical aspects discerned
A	Price reflects the *value or worth of the object*	Variation in the *characteristics of the object*
B	Price reflects the *demand conditions of the market* in which the object is situated	Variation in the *people who buy* such objects
C	Price reflects the *supply conditions of the market* in which the object is situated	Variation in the *people who sell* such objects (or the places where they are sold)
D	Price reflects the *opposing demand and supply conditions* of the market in which the object is situated	Variation in *both the people who buy and the people who sell* such objects (or the places where they are sold)

But other forms of presentation may also be used, for example the more visual approach by Lupton (2004) shown in Table 7.3.

Table 7.3 An example of structural (part-whole) relationships between different categories in an outcome space, based on a study of the different ways in which students can experience 'information literacy when researching an essay' (adapted from Lupton, 2004, pp. 53–54)

Ways of experiencing 'information literacy'	Critical aspects discerned
Category 1: Information literacy when researching an essay involves *seeking information to backup a pre-existing argument* for the essay. • Primary focus of attention is on meeting the requirements of the essay task.	Information / Essay task (nested circles)

Category B: Information literacy when researching an essay involves *using background information to develop an argument* for the essay. • Primary focus of attention is on the learning that occurs from the essay task.	
Category 3: Information literacy when researching an essay involves *applying learning to help solve problems* posed by the essay. • Primary focus of attention is on applying one's learning.	

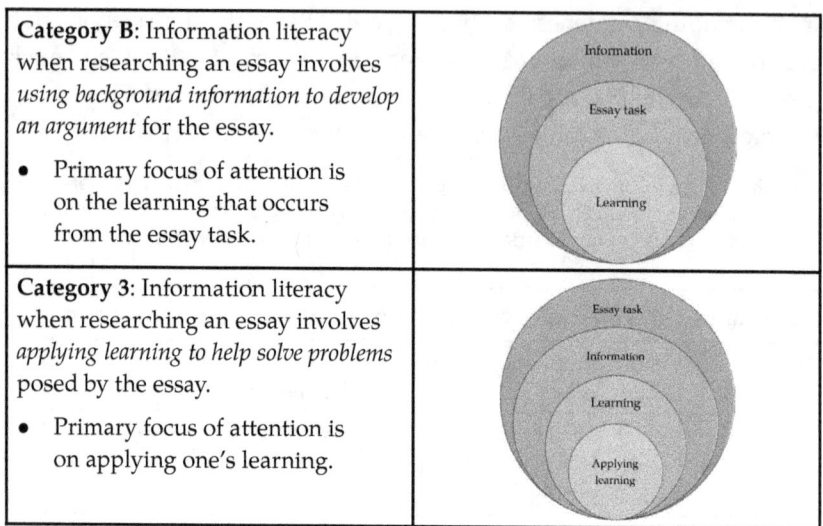

Labelling

Once the categories of description, associated critical aspects and relationships between categories have been clarified (i.e., checked and re-checked against the original transcript data and for consistency with the interpretations arising from each stage of the analysis), the categories are ready to be labelled. Of course, informal labels for different groupings may have been used during the analysis process as an aide-memoire for the researcher, but we are now talking about the formal labels that will be used in presenting the research to others. The labelling of categories is not about the comprehensive description of the category that will accompany the reporting of results, but about the succinct heading or descriptive title given to categories in phenomenographic outcomes.

Dahlgren and Fallsberg (1991) are unique in the literature in highlighting Labelling as a distinct stage in the analysis. The process of Labelling is normally left implicit in descriptions of phenomenographic analysis, but I would argue that the choice of labels for the categories is a complicated process and an interpretive act in its own right, in that the label inevitably highlights some things about the category but not others. This is why I have included it here as part of the analytic or interpretive process, rather than something that happens after the interpretation is complete.

Meanwhile, what the researcher decides to highlight and not highlight about a category through their choice of a label is likely to have a big impact on wider understanding of the research outcomes amongst readers of the research. When citing a phenomenographic study in the literature, it is common for authors to describe only the category labels used in the study, and these then become the main way in which the research outcomes are then spread and summarised. Whilst Collier-Reed and Ingerman (2013) rightly argue that "referring to the outcome of a phenomenographic study simply in terms of the titles of the categories is fairly meaningless" (p. 246), unfortunately, it is still common.

The starting question for the process of Labelling is, 'What do you want to highlight about the categories through the Labelling process?'. Some researchers focus on highlighting distinctive meaning. This acts to highlight what is different about each category. Other researchers focus on highlighting structural relationships between categories. This acts to highlight what is similar as well as different about each category, as illustrated in the 'concrete example' below. Because the process of Labelling has been uniformly neglected in the phenomenographic literature, I draw on the work of one of my research students, Laura Killam, to illustrate the process.

Concrete example of Labelling:

Categories of description

Early and final stages in the process of Labelling four categories of description are presented below, based on Laura Killam's study of different ways of experiencing 'learner-educator co-construction' of course assessment.

Early version:

1. A way to get help meeting course requirements.
2. A way of learning more during the course.
3. Working together to change aspects of the course.
4. An empowering learning environment.

Final version (Killam et al., 2024):

1. Educators supporting students to make consistent progress towards course goals.

> 2. Educators working with students on amending the course to promote learner access.
>
> 3. Educators and students sharing course decision-making to create power equity.
>
> 4. Educators and students sharing course decision-making to foster mutual growth.
>
> Both versions in the example present perfectly acceptable labels for the four categories. The early version focuses more on highlighting holistic meaning and differences in focus between the categories—it gives a 'feel' for the qualitative differences between categories. The final version places more emphasis on structure, highlighting critical parts that make up the whole. This enables a direct comparison between the category labels in terms differences between the categories in (a) what educators are seen to do; (b) what students are seen to do; and (c) the underlying purpose of what they do in co-constructing course assessment. However, some researchers may feel that the sense of holistic meaning is somewhat lost in this structural/relational emphasis, which reads more as a series of parts, and thus prefer the early version of the labels. Either way, putting thought and time into the process of Labelling can help increase clarity and precision for researchers in their interpretations of categories.

Critical aspects or dimensions of variation also need to be labelled, but that process is less complicated than labelling categories, because critical aspects can represent aspects of either structure or meaning, whilst categories of description always represent both structure and meaning (Collier-Reed and Ingerman, 2013).

> **Concrete example of Labelling:**
>
> **Critical aspects**
>
> Early and final stages in the process of Labelling critical aspects are illustrated below, based on my study of different ways of understanding 'phenomenography' described in Chapter 3.
>
> Early version:
>
> 1. Educational literature.
>
> 2. Research methods.
>
> 3. Focus on variation.
>
> 4. Focus on relationships.

5. Pedagogical utility.

6. Everyday thinking.

Final version (Chapter 3):

1. Contribution to literature.

2. Research methods used.

3. Research outcomes produced—variation.

4. Research outcomes produced—relationships.

5. Pedagogical applications.

6. Everyday applications.

Again, both sets of labels are perfectly acceptable, but I thought that the final version was more meaningful than the early version, especially when read in isolation from the larger description of research outcomes in Chapter 3, which is something that often happens when one's research outcomes are referred to in a subsequent paper.

Bringing all the steps together

As I have said a number of times throughout the description of these analytic guidelines, the steps are not undertaken in a linear and independent way, but iteratively and simultaneously. Even Familiarising and Condensing, which are largely done at the beginning of the analysis, are revisited as you proceed. Similarly, Relating and Labelling, in the form of building an outcome space, which are largely done towards the end of the analysis, may still lead to questions and insights that send you back to early stages of analysis for purposes of Checking and possible revisions to the final interpretation. For example,

> In summary, in trying to understand the transcripts, I was working on several different fronts at once: reading my transcripts [Familiarising]; reading my notes [on the transcripts] [Condensing]; working with individual transcripts and with preliminary groupings of transcripts [Grouping]; asking myself what was similar and what was different between transcripts [Comparing]... and between tentative groupings of transcripts [Delimiting]; focusing on similarities and differences in terms of a sense of more holistic meanings that emerged for me from the transcripts [Grouping]... and looking for dimensions and themes that would provide the basic structure or structural relationships between

the different ways of understanding that were emerging [Discerning and Relating]. More separated in the early stages of analysis, these different perspectives [or analytic steps] became increasingly integrated over time. (Åkerlind, 2005c, pp. 121–122)

This raises the issue of when you decide that the analysis is complete. In short, this occurs when the outcomes of the iterations form a coherent and integrated pattern, when all variation in the data has been accounted for within that pattern, and no new questions or insights into the data emerge from continuing iterations.

> **Another form of Labelling:**
>
> **What to call the unit of description in your study**
>
> I have already discussed decisions to be made when Labelling categories of description and critical aspects. But there is also a decision to be made about what label or term to use for the unit of description in your study— that is, what term you use to explain to others what is being represented by a category of description. As discussed in Chapter 6, 'conceptions', 'ways of understanding', 'ways of experiencing', 'ways of seeing', 'ways of making sense of' and 'ways of perceiving' a phenomenon are all terms that have been used.
>
> I suggest that your decision on which term, or label, to use to describe what you are studying should be made with both your object of study and the intended audience for the research in mind. For example, when the object of study is Newton's 3rd law of physics, it sounds more natural to refer to different ways of 'understanding' the law than to different ways of 'experiencing' it. But the word 'experiencing' feels perfectly appropriate when the phenomenon being studied is something like 'being a teacher'. In addition, because this decision is about how best to communicate your research outcomes to others, I also take the varied audience for my research into account, in terms of what label I think will be most meaningful to readers of the journal I am aiming to publish in (inevitably, most readers will not be familiar with phenomenographic research). For example, I am more likely to use the label 'conception' when writing for journals that are more oriented towards quantitative research, 'way of experiencing' when writing for journals that are more oriented towards qualitative research, and 'way of understanding' when writing for education journals.

Research rigour

In qualitative research of an interpretive nature, discussions of the quality and rigour of research primarily address issues of the 'trustworthiness' of the interpretive process and 'credibility' of the research outcomes. Different interpretive research traditions have developed different practices for establishing rigour (e.g., Denzin and Lincoln, 2000 [1994]; Bowden and Green, 2005; Sandberg, 2005; Higgs et al., 2010). This is because rigour is not an epistemology-free zone, so there are no universal definitions. Attempts to ensure rigour have to be consistent with both the methods used and the epistemological assumptions that underlie those methods. This means that what is regarded as evidence of rigour, and what constitutes accepted practices for ensuring rigour, varies with the methodology.

Phenomenography has its own set of practices for ensuring rigour, as will be described below. And whilst there is much in common between phenomenography's practices and those of other interpretive research traditions, there are also areas of difference. Meanwhile, even within phenomenography, there is not universal agreement amongst all researchers about appropriate indicators of rigour (as I have described previously—Åkerlind, 2022, 2012 [2005]). So, with room to argue for different approaches to rigour in phenomenographic research, the most important thing in deciding on your own approach is to be thoughtful and reflective about it. The practices you select have to make sense to you within your own understanding of phenomenographic research, and you need to be prepared to describe how your practices are internally consistent with phenomenographic methods and epistemology, as you understand them.

Although my primary discussion of research rigour is contained within this chapter, it is important to note that rigour is just as relevant to the decisions and procedures of gathering data, which were discussed in the previous chapter. The discussion in Chapter 6 of the importance of clarifying the phenomenon being investigated, ensuring as much as possible that participants are focusing on the same phenomenon and grounding their reflections on the phenomenon in concrete examples of their interactions with the phenomenon, the piloting of research questions, and the emphasis on follow-up questions that are as non-leading as possible, are all aspects of rigour. In addition, internal consistency (both methodologically and epistemologically) between the purpose(s) of the research, the research question(s), selection of participants, methods used to gather data and methods used to analyse data is vital in ensuring rigour.

Common practices for establishing rigour in phenomenography have changed over time in response to the rise in recognition over the 1970s–1990s that interpretive qualitative research is paradigmatically different to objectivist quantitative research and so should be judged by different criteria (Guba, 1981; Guba and Lincoln, 1994; Denzin, 2009). In the early days of phenomenography, the objectivist epistemology associated with quantitative research was more dominant than today, and its associated expectations of validity, reliability and generalisability of research were still the gold standard as indicators of research quality. Consequently, early phenomenography tended to position its research rigour with respect to these indicators. But over time, as interpretive research came to be more mainstream, more appropriate indicators have developed.

There are a number of publications specifically focused on aspects of rigour in phenomenographic research (Svensson and Theman, 1983; Sandberg, 1997; Ashworth and Lucas, 1998, 2000; Cope, 2004; Bowden and Green, 2005; Collier-Reed, Ingerman and Berglund, 2009; Green and Bowden, 2009; Bowden and Green, 2010; Sin, 2010; Collier-Reed and Ingerman, 2013; Straub and Maynes, 2021;[4] Rotar, 2024), as well as rigour being a sub-topic in many other papers. So, I do not intend to approach the topic afresh here. As I said earlier, there is not universal agreement amongst phenomenographers about what constitutes rigour in research, and I do not necessarily agree with everything proposed in the articles cited above, but I do think that it is worth reading a variety of views on the issue (including literature from interpretive research traditions other than phenomenography) in order to form your own thinking on the matter. But in this chapter, I will focus on describing the practices that I personally use.

---

4   Although Straub and Maynes (2021) make many useful points about phenomenographic analysis, I have to note my concerns with the inappropriate cognitivist and quantitative perspectives that they introduce at times into their discussion of phenomenographic analysis and research rigour.

I find it conceptually useful to think of rigour, or research quality, in terms of the trustworthiness of the *processes* of research and the credibility of the *outcomes* of research—although the distinction is somewhat artificial, because credibility of research outcomes is impossible without trustworthiness of research processes. To develop the trustworthiness of my research process, I make particular use of 'interpretive awareness' (including what has been called 'devil's advocacy' and 'dialogic consensus'). To develop the credibility of my research outcomes, I make particular use of communicative validity, although I prefer to call it 'communicative credibility' to remove associations with objectivist notions of validity.

However, as I said previously, separation of the quality of the process and the quality of the outcomes of research is somewhat artificial, and feedback on communicative credibility can also be used to refine the outcomes, making it simultaneously a potential part of the interpretive process as well as the assessment of credibility of outcomes. Meanwhile, the terms are used with different meanings in different articles so, to avoid confusion, I will explain what I personally mean by them.

Trustworthiness of the research process

With any interpretive research there are always concerns about how best to handle the researcher's subjective input into the analysis and outcomes. From an objectivist position, subjectivity is something to be avoided, but from an interpretivist position, it is something to be acknowledged and managed. But in order to manage subjectivity during the phenomenographic interpretive process, it first needs to be understood from a phenomenographic perspective, and phenomenographers think not so much in terms of subjectivity (which reflects a dualistic perspective), but relationality (which reflects a non-dualistic perspective).

Relational role of the researcher—Because phenomenography adopts a non-dualistic position on human experience of the world (as described in Chapter 5), in which experience is seen as a relation between the experiencer and the phenomenon being experienced, this must also apply to the relation between the researcher and their experience of the research data. Figure 7.1, from Bowden (2005), summarises the relational role of the researcher during data analysis, as seen from a phenomenographic epistemological perspective.

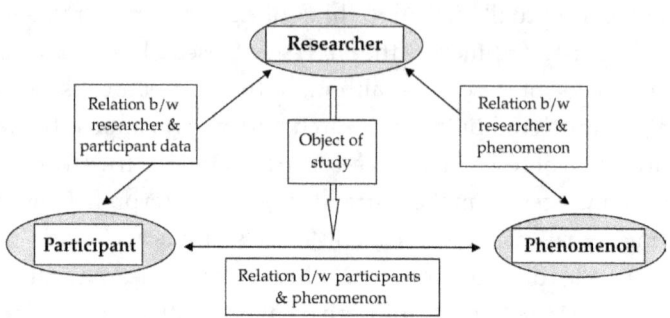

Fig. 7.1 Relational role of the researcher during analysis (adapted from Bowden, 2005, p. 13)

So, from a phenomenographic perspective, researchers are seen as inevitably bringing to their interpretation of the research their relationship with the phenomenon, with the data, and with the community participants represent. These aspects of researchers' relationality must be acknowledged by the researcher, and their potential impact upon interpretation of the data (and indeed gathering of the data) actively considered during the research process.

Interpretive awareness—As part of this consideration, the researcher needs to engage in activities that will provide checks and balances on the potential impact of their relationality on research interpretation and outcomes. This sensitivity to the potential for researcher impact, combined with attempts to mitigate these impacts, has been called 'interpretive awareness' (Sandberg, 1994, 1996, 1997), which is similar to the concept of 'researcher reflexivity' used in other traditions.[5] As described by Sandberg (2005),

> [interpretive awareness] implies first and foremost that researchers must demonstrate how they have dealt with their intentional relation to the lived [sic] experience studied. That is, researchers must demonstrate how they have controlled and checked their interpretations throughout the research process: from formulating the research question, selecting individuals to be studied, obtaining data from those individuals, analyzing the data obtained, and reporting the results. (p. 59)

---

5   This is related to, but goes beyond, the notion used in other traditions of the researcher's 'positionality', which focuses on the researcher becoming aware of and describing their social connections and identities, with a sensitivity to how this may influence their interpretations.

To maintain interpretive awareness during analysis means to acknowledge and explicitly deal with your relationality throughout the research process, rather than leaving the process implicit. This includes:

> ...documenting how researchers have adopted a critical attitude towards their own interpretations, that is, how they have analysed their own presuppositions, and the checks and balances that they have employed to help counteract the impact of their particular perspectives on the research outcomes. (Åkerlind, 2012 [2005], p. 125)

So, whilst relationality is inevitable, and in many ways even desirable (for example, through the expertise and specialised knowledge that the researcher brings to the analysis), it also needs to be monitored and balanced.

Drawing on other traditions, Rotar (2024) has developed a comprehensive list of ways of considering and documenting reflexivity as a researcher during phenomenographic data analysis. This provides a useful source of potential ideas and practices when thinking about researcher reflexivity and interpretive awareness. However, as Rotar acknowledges herself, if you were to undertake everything on her list, there would be no time left for the research itself! So, interpretive checks and balances need to be undertaken thoughtfully and pragmatically.

Meanwhile, there is a difference between the assumption of researcher relationality and simple researcher bias. Biased researchers selectively interpret statements to justify their own conclusions, including taking particular note of statements that support their own opinions, and tending to ignore counterevidence (without necessarily even being aware that they are doing so). In contrast, researchers exercising interpretive awareness are attentive to how their own interpretations may be influenced by their relationship to the research, and attempt to take this into account during their data gathering, analysis and reporting.

Interpretive checks and balances—One obvious way in which our interpretations may be influenced by our pre-existing understandings is the potential they create for 'blinding' us to understandings that we have not ourselves previously experienced, and to variation that we have not ourselves previously discerned (i.e., the potential to miss something in the data). During data analysis, I attempt to overcome this potential limitation in the following ways:

1. By actively comparing and contrasting participant responses in the data, explicitly looking for *all* variation, not just particular types of variation.

2. By approaching the data with active curiosity, very open to the possibility of finding something that I had not noticed about the object of study before. (Indeed, I would say that I am always hopeful of doing so, because I find that exciting.)

3. By bringing someone else's perspective into the interpretation. For instance, phenomenographic research is often undertaken by a group of two or more researchers, which automatically brings in more than one perspective during the interpretive process. But even as a single researcher, it is possible to consult colleagues about particular aspects of your analysis and share at least small amounts of data with them, in particular in areas where you feel uncertain of your interpretations. Reaching a joint decision on an interpretation in this way has been called dialogic reliability, but I prefer 'dialogic consensus', to avoid the objectivist associations with the term reliability.

> **Analytical aside:**
>
> **Data analysis as a single researcher vs group of researchers**
>
> The only literature where I have seen a discussion of data analysis undertaken by a lone researcher *vs* a group of researchers is in Bowden and Green's (2005) book. Amongst other things, this book actively compares the experience of a single researcher (myself) with that of a group of researchers (John Bowden, Pam Green, Robyn Barnacle, Nita Cherry and Robin Usher) in undertaking phenomengraphic research on a similar object of study ('Being a researcher' and 'Success as a researcher'). Below, I quote from their section on 'Should phenomenographic analysis be done individually, or as a team?'
>
> "The relative confidence one could feel in the outcomes of individual versus team phenomenographic analysis was explicitly discussed by the contributors to this monograph... Although the decision on this issue is often made as much on practical grounds of feasible research resources as on logical argument for the 'best' approach.

Both Gerlese, with her extensive experience of individual analysis, and Robyn, who was currently involved in conducting primarily individual analyses... expressed confidence as individual researchers. One of the advantages they experienced as individual researchers was becoming more deeply familiar with the data than was possible for each member of a team research project. Furthermore, as an individual researcher, one can still seek feedback from others during the analysis, and both had done so. Nevertheless, because such feedback would be more regular and systematic with team research, it seems likely that team research might be more rigorous, in general.

Robyn suggests that: 'The process of team analysis highlights the crisis involved in all interpretation: the challenge of realising difference, bringing it to the fore. But within a team situation there is also more because it is not just agreement between text and interpreter that is sought but agreement between text and multiple interpreters. In order to reach consensus one must convince others of the credibility of one's interpretation. A case needs to be made and defended... I found the process of team analysis provided a rare opportunity to gain insight into, as well as critique, my own interpretive habits. This may have made the analysis process longer than it might otherwise have been, but it was certainly more rewarding.'

While team analysis may seem inevitably more rigorous than individual analysis, Gerlese highlights in her story that 'the large number of existing phenomenographic doctoral theses indicates that high quality phenomenographic research can be accomplished as an individual researcher working largely on one's own'. She also points out that 'any outcome space is inevitably partial, with respect to the hypothetically complete range of ways of experiencing a phenomenon'. Consequently, the contrast between different phenomenographic approaches should not be considered in terms of what is most likely to produce 'right' or 'wrong' outcomes, but rather, more or less complete outcomes. 'Thus, an individual researcher can, at the least, make a substantial contribution to our understanding of the phenomenon, even if team research might have taken that understanding further'" (pp. 92–93).

Given that group analysis is also a social process, in another section of the book Bowden talks about the need for mutual trust amongst an analytic team. He notes that comparing and questioning each others' interpretations can be a vulnerable process, and there is a need for sensitivity to the potential for members of the team to feel that their

> interpretations have been not just critiqued, but criticised: "all members of the team need to be continually sensitive to their colleagues' feelings—not to change what the group does (that would defeat the purpose) but to change how they do it (perhaps by making the process...more explicit) whenever one of their colleagues appears more vulnerable than usual" (p. 31).

When reflecting on potential limitations placed on the interpretive process by researchers' pre-existing understandings of the phenomenon being studied, it is also important to note that researchers' understanding of the phenomenon at the end of the analysis process is likely to be different to their understanding at the beginning. The process of engaging with the data is likely to expose them to variation in aspects of the phenomenon that they might not have previously discerned, and in this way change their way of understanding it. In this sense, any initial limitations on the researcher's capacity to 'see' variation in the data may well reduce over the course of the analysis.

Meanwhile, an alternative way in which researcher interpretations may be unduly influenced by pre-existing understandings is the potential they create for unintentionally 'imposing' our understandings on interpretations of the data (i.e., distorting the data). As a single researcher, I attempt to overcome this potential limitation in the following ways:

1. By actively comparing every response that I allocate to a particular category with every other response allocated to that category, actively checking that they are indeed saying similar things, and that there is not internal variation in what they are saying that I have so far missed.

2. By employing what Bowden has called a 'devil's advocacy' approach to my own interpretations (Bowden, 2005; Bowden and Green, 2010; Green and Bowden, 2009), that is, explicitly looking for evidence that challenges the interpretations, not just evidence that supports it (which has much in common with what other traditions call 'negative case analysis').

3. By careful checking of the hierarchically inclusive nature of the different categories presented in the outcome space. If

what I have interpreted as a critical aspect of the phenomenon does not distinguish between different categories, then it has to be reconsidered. And if the proposed critical aspects do not distinguish categories in an inclusively expanding way, then they again have to be reconsidered.

> **A concrete example of an act of interpretive awareness**
>
> I will draw on the study I presented in Chapter 4 of educational researchers' varied understandings of 'structural relationships' in phenomenography to provide a concrete example of an approach to interpretive awareness during research.
>
> First, before looking at any data, I completed the same survey that I used for gathering the data, so that I could record and, later, consider potential limitations that my own initial understanding of structural relationships in phenomenography may have placed on my interpretation of the data. Many qualitative researchers talk about considering the potential influence of researchers' social, cultural and professional context (positionality) on their interpretations, but I think that the phenomenographic focus on investigating different ways of understanding phenomena makes the potential influence of the researcher's understanding of the object of study even more important to consider.
>
> To help explain how I used my own survey response as a source of interpretive awareness, I need to share my response with you. The relevant question was, 'Phenomenography is often described as focusing on structural relationships—what does that mean to you (if anything)?'
>
> *My response*: "The focus on structure is the most defining and most powerful aspect of phenomenography; it is what makes it most useful/insightful. Although the form taken by the phenomenographic focus on structure has varied over time, I think a focus on part-whole relationships is at its core, including:
>
> - The theoretical structure of awareness—internal/external horizons; theme, thematic field, and margin of awareness.
>
> - The part-whole structure of different categories of description that make up the total outcome space, i.e., the relationship of specific/qualitatively different ways of experiencing to the collective whole.

- The part-whole structure of the critical aspects of a phenomenon discerned to the overall meaning/experience of that phenomenon as a whole.

- The dialectical nature of meaning and structure, i.e., the what and how of the experience of phenomena" (Gerlese Åkerlind, 5 December, 2018).

After completing my response, I did not look at it again until I had finished analysing the data (some time later), because what is significant in my response could only be understood within the context of comparison with other responses, which requires at least a preliminary data analysis. So, at an advanced stage of analysis, I used my response to consider how my understanding of structural relationships may have influenced my interpretations and constitution of the outcomes to date.

At this point, it was apparent from my survey response that what had been available within my own personal understanding to then readily experience in the data was a focus on (1) what I called theoretical structures (but what would be better called figure-ground structures) in awareness; (2) two types of part-whole structures in awareness; and (3) the dialectical nature of meaning and structure in human experience. So, it may not be surprising that I also saw these elements in the data.

But I could also see that, in my own survey response, I did not highlight hierarchical structures, even though this was a theme that emerged strongly in the data. (This was because I, personally, saw part-whole structures as inclusive of hierarchical structures, in that they provide the basis for constituting hierarchical structures, rather than because I was completely unaware of hierarchical structures.) Nevertheless, it is clear that during the analysis I was able to highlight critical aspects of structural relationships in the data that I had not personally highlighted in my own response (i.e., hierarchical structures)—which is an encouraging indication that I was not unduly limited by my pre-existing understandings in my ability to discern variation in the data. (Though there is always the possibility that there were other aspects of structure represented in the data that I did not notice, because they were outside my own experience.)

At the same time, there were also aspects of structure that I highlighted in my survey response, but which did not form part of the outcome space—which is an encouraging indication that I did not actively impose my pre-existing understandings on the data. Specifically, my response drew an explicit distinction between two types of part-whole structures: (1) the way in which awareness of different critical aspects form the parts that constitute a holistic category of meaning; and (2) the way in which different categories of meaning combine to form the parts that constitute collective meaning. Whilst I could see both types of part-whole structures in the data, I did not see them mentioned simultaneously in the survey responses in the way they were in my response. That is, while respondents mentioned one or the other type of part-whole structure, no respondent mentioned both types. So, I could not say that the distinction in type of part-whole structures was critical to distinguishing one way of experiencing structural relationships from another way in this dataset (even though I personally think the distinction is important). In this way at least, I could see that I did not impose my expectations on the data interpretation.

Lastly, I would like to acknowledge a particular way in which I could see that my own understanding *did* influence my interpretation of the findings. In my own response, I had highlighted figure-ground structures as an aspect of 'structural relationships'. But this aspect was not strongly evident in the data (being referred to only once in the whole data set). Nevertheless, it could be seen in the data, even though in only one instance. During my analysis, this weak presence of references to figure-ground structures in the data, but strong presence in my own understanding, led me to question whether I should interpret awareness of figure-ground structures as a critical aspect of the collective understanding of structural relationships or not.

What made me hesitate to interpret figure-ground structures as a critical aspect was not so much that it had only been mentioned once, but the relatively off-hand way in which it seemed to be mentioned by that respondent, as an unelaborated comment at the end of the respondent's overall response, i.e., "There are different ways of handling structure. I tend to lean towards expanding awareness ... theme, thematic field, etc." (Response 17).

What made me decide, in the end, to include it as a separate category is that (a) the respondent said that they personally tend towards using this structure, so even though it seemed to be mentioned in an offhand way it was clearly of significance to them; (b) this highlighting of what I called figure-ground structures in phenomenography occurred in a response that also mentioned every other critical aspect discerned across the sample, so it was clearly inclusive in complexity; and lastly (3) I

> was influenced by my own understanding of structural relationships in phenomenography, based on my reading of Marton and Booth (1997).
>
> So, here is a clear example of where my own knowledge and understanding of the phenomenon influenced my analysis. Whether one would argue that this was a negative influence (i.e., that I potentially 'imposed' this understanding on the data) or a positive influence (i.e., that my extensive knowledge of phenomenography enabled me to discern a variation in the data that someone with a less extensive knowledge may have missed) is beside the point. The important point is that interpretive awareness is maintained and documented during the analysis, so that such influences can be taken into account as much as possible during the analysis and in reporting the research outcomes.

Bracketing—Although my primary focus in ensuring trustworthiness is on employing interpretive awareness, many phenomenographic researchers suggest using 'bracketing', so let me discuss how this fits with the notion of interpretive awareness. Although, in practice, researchers typically focus on one or the other process (i.e., on either bracketing or interpretive awareness), I regard interpretive awareness as the more encompassing concept. So, I see bracketing as something that could potentially be undertaken as part of the checks and balances involved in interpretive awareness, but I do not think bracketing is adequate on its own for ensuring interpretive rigour.

But first, let me explain the notion of bracketing in more detail. Bracketing is the attempt to put to one side (or bracket) one's pre-existing assumptions about participants, the phenomenon and different ways of understanding the phenomenon during data collection and analysis. The notion is derived from phenomenology, and was first suggested as also appropriate for phenomenography by Marton (1994). It was then substantially elaborated within the phenomenographic research context by Ashworth and Lucas (2000). In contrasting bracketing with interpretive awareness, I would say that bracketing emphasises controlling the researchers' subjectivity, while interpretive awareness emphasises acknowledging the researchers' subjectivity. And bracketing emphasises trying to stop something (i.e., the interference of pre-existing assumptions), while interpretive awareness emphasises trying to do something (i.e., engage in interpretive checks and balances).

However, in saying this, I am focusing on the way in which bracketing is commonly described in phenomenographic research studies. But in these descriptions, much of the complexity of Ashworth and Lucas's initial description seems to have been lost. For instance, it is very common to see published studies that contain the simple statement that bracketing was employed during the study, with no description of how bracketing was undertaken or the limitations of bracketing. So, I would suggest that researchers who are drawn to the concept of bracketing should ensure that they include some of the nuances of Ashworth and Lucas' description of bracketing in their research practice (and in their descriptions of that practice when publishing their research).

First, there is the need to acknowledge that complete bracketing of one's own prior experience and assumptions is, of course, impossible—especially within phenomenography's epistemological assumption of relationality (see Figure 7.1 above). Then, there is a need to describe the process by which one has attempted to achieve bracketing—a simple claim that one has engaged in bracketing is worth little. For example, Ashworth and Lucas describe a set of guidelines that they created and followed during their research, and while I am not advocating those guidelines in particular, what I am advocating is the need to think clearly about what the process of bracketing involves from the researcher's perspective.[6]

Empathy for participants' perspectives—Further, where bracketing fits into the research aims of phenomenography also needs to be clarified. A primary aim during phenomenographic data collection and analysis is to attempt to see the phenomenon from the perspective of participants. This involves not just attempts to control or mitigate any assumptions that might interfere with seeing the phenomenon from participants' perspectives, but also corresponding attempts to be actively sensitive to participants' perspectives. (The first approach emphasises stopping something, while the second emphasises doing something.)

---

6   This includes the range of aspects of the research where bracketing is relevant. This includes not just the researcher's prior assumptions about the phenomenon under study, but also about participants and their characteristics, the likely meaning of the phenomenon for different participants, likely variation in collective meaning, and the intended meaning of particular statements made by participants during the interview (these can never be taken-for-granted).

The need to combine both approaches was also reflected in Ashworth and Lucas' article, where they emphasise the need to combine bracketing with development of what they called an 'attitude of empathy':

> ...the researcher who adopts an attitude of empathy with the [participant] should find [their] views and factual claims of *immense interest* (cf Wertz, 1983). The researcher begins to be taken up with questions such as, What does the espousal of such notions mean—what does it say about the [participant's] experience? ... Empathy in this context involves imaginative engagement with the world that is being described by the [participant]. (Ashworth and Lucas, 2000, p. 299)

As I said above, I personally place more emphasis on interpretive awareness than bracketing, especially given the way that the notion of bracketing has so often been simplified in the literature. But bracketing is something that could potentially be undertaken as part of the checks and balances of interpretive awareness. Meanwhile, Ashworth and Lucas' notion of an attitude of empathy for participants' experiences is related to what I have described above as 'active curiosity' and Bowden and Marton (1998) have described as 'interest and respect' for other people's ways of seeing the world (see Chapter 10). This attitude of empathy, curiosity and respect could usefully be re-introduced into descriptions of approaches to ensuring rigour in phenomenographic research.

Research outcomes as constituted—Acknowledgement of the relational role played by the researcher is also what underlies the common use of the term 'constitute' in reporting phenomenographic outcomes. Formally, in phenomenography different categories of descriptions are 'constituted'—not constructed, created, found or discovered. This is despite early references in the literature to phenomenographic analysis as a process of 'discovery' (Marton, 1986) and later debate as to whether it is a process of 'discovery' or 'construction' (Walsh, 1994 [2000]). Such debate has since been overtaken by the understanding that phenomenographic analysis is a relational process of 'constituting' research outcomes, based on phenomenography's non-dualistic ontology:

> There is not a real world 'out there' and a subjective world 'in her'. The world [as experienced] is not constructed by the learner, nor is it imposed upon her; it is *constituted* as an internal relation between them. (Marton and Booth, 1997, p. 13, italics added)

> Our position is not that the reality we experience is just our construction (this would be the thesis advocated by the constructivists). Reality is, in our view, *constituted* through the mutual and intertwined emergence of humans and their world. (Bowden and Marton, 1998, p. 206)

Where terms like 'constructed' or 'created' are seen as implying a dualistic focus on the subjective side of a person-world border, and terms like 'found' and 'discovered' are seen as implying a dualistic focus on the objective side of the person-world border, the term 'constitute' is regarded as implying a non-dualistic or relational focus. In effect, the term, constitute, is seen as short for 'constituted by the researcher in relationship with the data', 'constituted as a relationship between the researcher and the data' or 'mutually constituted by the researcher and the data'.

However, 'constitute' is also an esoteric term, of little meaning to readers of one's research who have no training in phenomenography, so I often also use dualistic terms when reporting my research because they represent more natural language and make the article easier to read, even if less precise.

Credibility of the research outcomes

Marton and Booth (1997) argue that the final interpretation of outcomes needs to provide a meaningful pattern to the data that is coherent, internally consistent and empirically supported. They present three primary criteria for judging the quality of a phenomenographic outcome space:

1. that each category in the outcome space reveals something distinctive about a way of understanding the phenomenon;
2. that the categories are logically related, typically as a hierarchy of structurally inclusive relationships; and
3. that the outcomes are parsimonious, i.e., that the critical variation in experience observed in the data be represented by a set of as few categories and dimensions of variation as possible.

Communicative credibility—Other criteria for establishing the credibility of one's research outcomes include what has been called communicative validity (Kvale, 1996; Sandberg, 2005), though I prefer the term 'communicative credibility' to remove associations with objectivist notions of validity. Given the assumption of researchers' relationality with their data, the idea that different researchers will arrive at different interpretations of the same data is to be expected (though it is also expected that the different interpretations will be related, due to the common phenomenon being interpreted, but just not identical). Meanwhile, when research outcomes can no longer be assessed according to objective criteria, it becomes vital for researchers to formulate evidence and arguments for the credibility of their interpretations.

Such evidence includes providing illustrative extracts from the raw data to demonstrate how the data have been interpreted by the researcher. The quotes from transcripts typically included when reporting phenomenographic outcomes provide a means for readers to assess the credibility of the researchers' interpretations, by showing the type of data regarded as indicative of different categories and critical aspects (as illustrated in Chapter 3 and Chapter 4).

Another source of credibility includes checking the meaningfulness of one's outcomes with different communities relevant to the study (Kvale, 1996; Uljens, 1996; Sandberg, 2005). In effect, we are asking these communities whether the outcomes look plausible, insightful and/ or useful to them. Such communities would include other researchers in the area (e.g., educational and phenomenographic researchers), communities you expect to make use of the results (e.g., teachers) and members of the population from which the sample was selected. This can occur through, for example, workshops with practitioners, seminar and conference presentations to other researchers, and circulation of draft research outcomes amongst those interviewed[7] and/or other members of that community.

---

7   Although research participants can give useful feedback on the meaningfulness of the research outcomes for members of their community, phenomenographers would generally not seek feedback from participants on the transcript of their particular interview, as some other traditions do (i.e., phenomenographers do not engage in 'member checking' of transcripts). This is primarily because ways of experiencing a phenomenon can change with context (as described in Chapter 5), and participants will be in a different context when checking the transcript of their interview than they were during the conduct of the interview.

Each community will have a different perspective from which to judge the outcomes in relation to their field of knowledge, such as knowledge of phenomenographic methods, knowledge of the object of study, knowledge of the participant community, etc. These communities can also be used to check the credibility of research methods, as well as outcomes—because no outcomes can be credible if the methods used to constitute those outcomes are not. Relating one's research outcomes to the outcomes published by other researchers studying similar phenomena, or the same phenomenon with different research participants, is also a way of increasing credibility (because we would expect our outcomes and their outcomes to be related through the common phenomenon being studied, as stated above).

Credibility of the inclusive hierarchy—I, personally, also feel a strong obligation to demonstrate the credibility of the inclusive hierarchy constituted in my outcome spaces. In fact, I would say that I pay more attention to this than any other phenomenographic researcher that I know. I do this because the hierarchy in phenomenographic outcomes is perhaps the aspect of phenomenographic research that is most frequently questioned by others (Akerlind, 2024a). This questioning started with early phenomenographic claims that the inclusive hierarchy was constituted on a 'logical' basis (e.g., Marton, 1986, 1994), with inclusivity logically implied in the categories. But the logic was rarely justified, being regarded as obvious in the description of categories. This made the credibility of the hierarchy particularly open to challenge.

In contrast, 21st-century phenomenography provides a much stronger basis for the credibility of an inclusive hierarchy, by justifying the inclusive nature of the hierarchy in terms of the critical aspects of the phenomenon discerned within each category of description. But to further enhance the credibility of my claims of inclusivity across categories, something that I routinely do (but that I have not seen other phenomenographers do) is attempt to demonstrate the inclusive nature of my categories through quotes from transcripts. I select extended quotes that illustrate how transcripts representing categories higher in the hierarchy also show awareness of the meaning and critical aspects apparent in categories lower in the hierarchy. This is illustrated in Chapters 3 and 4, where I present the outcomes of my studies of different understandings of 'phenomenography' and 'structural relationships in phenomenography'.

In checking the ordering of categories in the hierarchy, I ensure that each grouping of transcripts (i.e., each category) shows evidence of awareness of all of the critical aspects that demarcate categories lower in the hierarchy. Not every single transcript in a grouping needs to do so, but the set of transcripts in the grouping as a whole must do so. Otherwise, I need to reconsider the ordering or the groupings.

Common challenges to the trustworthiness and credibility of phenomenographic research

A concern with the credibility of phenomenographic outcomes commonly raised by other qualitative researchers is the 'neatness' of the outcomes. My response is that, in analysing the data, we are seeking for patterns in the data, and whilst it is true that all pattern-seeking is inevitably reductive to some degree, it is in finding patterns in the data that the research outcomes become most useful. In other words, finding 'neat' patterns in the data increases the utility of the outcomes. It is this that enables us to identify what critical aspects of a phenomenon need to be discerned in order to move from one way of understanding to a more complex way of understanding the phenomenon, for instance.

Underlying this concern with the neatness of outcomes is the implication that the researcher must have ignored aspects of the data in order to reach such a neat outcome space. My response is that we have not 'ignored' variation in the data, but have foregrounded some aspects (interpreted as critical aspects) and backgrounded other aspects (interpreted as non-critical aspects) as part of the pattern-seeking process. Consequently, I think that an important part of rigour is to acknowledge and briefly document the non-critical variation that was seen in the data when reporting the outcomes. For example, in a study of variation in understandings of academic freedom (Åkerlind and Kayrooz, 2003), in addition to presenting critical aspects of variation as part of the outcome space, we also briefly described non-critical variation:

> The social scientists surveyed in this study [also] described academic freedom as applying to one or more of the following areas of activity:

> research, teaching, freedom of speech and expression, and/or the pursuit of knowledge and truth to inform social debate and social good. ... [But] based on the analysis reported in this paper, the type of activity to which academic freedom is seen as relevant is not a critical aspect of the meaning of academic freedom, as the range of possible activities was found equally in each category and did not distinguish between them.
> (Åkerlind and Kayrooz, 2003, pp. 341–342)

Another challenge to the credibility of phenomenographic outcomes (though more commonly raised by quantitative researchers than qualitative ones) is that the research has only looked at what people say, not what they do—so how can we know that the outcomes have any implications for people's behaviour and actions? My response is that, first, phenomenographic research is not really looking at what people say, but at the understanding of the phenomenon that underlies what they say. Secondly, the research grounds such understandings in behaviour and actions, in the sense that interviews explore descriptions of what participants do or have done, in the form of concrete examples of the ways in which they interact with the phenomenon.

But more importantly, the significance of phenomenographic outcomes for people's potential behaviour is that it is not possible for people to act outside the limits of their understanding of a phenomenon. So, each way of understanding described in the outcome space tells us something important about what sort of actions the understanding enables. Each way of understanding the phenomenon simultaneously opens up certain possibilities for action and limits other possibilities, and the most complex way of understanding opens up the greatest range of possibilities for action. The research outcomes thus have implications, not so much for what people will actually do in any one situation, but for what it is *possible* for them to do. This is often referred to in phenomenography as a 'capability' for acting.

There are also challenges that come from other qualitative researchers who support different epistemological perspectives to phenomenography. Most commonly, social theorists may express concern that phenomenographic research is based on the experience of individuals and has ignored the socially-based foundations of human experience of the world. My response is that, first, phenomenography is not describing individual experience, but collective experience. And in that description, we do not reject social underpinnings of experience, we simply do not comment on them. This is because our research interest is a descriptive one, not a causal one; we aim to describe the variation in ways of understanding the same phenomenon within a particular community, not to investigate what causes that variation (other than in terms of discernment and non-discernment of critical aspects). Whilst arguing that discernment is based on exposure to variation in different aspects of the phenomenon, we do not investigate or postulate how that exposure to variation has come about. It may well be a socially-based exposure, in which case our outcomes could be regarded as showing the variation in understanding that can occur within a particular social community.

Another response that I make to challenges to phenomenographic research from other epistemological perspectives is that there is room for a multiplicity of perspectives on any one topic of research. If all research into human experience came from the same theoretical perspective, that would sadly limit potential insight into the topic.

Transferability of outcomes

A key question asked of all research is to what extent the outcomes of the research are relevant, applicable or transferable to other groups and settings. At one level, transferability can be inferred from the characteristics of the sample. To the extent that similar demographic characteristics are likely to reflect similar exposure to patterns of variation in the phenomenon, groups of people with similar characteristics can be expected to experience a similar range of ways of understanding the phenomenon. This is why it is important to describe the characteristics of the sample as part of the research report. Then, users of the research can make their own assessment as to the relevance of the sample group to the group of people they are interested in.

In addition, the phenomenographic focus on describing collective experience rather than individual experience of a phenomenon also has implications for transferability. For any individual, phenomenographers expect their experience of a phenomenon to change with changes in context, potentially even moment to moment changes. But the *range* of possible ways of experiencing the phenomenon within a particular group at a particular point in time is expected to be more stable, and thus more transferable to different settings. In other words, collective experience is transferable to different contexts in a way that individual experience is not.

Lastly, the phenomenographic assumption that human experience represents a non-dualistic relationship between the experiencer and the phenomenon being experienced means that it is theoretically impossible for the ways of experiencing a phenomenon evident in one group of people to be completely unrelated to the ways of experiencing the same phenomenon evident in another group of people, despite substantial changes in characteristics. So, all ways of experiencing the same phenomenon can be expected to be related at some level (as described in Chapter 5). This means that, if we were to consider the same phenomenon in a substantially different population and context to the original research, the ways of experiencing present in the new population would be expected to bear at least a partial relationship to those found in the original research. Put simply, members of a substantially different community are likely to show a smaller or larger range of ways of experiencing the phenomenon to that found in the original research, rather than a completely unrelated range of ways of experiencing. In this sense, all phenomenographic outcomes must be at least partially transferable to other settings.

Of course, when I say smaller or larger range of ways of experiencing, I do not mean to imply that overlaps in ways of experiencing between the two groups would be described in exactly the same terms by a different researcher. As described above, no researcher would constitute exactly the same descriptions of ways of experiencing a phenomenon as another researcher, even if working with the same dataset. This is because each researcher will form their own relationship with the data. Nevertheless, the ways of experiencing that they do constitute should be related, because they are all of the same phenomenon.

Chapter summary

This chapter described the processes of data analysis in phenomenographic research, presenting a ten-step set of guidelines, with concrete illustrations of what each step involves and how it might vary between individual researchers:

1. Familiarising oneself with the data.
2. Condensing the data.
3. Comparing the data.
4. Grouping the data into categories.
5. Delimiting different categories.
6. Discerning critical aspects.
7. Articulating the parts and whole of each category.
8. Checking interpretations.
9. Relating the categories in an outcome space.
10. Labelling the categories and critical aspects.

The relational role of the researcher in interpreting the data was then outlined and the implications for ensuring quality and rigour in research discussed. Particular approaches to ensuring the trustworthiness of the research process and credibility of the research outcomes in phenomenography were outlined, again with concrete examples of practice. A particular focus was placed on maintaining interpretive awareness throughout the research processes and on the communicative credibility of research outcomes. Although my primary discussion of research rigour is contained within this chapter, rigour is just as relevant to the decisions and procedures of data gathering (Chapter 6), with an emphasis on ensuring internal consistency (in both methodological and epistemological terms) between the purpose(s) of the research, the research question(s), selection of participants, methods used to gather data and data analysis.

This chapter has focused on mainstream approaches to phenomenographic analysis. The next chapter describes a less traditional approach to constituting critical aspects of phenomena that has developed in the 2000s and is reflected in a search for 'themes of expanding awareness' that run across the different categories in an outcome space and act to highlight structural relationships between critical aspects of a phenomenon.

8. Adding further structure to the outcome space: Structural relationships between dimensions of variation

At this point in the book, I have already described several times the key role played in 21st-century phenomenography by the notion of 'critical aspects' and associated 'dimensions of variation' in our experience of phenomena, based on the theoretical description of these notions in Marton and Booth's (1997) book, *Learning and Awareness*. In brief, Marton and Booth argue that the different ways in which the same phenomenon can be experienced arise from discernment of different aspects of the phenomenon. They call these aspects 'critical aspects', because they are critical in distinguishing one way of experiencing a phenomenon from a qualitatively different way of experiencing it.

They go on to argue that it is the experience of variation in an aspect of a phenomenon that enables that aspect to be discerned. They call this discernment the opening up of a 'dimension of variation'.[1] As described in Chapter 2 and Chapter 7, this claim has led to a 21st-century focus in phenomenographic research on identifying different dimensions of variation in awareness of a phenomenon, in order to identify critical aspects of human experience of the phenomenon.

But what I have *not* so far described is that an alternative way of identifying and describing critical aspects in phenomenographic research has also emerged in the literature, based on 'themes of expanding awareness' (e.g., Åkerlind, 2003a [2011], 2005c, 2005d, 2005e, 2011, 2018; Bowden et al., 2005; Paakkari et al., 2010; Kettunen, 2024). The main difference between the two analytical approaches is

---

[1] The term 'dimension of variation' may be considered as short for 'dimension of variation in awareness', which is short for 'dimension of variation in awareness of a phenomenon'.

that, in the traditional approach, dimensions of variation (and thus critical aspects) are constituted independently of each other, whilst in the alternative approach, dimensions of variation (and thus critical aspects) are constituted in a structurally related way along common themes of meaning, called 'themes of expanding awareness'.[2]

Although based on the same theoretical assumptions about the nature of a dimension of variation as the traditional approach, this alternative approach adds additional structural complexity to the analytic identification of critical aspects of phenomena, by looking for structural relationships between different dimensions of variation, and thus between different critical aspects of a phenomenon.

> With a focus on themes of expanding awareness, instead of identifying the critical aspects that make up each way of experiencing *in isolation from* each other... there is a search for logical relationships between the critical aspects that emerge during data analysis. These logical relationships allow the critical aspects to be grouped into themes that run across all of the ways of experiencing, showing how awareness is expanding along that theme as one moves from less complete to more complete ways of experiencing the phenomenon. (Åkerlind, 2018, p. 956, italics added)

Originally devised during my doctoral research (2003a [2011]), the notion of themes of expanding awareness has since been taken up in other doctoral dissertations (e.g., Collier-Reed, 2006; Daly 2008; Lupton, 2008; Nelson, 2012; Paakkari, 2012; Cutajar, 2014; Yu 2019), as well as published studies (e.g., Bowden et al., 2005; Åkerlind, 2005d, 2005e; Paakkari et al., 2010; Kettunen, 2024).

In addition, there are a growing number of published studies that claim to describe dimensions of variation, but are actually describing themes of expanding awareness (e.g., Lupton, 2004; Gonzalez, 2011; Light and Calkins, 2015; Täks et al., 2016; Töytäri et al., 2016; Khan et al., 2019; Mimirinis, 2018; Mimirinis et al., 2023; Kettunen et al., 2020; Kettunen and Tynjälä, 2022; Wilson et al., 2021; Stoffels et al., 2021; Wardak et al., 2023; Brauer et al., 2023). This growth in studies that are constituting 'themes of expanding awareness' but calling them 'dimensions of variation' is of concern, because it means that there are two analytic

---

2 'Themes of expanding awareness' could just a readily have been called 'themes of increasing differentiation'.

approaches to constituting critical aspects of phenomena circulating in the literature, but with few researchers explicitly discerning that there is a difference between the two. This is bound to lead to confusion over time, which I hope this chapter will help to avoid.

The aim of this chapter is to:

- clarify the difference between constituting critical aspects as independent dimensions of variation *vs* constituting critical aspects as related dimensions of variation structured along a theme of expanding awareness;
- provide concrete illustrations of the research outcomes that result from the two analytic approaches; and
- discuss the different insights that each approach provides to our understanding of critical aspects of human experience of phenomena.

How the notion of 'themes of expanding awareness' developed

I would like to start by noting that during my doctoral work I was not attempting to develop a different analytical approach to constituting critical aspects; I was simply following Marton and Booth's description of how to identify dimensions of variation and constitute critical aspects to the best of my ability—but, in doing so, constituted themes of expanding awareness instead. There appears to be some ambiguity in Marton and Booth's description of dimensions of variation, because unintentional constitution of themes of expanding awareness is a process that has since been replicated numerous times by other researchers, as reported above.

In my case, what I initially envisioned as representing different values along a dimension of variation, I subsequently came to realise represented different dimensions of variation along a common theme of meaning that ran through all of the ways of experiencing the phenomenon under study. My research outcomes were already well developed by the time I realised this, and after discussions with Ference Marton and other colleagues at the 2002 Phenomenography SIG conference, I decided to maintain my approach to analysis and call the common themes of meaning 'themes of expanding awareness' (Åkerlind, 2003a). And as an examiner of my dissertation, Ference was supportive of my approach to analysis.

It is important to remember that at the time *Learning and Awareness* was published, there were no widely available examples of phenomenographic studies using the notion of dimensions of variation as critical aspects of phenomena, because the theoretical framework was so new. This meant that there was a cadre of doctoral students using phenomenography in the late 1990s (of whom I was one) who were attempting to implement the new approach to looking at critical aspects and dimensions of variation into their research, but without any illustrative examples to draw on.[3]

Meanwhile, the approach I took to analysis in my doctoral research turned out to have a fortuitous outcome, because I (and others) have since found that constituting dimensions of variation as structurally related along a theme of expanding awareness is a very useful approach to examining variation in ways of experiencing phenomena, as I describe further below.

The traditional approach—independently constituted dimensions of variation

To help explain the approach of constituting dimensions of variation along themes of expanding awareness, I will start by comparing the type of outcomes to be expected from this approach with the type of outcomes to be expected from the traditional approach to constituting dimensions of variation. This comparison should act to improve not only our understanding of themes of expanding awareness, but also our understanding of traditional dimensions of variation, due to

---

3   The ambiguities and uncertainties that can arise from a lack of illustrative examples was also described by Harris (2011) with respect to Marton and Booth's (1997) explanation of the relationship between the what/how and structural/referential frameworks in *Learning and Awareness* (see chapter 5): "[descriptions] relating to the frameworks were primarily concerned with explaining them and providing hypothetical examples of their uses drawing on pre-existing data sets, questions about how these would apply in real research scenarios remained unanswered..." (Harris, 2011, p. 113).

Marton and Booth's (1997) principle of 'contrast' (also see Chapter 9). This is the theoretical assumption that the different contexts in which we experience a phenomenon will act to highlight different aspects of the phenomenon. And when we contrast one phenomenon with another, we change the context in which the phenomenon is being experienced. So, contrasting phenomena can be expected to bring different aspects of each phenomenon to the foreground of our awareness. For example, it had not struck me that dimensions of variation are traditionally constituted independently of each other until I explicitly compared the traditional approach with the themes of expanding awareness approach when writing this chapter. Prior to that, it was a taken-for-granted aspect of traditionally constituted dimensions of variation for me.

Now, let me illustrate the type of outcomes that result from the way in which dimensions of variation are traditionally constituted during data analysis. I have chosen Marton and Pong's (2005) study as my first example, because the explicit aim of their paper was to explain the then 'new' way of looking at different ways of understanding a phenomenon (i.e., via dimensions of variation). The phenomenon being explored in their study was the experience of 'price' in economics. Marton and Pong describe what is meant by a dimension of variation through an illustration,

> ...every feature [critical aspect] discerned corresponds to a certain dimension of variation. ...discernment originates from the experience of variation. (p. 336) ... For example, one interviewee said that "The condo is older than it used to be when she bought it, so the price goes down". ... Such explicit [awareness of] variation can indeed be found in every conception. (p. 346)

So, awareness of variation in aspects of the phenomenon of 'price' (like variation in the 'age' of the object being sold) constitutes a dimension of variation (and thus critical aspect) in the experience of the phenomenon. Awareness of this dimension is associated with a particular way of experiencing price, and awareness of other dimensions with other ways of experiencing price (see Table 8.1).[4]

---

4 The information in Table 8.1 was also presented, in slightly modified form, as Table 7.2 in the previous chapter.

Table 8.1 An example of an outcome space that constitutes dimensions of variation in the traditional way—constituted independently from each other (adapted from Marton and Pong, 2005, p. 342)

Categories of description	Dimensions of variation discerned	Ways of experiencing price
A	Discernment of variation in the *characteristics of the object*	Price reflects the value or worth of the object
B	Discernment of variation in the *people who buy* such objects	Price is related to the *demand conditions of the market* in which the object is situated
C	Discernment of variation in the *people who sell* such objects (or the places where they are sold)	Price is related to the *supply conditions of the market* in which the object is situated
D	Discernment of variation in *both the people who buy and the people who sell* such objects (or the places where they are sold)	Price is related to the *opposing demand and supply conditions* of the market in which the object is situated

As can be seen from the table, each way of experiencing is marked by awareness of a different dimension of variation or critical aspect of the phenomenon. So, an understanding of price as reflecting the inherent 'value of an object' (Category A) is marked by discernment of variation in 'characteristics of objects', an understanding of price as reflecting the 'demand for an object' (Category B) is marked by discernment of variation in 'people who buy objects', and so on. For the most part, these dimensions are constituted independently of each other, in that the dimensions are not related to each other (with the exception of Category D).

But there are other ways of representing the outcomes of traditional analyses for dimensions of variation — for example, in Åkerlind (2003b), where I identified four different ways of experiencing the phenomenon of 'development as a university teacher', each defined by awareness of variation in a different dimension of teacher development. But first, I will present my outcomes following the format of Marton and Pong's table above (see Table 8.2 below).

Table 8.2 Another example of an outcome space that constitutes dimensions of variation in the traditional way (derived from Åkerlind, 2003b)

Categories of description	Dimensions of variation discerned	Ways of experiencing teacher development
1(A)	Discernment of variation in *teachers' comfort* with teaching (ease)	Development as a university teacher is experienced as *teaching becoming easier*
1(B)	Discernment of variation in *teachers' comfort* with teaching (confidence)	Development as a university teacher is experienced as *becoming more confident as a teacher*
2	Discernment of variation in *teaching practice*; what one does as a teacher	Development as a university teacher is experienced as *improvement in teachers' knowledge and skills*
3	Discernment of variation in the *students' learning* outcomes associated with one's teaching	Development as a university teacher is experienced as *improvement in students' learning and development*

As with Marton and Pong's study, each way of experiencing 'development as a university teacher' is marked by awareness of a different dimension of variation or critical aspect of the phenomenon. So, an understanding of development as 'teaching becoming easier' is marked by discernment of variation in 'comfort while teaching'; an understanding of development as 'improvement in teachers' knowledge and skills' is marked by discernment of variation in 'teaching practice'; and so on. And again, these dimensions are constituted independently of each other, in that the dimensions are not related to each other (with the exception of the sub-categories 1(A) and 1(B)—which is why they are constituted as sub-categories rather than separate categories).

Different ways of showing the relationship between dimensions of variation and ways of experiencing

But the format shown in Table 8.2 is not how I actually presented the table of outcomes in my 2003b paper. I only provide Table 8.2 here to demonstrate the equivalence between the way I constituted dimensions of variation in my research, with the way Marton and Pong did. It is important for the equivalence to be clear before I illustrate an alternative way to present the relationship between discernment of different dimensions of variation and the way the phenomenon is experienced (see Table 8.3). Table 8.3 is the way in which I originally presented my outcomes in the 2003b article.

Table 8.3 An alternative format for presenting the relationship between traditionally constituted dimensions of variation and different ways of experiencing a phenomenon (adapted from Åkerlind, 2003b, p. 384)

	Dimensions of Variation		
Ways of experiencing development as a university teacher	*Awareness of variation in:*		
	• Teacher comfort	• Teaching practice	• Student learning
1(A) Ease of teaching	X*		
1(B) Confidence as a teacher	X		
2 Teacher's knowledge and skills	X	X	
3 Students' learning and development	X	X	X

*X indicates that awareness of the dimension is present in the relevant way of experiencing

From my perspective, the advantage of the format of Table 8.3 is that it not only shows that different ways of experiencing development as a university teacher are marked by discernment of different dimensions of variation, but it also shows that the dimensions of variation are discerned in an inclusive way across the different ways of experiencing 'development as a university teacher'. If you look across each row of Table 8.3, you can see that the most complex way of experiencing (row 5) discerns three dimensions of variation, the next most complex (row 4) discerns two dimensions, and the least complex ways of experiencing (rows 2 and 3) discern only one dimension of variation.

So, this format provides greater justification for the hierarchical ordering of the different ways of experiencing that are constituted.[5] Whilst the format of Table 8.1 and 8.2 highlights the role played by dimensions of variation and critical aspects in the part-whole structure of each way of experiencing, the format of Table 8.3 highlights both this and also the hierarchically inclusive structure that links the different ways of experiencing, through inclusive discernment of an increasing number of dimensions of variation or critical aspects of the phenomenon.

I also think there is a value in illustrating variation in practice within phenomenography, so that novice researchers can gain a sense of the flexibility they have to undertake and present their research in novel ways (whilst still maintaining the core principles of phenomenographic research, of course).

The themes of expanding awareness approach— relationally constituted dimensions of variation

Moving now to the type of outcomes to be expected from constitution of dimensions of variation along themes of expanding awareness, I draw again on my own research (see Table 8.4), this time into different ways of understanding 'development as an academic' (Åkerlind, 2005e). I use my own research for the example here because it enables a more direct comparison between the outcomes presented here and the traditional outcomes illustrated in Tables 8.2 and 8.3. By using my own research, I am able to remove extraneous variation from the comparison, because it makes it possible to compare the two forms of analysis based on the same researcher, the same set of research participants and very similar phenomena (development as a university teacher *vs* development as a university academic). In this way, the variation in outcomes becomes clearer, by being experienced against 'a background of sameness' (see Chapter 9).

---

5   Table 8.3 also provides an example of an outcome space that is not a simple linear hierarchy. As mentioned in previous chapters, whilst a simple hierarchy is the norm for phenomenographic outcomes, it is not inevitable. Whilst Category 3 is regarded as inclusive of Category 2, and Category 2 inclusive of Categories 1(A) and 1(B), Categories 1(A) and 1(B) are not inclusive of each other.

Table 8.4 An example of an outcome space that constitutes dimensions of variation along themes of expanding awareness (adapted from Åkerlind, 2005e, p. 18)[6]

	Themes of expanding awareness			
Ways of experiencing academic development	*Impact of development*	*Potential for development*	*Validation that development has occurred*	*Nature of development*
1 Increase in work productivity	Improves work performance	Has an endpoint	Externally validated	Quantitative (re. work performance)*
2 Improvement in academic standing	Improves work performance	Has an endpoint	Externally validated	Qualitative
3 Improvement in work quality	Improves work performance	Has an endpoint	Externally validated	Qualitative
4 Breadth of knowledge/ skills	Improves own learning	Potentially endless	Internally validated	Quantitative (re. own learning)*
5 Depth of own understanding	Improves own learning	Potentially endless	Internally validated	Qualitative
6 Contribution to field/society	Creates disciplinary change	Potentially endless	Internally validated	Qualitative

*Awareness of the nature of development expands from quantitative to qualitative with respect to 'work performance'. Then the same expansion in awareness is seen again for the nature of development with respect to 'own learning'

As can be seen in the table, the themes are constituted independently of each other, but within each theme, dimensions of variation are constituted in a structurally related way that distinguishes between different ways of experiencing the phenomenon. This focus on constituting dimensions of variation along common themes of meaning maintains the phenomenographic focus on experience at the collective level, through its focus on common themes in collective experience. Each column of Table 8.4 shows how awareness is expanding (in the

---

6 The original study identified five themes, but these have been reduced to four in Table 8.4 to simplify the illustration.

sense that additional dimensions of variation are discerned) along each collective theme as one moves from less complex to more complex ways of experiencing the phenomenon.

Analytically, this requires a search for logical relationships between the dimensions of variation that emerge during data analysis. These logical relationships allow the dimensions to be grouped into themes that span all the ways of experiencing, as a collective group.

> My initial search ... focused on identifying different aspects of the phenomenon that were referred to in some transcripts but not in others. In this way, I started to tentatively identify dimensions that appeared critical in distinguishing between transcripts and between emerging categories of description. At the same time, I looked to see whether these tentative dimensions of variation could be systematically grouped into themes of expanding awareness running through *all* of the ... tentative categories of description... In the final constitution of each theme, I required that it [the theme] be apparent in *each* category of description constituted, and that different levels along the theme (where each level typically represented a dimension of variation) *distinguish between* each category of description in an *inclusively ordered* way... The consistent occurrence of a theme across all transcripts or categories was used as my primary criterion for identifying variation that appeared *critical* to distinguishing qualitatively different ways of experiencing [the phenomenon]. (Åkerlind, 2005c, p. 122)

Further clarification of the nature of themes of expanding awareness and their relationship to dimensions of variation can be gained by contrasting Table 8.4 with Tables 8.1–8.3, based on the traditional approach to constituting dimensions of variation. By contrasting the outcomes of the traditional approach to analysis (Tables 8.1 and 8.2) with this alternative approach to analysis (Table 8.4) you can see that the alternative approach brings an additional component to the data analysis and outcomes, with three components to the outcome space instead of just two:

1. ways of experiencing (and the associated category of description);
2. themes of expanding awareness that run across each way of experiencing; and
3. dimensions of variation discerned within each theme and way of experiencing.

In contrast, in Tables 8.1 and 8.2, there are only two components: (1) ways of experiencing (and the associated category of description); and (2) dimensions of variation discerned in way of experiencing.

It is also useful to compare Table 8.4 with Table 8.3. Both tables show how dimensions of variation (and thus critical aspects) are discerned in an inclusive way across the different ways of experiencing the phenomenon. But in Table 8.3, each dimension is represented by a column, whereas in Table 8.4 each dimension is represented by a cell, with the columns representing themes of expanding awareness. This highlights that (unlike Table 8.3) the dimensions presented in Table 8.4 are structurally related, representing different 'values' along the themes.

The number of critical aspects discerned in each category

When dimensions of variation are constituted in the traditional way, each new category of description is normally marked by awareness of one new dimension of variation (as seen in Tables 8.1–8.3 above, for example). This can also be the case when dimensions of variation are constituted along themes of expanding awareness (as illustrated by Table 8.4 above). But, more commonly when using themes of expanding awareness, each new category is marked by discernment of multiple new dimensions of variation, often one new dimension for each theme. As there are always multiple themes, this means that multiple new dimensions of variation may be apparent in each new category or way of experiencing. To illustrate this, I will initially draw again on my own research, with the same aim of reducing extraneous variation in the comparison with previous examples. Then, I will broaden the focus to illustrations from other people's research.

In my study of different ways of experiencing 'being a university researcher' (Åkerlind, 2005d), every category of description, or way of experiencing, was marked by awareness of four new dimensions of variation—one for each of the four themes of expanding awareness constituted in the outcome space (see Table 8.5). This is a common outcome when constituting themes of expanding awareness (e.g., Bowden et al., 2005; Pakkarri et al., 2010; Kettunen, 2024).

Table 8.5 Another example of an outcome space that constitutes dimensions of variation along themes of expanding awareness (adapted from Åkerlind, 2005d, p. 152)[7]

	Themes of expanding awareness			
Ways of experiencing being a university researcher	*Research aims*	*Research process*	*Research outcomes*	*Purpose of publication*
1 Academic duty	To fulfil academic role	To identify and solve a problem	Concrete products	Satisfy expectations
2 Personal achievement	To become well-known	To discover something new	Academic credibility	Make work known
3 Personal understanding	To solve a puzzle	To investigate an interesting question	Personal understanding	Gain feedback on work
4 Benefiting a community	To make a contribution	To address broad issues in community	Benefits to community	Encourage change

On the surface, each cell in Table 8.5 may not read like a dimension of variation, but this is because the dimensions of variation have been labelled in a way that highlights the change in meaning that they represent more than the discernment of potential variation that they represent. But that is just the chosen label (see Chapter 7 for my discussion of considerations in choosing a label for critical aspects or dimensions of variation during the interpretive analysis). Underlying the label is discernment of potential variation. For example, the dimension labelled 'to fulfil academic role' involves discernment of the potential for variation in how well an academic performs their role. The dimension labelled 'to become well-known', involves discernment of the potential for variation in how well one is recognised by one's peers, and so on.

As discussed previously, discernment of a dimension of variation in a phenomenon is dialectically related to a change in the meaning of the

---

[7] The original paper identified five themes, but these have been reduced to four in Table 8.5 to simplify the illustration.

phenomenon. Table 8.5 highlights that the change in meaning occurs at the level of the parts as well as the whole of a phenomenon. That is, each theme reflects a part of the overall meaning of the phenomenon, just as each dimension does. In effect, when themes and dimensions are both constituted, two part-whole descriptions of the phenomenon eventuate:

- parts that vary between different ways of experiencing (the dimensions of variation discerned); and
- parts that are common to different ways of experiencing (common themes of meaning).[8]

When the outcome space combines both dimensions and themes, it highlights that, just as we can expect different parts of a phenomenon (dimensions of variation) to be discerned in different ways of experiencing it, so we can also expect similar parts (common themes of meaning) to be discerned in different ways of experiencing it. Plus, just as the whole meaning of the phenomenon will be experienced differently by different people and in different situations, so parts of the meaning will also be experienced differently (different values, or dimensions of variation, along each theme) when the whole meaning changes.

Examples of themes of expanding awareness constituted by other authors

Having presented examples of themes of expanding awareness with as little extraneous variation as possible, it is now time to present more varied examples, drawing on the work of other researchers. This is in line with the principle of 'generalisation' (see Chapter 9), where being exposed to varying instances of the same phenomenon is regarded as important for discerning critical aspects of the phenomenon. But it is also important that the broad degree of variation one is exposed to during 'generalisation' should follow, not precede, the controlled degree of variation one is exposed to during 'contrast' (as I have done in this chapter).

---

8   To reiterate, themes of expanding awareness can also be described as themes of meaning with respect to the phenomenon. What is common across different ways of experiencing is the focus of the theme, e.g. on aims, process, outcomes and purpose in being a researcher (see Table 8.5). What is different across different ways of experiencing are different values along the theme, representing expanding awareness of an increasing number of dimensions of variation.

The first example comes from Paakkari et al.'s (2010) study of ways of understanding health education as a school subject (see Table 8.6).

Table 8.6 Another example of themes of expanding awareness (adapted from Paakkari et al., 2010, p. 944)[9]

	Themes of expanding awareness				
Ways of experiencing health education	*Prerequisites*	*Perspective*	*Knowledge*	*Health concept*	*Representation of health concept*
1 A context for delivering theoretical knowledge	Knowledge capital	Individual	Objective facts	Multi-dimensional	Separately taught content entities
2 A channel for providing practical knowledge and skills	Abilities to apply knowledge	Individual	Practical and concrete	Multi-dimensional	Perspectives for other contents
3 A means to promote pupils' independent thinking	Self-reflective, metacognitive and independent thinking skills	Individual	Evaluative; personal	Perceived and diagnostic; positive and negative	How teacher looks at students; teaching methods
4 A context for personal growth	Courage to be oneself	Individual	Tacit; relational	Balance; personal resource	Strengthening self-esteem; finding positive sides of oneself
5 A means for developing responsible behaviour in society	Respect for and recognition of others; tolerance; sense of responsibility	Individual —society	Tacit; relational	Personal and societal matter; value; resource for others	Evaluation of health matters from perspective of society and individual

The next example comes from Kettunen's (2024) study of ways of understanding systems development in career guidance in schools (see Table 8.7).

---

9   The original study identified six themes, but these have been reduced to five in Table 8.6 to simplify the illustration.

Table 8.7 Another example of themes of expanding awareness (adapted from Kettunen, 2024, p. 76)

Ways of experiencing systems development	Themes of expanding awareness					
	Legislation	*Strategic leadership*	*Co-operation*	*Delivery*	*Profession-alisation*	*Evidence of impact*
1 *Minimal*	Non-existent	Missing	Lacking	Limited	Resistant	Not evaluated
2 *Aspirational*	Nominal	Scattered	Emerging	Fragmented	Aspirational	Desired
3 *Strategic*	Embedded in other policies	Devolved	Multi-lateral	Vertically coordinated	Partial	Ad hoc
4 *Systemic*	Explicit	Shared	Multi-sectoral	Horizontally coordinated	Regulated	Systemic

Having now looked at multiple examples of outcome spaces and dimensions of variation structured along themes of expanding awareness (Tables 8.4–8.7), I hope you have been able to 'generalise' the distinctive elements of this approach to analysis across the examples. Plus, having looked at multiple examples of outcome spaces arising from the more traditional approach to analysis (based on independently constituted dimensions of variation—see Tables 8.1–8.3), I hope you have been able to generalise the distinctive elements of that approach. Then, by contrasting Tables 8.1–8.3 with Tables 8.4–8.7, I hope the differences between the distinctive elements of the two approaches have become clear.

How to constitute themes of expanding awareness

To complement Chapter 7, which describes the analytic process of constituting dimensions of variation in the traditional way, I will now present a description of the analytic process I engaged in to constitute the themes of expanding awareness (and associated dimensions of variation) shown in Table 8.6 above, for different ways of experiencing 'being a researcher'. Uniquely, I will also show interim stages in my constitution of the outcomes over multiple analytic cycles with the data, drawing on the appendix I provided to my description of the outcomes in Åkerlind (2005d).

In line with the guidelines provided in Chapter 7, I started by Familiarising myself with the data, Condensing the data and then completed my first round of Comparing the data. I then made my first (very preliminary) attempt at Grouping the condensed data into categories and Delimiting the meaning represented by the tentative categories (see 'Preliminary categories of description: Version 1' in the box below). This first cycle of analysis was focused on variation in holistic meaning.

> **Preliminary categories of description—**
> **Version 1**
> Being a university researcher varyingly experienced as:
> - satisfying academic job requirements;
> - receiving external funding;
> - contributing to knowledge;
> - exploring the unknown;
> - solving a problem/puzzle;
> - finding out what works and doesn't work;
> - improving practice;
> - advancing your field;
> - a mission/project;
> - helping the community;
> - carving out your territory;
> - achieving credibility; and
> - satisfying your curiosity.

At this early stage in the analysis, the groupings were very preliminary. In a finalised outcome space, there are normally between three and six categories of description, so having thirteen initial groupings in my first round of interpretation shows that I was more struck by the differences than similarities in ways of experiencing at this early point. But the groupings become further refined with each future cycle of analysis, as shown below.

For my second round of analysis, I repeated the comparison process, but this time with a focus on variation in aspects or dimensions of meaning, rather than in holistic meaning. That is, I did another cycle of Comparing the data, but this time looking for variation in parts of the phenomenon that had been discerned in some transcripts but not in others. On this basis, I constituted the following preliminary themes and dimensions of variation (see 'Preliminary themes and dimensions: Version 1' in the box below). However, at this early stage in the analysis, the distinction between themes and dimensions is not very developed, nor trying to be.

> **Preliminary themes and dimensions:**
> **Version 1**
> 1. The nature of research as externally *vs* internally determined.
>   *External*, e.g.,
>   - satisfy job requirements;
>   - contribute to knowledge;
>   - solve a problem; and
>   - carve out a territory in the debate.
>
>   *Internal*, e.g.,
>   - personal understanding/use;
>   - own curiosity;
>   - own cultural mission; and
>   - interest/enthusiasm.
>
> 2. Research as impacting on the self *vs* others.
>   *Self*, e.g.,
>   - keep job;
>   - gain credibility/fame/promotion;
>   - satisfy curiosity/improve understanding;
>   - interest/enthusiasm;
>   - improve own practice; and
>   - carve out own territory.
>   *Other*, e.g.,
>   - advance field;
>   - contribute to knowledge;
>   - cultural project; and
>   - useful to community.

I then returned to the full transcripts and re-read them all, making a new set of summary notes (or condensed data) on each transcript. Based on the re-reading and subsequent analysis of the new summary notes, I constituted a new set of groupings of holistic meanings (see 'Preliminary categories of description: Version 2'), followed by a new set of themes and dimensions that showed variation in discernment of aspects, or parts, of the phenomenon (see 'Preliminary themes and dimensions: Version 2').

> **Preliminary categories of description:**
>
> **Version 2**
>
> Being a university researcher experienced as:
> - part of an academic job;
> - turning ideas into products;
> - solving a problem/puzzle;
> - carving out a territory in the debate;
> - improving practice — finding what works/doesn't work;
> - discovering something new — contributing to knowledge and exploring the unknown;
> - advancing the field/useful to community;
> - a project/mission;
> - understanding/discovery/pursuing lines of inquiry; and
> - following a personal interest.

> **Preliminary themes and dimensions:**
>
> **Version 2**
>
> Perceived variation within aspects of being a researcher:
> 1. personal changes in the academic *vs* the field *vs* the community;
> 2. working alone *vs* working together;
> 3. an intellectual *vs* social project; and
> 4. self *vs* other directed.

At this stage of the analysis, the original thirteen preliminary categories of description have been reduced to ten, and the original two preliminary themes or dimensions expanded to four. So, finer 'delimitation' of meaning and 'discernment' of variation are developing from the additional cycles of analysis.

I then repeated the iteration between transcripts, summary notes and preliminary outcomes again, leading to version 3 of the categories of description (see 'Preliminary categories of description: Version 3'). In versions 1 and 2, I had just been feeling my way and coming to terms with the data. But version 3 represents a qualitative leap in integration, clarity and parsimony of the groupings as compared to the previous two versions. Version 3 also represents my first to attempt to start Relating the categories of description, in the form of starting to identify inclusive relationships between the tentative categories. Although it may not be obvious in the version 3 Labelling of the categories, I see Category 2 as inclusive of Category 1, and Categories 3 and 4 as inclusive of Categories 1 and 2, but Category 4 is not inclusive of Category 3. In other words, in version 3, the inclusive structure forks at this point, but comes back together for Category 5, which is seen as inclusive of all previous categories.

Preliminary categories of description: Version 3

Being a university researcher experienced as:

1. research as an academic duty;
2. research as discovering something new (in order to establish fame/credibility);
3. research as personal, lifetime education;
4. research as contributing to a community (academic or societal); and
5. research as contribution *and* lifetime education.

Whilst the lack of a neat hierarchy is a sign that further rounds of Checking my interpretations need to occur, the lack of neatness is also not preclusive of a final outcome. As mentioned earlier in the chapter (and in previous chapters), not all outcome spaces are simple linear hierarchies (e.g., see Table 8.3 above and Bowden et al., 2005). Meanwhile, version 3 represents a significant advancement in my analysis because meaning and structure (relationship between categories) are starting to come together. As described in previous chapters, meaning and structure need to align in phenomenographic outcomes. This means that they have to be considered together, with both meaning *and* structure taken into account in interpreting the data (also see the discussion of this issue in Åkerlind et al., 2005).

Continuing my alternation between focusing on Grouping data to develop categories of description and Discerning variation in different aspects of the phenomenon to develop themes and dimensions, I then developed version 3 of the themes and dimensions (see 'Preliminary themes and dimensions: Version 3'). As with version 3 of the categories of description, version 3 of the themes and dimensions represents a substantial increase in the sophistication of my interpretations, attempting for the first time to capture systematic variation across the revised set of categories of description in *each* of the themes proposed. In addition, version 3 distinguishes between variation in dimensions and variation in themes for the first time, with each of the four preliminary themes defined by associated dimensions of variation.

Preliminary themes and dimensions :
Version 3

1. *Nature of research*:
   - Solving problems *vs*
   - Finding something new *vs*
   - Advancing field *vs*
   - Contributing to self-development *vs*
   - Contributing to community

2. *Research process*:
   - Individual *vs*
   - Combined (i.e., research community or social community)

3. *Research outcomes*:
   - Theoretical *vs*
   - Applied/useful (to self or others; field or society)

OR

3. *Research outcomes*:
- Products *vs*
- Theoretical understanding *vs*
- Personal understanding *vs*
- Changes in practice

4. *Role of publication*:
- A requirement *vs*
- A source of fame/becoming known *vs*
- A source of feedback to improve work *vs*
- A source of communication with others

Version 3 of the categories of description was the first version to be elaborate enough to allow a systematic approach to confirming or refuting the proposed categories against the transcript data (Checking). To facilitate this process of Checking and Delimiting the groupings/ categories, I then took the full transcripts (not just my summaries of the transcripts), grouped them according to the category that they best represented, then re-read the transcripts *in these groupings* in order to constitute version 4 of the categories (see 'Preliminary categories of description: Version 4').

Preliminary categories of description :

Version 4

Being a university researcher experienced as:

1. An academic duty
   Dimensions discerned in this category include awareness of external/ tangible products of research, e.g., grants, publications.

2. Discovering something new
   The transcripts reflecting this category include reference to academic duty, indicating Category 2 is inclusive of Category 1. New dimensions discerned in this category include awareness of practical (vs theoretical) outcomes and academic prestige.

3. An act of discovery (personal understanding/puzzle solving; includes lifetime education)

> The transcripts reflecting this category include references to practical outcomes and academic prestige. This indicates that this category is either inclusive of Category 2, subsumed under Category 2 or (given the apparent absence of additional dimensions of variation) the same as Category 2.
>
> 4. Advancing the field/society
> The transcripts reflecting this category include references to practical outcomes and academic prestige, indicating inclusiveness of Categories 2 and 3. Additional dimensions of variation discerned include a focus on advancing the field and having a larger mission.

Version 4 is marked by a simpler structure than version 3, with the proposed outcome space now forming a linear hierarchy of inclusiveness. Categories 1 and 2 are essentially the same in both versions, but Categories 3–5 in version 3 have been condensed into two categories in version 4, enabling the simpler hierarchy. Version 4 also began the process of Articulating the part-whole relationships within categories, in terms of discernment of different dimensions of variation in different categories.

For the next round of analysis, the transcripts and transcript summaries were again grouped according to the latest version of the categories of description. With each re-grouping of the data, I was able to pick up finer discriminations in my ongoing Checking for:

- any transcripts which did not align with the proposed categories—which would indicate that there were aspects of the data that had not been accounted for by the categories;
- within group similarities and differences—which might support my proposal that a grouping of transcripts reflects the same way of experiencing or, alternatively, clarify differences which might suggest a group should be divided into separate categories; and
- between group similarities and differences—which might support or challenge my proposed categories, as well as indicating the presence or absence of inclusive relationships between categories.

At this advanced stage of the analysis, I became even more systematic about the use of the proposed themes of expanding awareness to help finalise the categories and category descriptions, looking for confirmation or refutation that each proposed theme was evident in the description of each category. On this basis, the categories, themes and dimensions were finally integrated into a combined outcome space, containing a coherent set of themes, and with each category marked by discernment of a different dimension of variation along each theme (see 'Integration of categories, themes and dimensions').

Integration of categories, themes and dimensions

Categories of description: Version 5

1. Research as an academic duty
2. Research as a personal discovery
3. Research as enhancing personal understanding
4. Research as benefiting a larger community (includes benefits to the researchers' own ongoing learning and development)

Themes and dimensions: Version 4

1. *Aim:*

    Category 1—fulfil role/keep job;

    Category 2—personal sense of achievement, to be famous/amongst top in field;

    Category 3—solve a puzzle/find out what works and what doesn't work; and

    Category 4— advance your cause/make a contribution to change/follow your personal ideology/values.

2. *Process:*

    Category 1—identify and solve a problem through a set of research procedures/skills;

    Category 2—discover something new and substantial in the field;

    Category 3—investigate questions of personal interest to the researcher; and

    Category 4—use research to address broader issues of importance to the field or society (includes identify different world views).

3. *Outcomes:*

   Category 1—solve a problem/complete PhD/publication (i.e., concrete products);

   Category 2—become well known (also understand it yourself?);

   Category 3—personal understanding; and

   Category 4—produce material of value, which will enable significant resolutions to the research/social group (includes change in world views).

4. *Publication:*

   Category 1—requirement of job, establish credibility, increase chances of funding (i.e., extrinsic benefits);

   Category 2—make your research known to others, gain credibility/fame;

   Category 3—gain feedback to improve work (or not relevant to the research process); and

   Category 4—spread the message/encourage change (or not relevant).

Version 5 of the categories of description is only slightly different to version 4, being more concisely described. However, as I did not revisit the themes of expanding awareness when I constituted version 4 of the categories of description, the themes show more substantial modifications here than in their previous version (version 3). Some of the themes, such as the ones labelled 'outcomes' and 'publication' have simply been further clarified. Others, such as the one labelled 'nature/aims of research' have been more substantially revised, with a stronger focus being placed on highlighting the intentional nature of the experience. The 'process' theme, in particular, looks very different to the previous version, although the dimensions of variation in awareness represented within the theme reflect the previous version. So, the dimensions have continued between versions, but been 'labelled' differently to better align with the themes. This represents an attempt on my part to further elaborate and integrate the dimensions across different themes. It also represents, once again, a more intentional focus to my descriptions of variation in awareness.

Perhaps the largest modification to the proposed themes of expanding awareness in this version is the apparent disappearance of the variation in focus on 'theoretical *vs* useful' research outcomes and 'individual *vs* combined' research processes, seen in earlier versions of the themes. This is because, after carefully Checking the groups of transcripts representing each proposed category of description, I found evidence of variation along these lines in *each* category, not just some categories. This means that the variation did not discriminate between the proposed categories of description and, thus, did not form part of what makes the categories qualitatively distinct. Thus, although the variation was still evident to me, I came to see it as representing non-critical variation (i.e., within-category variation), rather than critical variation (i.e., between-category variation).

In summary, over the course of the analysis, certain themes of expanding awareness were apparent from the beginning, but over repeated cycles of analysis become more precisely, concisely and systematically defined, more intentionally focused, more coherent and integrated, clearly structured and better justified in the transcript data. At the same time, new themes not apparent at the beginning also emerged over the course of the analysis. At this stage, I took a break of several months in order to return to the analysis with a more open mind. After repeating the iterative process described in my last round of analysis, I arrived at the final outcome space described in Table 8.6.

Not just variation in values along a dimension, but also variation in dimensions along a theme

Having described how to constitute dimensions of variation along themes of expanding awareness, let me now turn to summarising the potential value in doing so. The constitution of themes of expanding awareness furthers many of the key distinguishing features of phenomenographic research. In particular, this form of analysis and outcomes further emphasises the phenomenographic focus on:

- *viewing human experience from a collective perspective*, by constituting collective themes of meaning that are common across all ways of experiencing a phenomenon;

- *variation in human experience of phenomena*, by being able to constitute not just variation in different values along a dimension of variation but also variation in different dimensions of variation along a theme of meaning;
- *structural relationships between different ways of experiencing*, with the different dimensions of variation discerned in each way of experiencing being structurally related along each theme; and
- *the dialectical relationship between meaning and structure*, in that, while each way of experiencing the same phenomenon shares common themes of meaning, these themes will be experienced differently (carry different meanings) in different ways of experiencing the phenomenon.

Thus, in my opinion, constitution of dimensions of variation along themes of expanding awareness further enhances both structure and meaning in the study of collective experience of phenomena. It adds additional structural complexity to the analytic identification of critical aspects of phenomena, by looking for structural relationships between different dimensions of variation. It also adds additional meaning to the final outcome space, by showing how the same themes carry different meanings in different ways of experiencing a phenomenon. In the process, it also highlights an additional layer to variation in meaning, by making it possible to constitute both different values along a dimension of variation and different dimensions of variation along a theme.

Both analytic approaches are based on the same theoretical assumptions about the nature of a dimension of variation and critical aspect, but we can expect the dimensions constituted via themes of expanding awareness to differ somewhat from those constituted without using themes, due to the expectation when constituting themes that each dimension in a theme be logically and structurally connected to other dimensions in the theme. One outcome of this is that it is not unusual, when constituting dimensions of variation along themes of expanding awareness, for each way of experiencing to be distinguished by discernment of a number of different dimensions of variation, not by just one dimension, as is typical of the traditional approach.

For some researchers, the traditional way of constituting dimensions of variation may be more appealing, due to the parsimony of distinguishing between different ways of experiencing in terms of discernment of just *one* new dimension of variation or critical aspect of a phenomenon. However, for other researchers, constituting dimensions of variation along themes of expanding awareness is more appealing, because it further highlights the intricate, but logical, nature of variation in and relationships between different meanings of a phenomenon in a way not possible with the traditional approach.

Chapter summary

This chapter describes two forms of analysis for dimensions of variation and critical aspects of phenomena that have developed in phenomenography since the notions were first introduced by Marton and Booth (1997):

1. the traditional approach of constituting dimensions of variation independently of each other; and

2. an alternative approach of constituting dimensions of variation in a logically and structurally related way, linked along themes of expanding awareness.

This chapter clarifies the difference between the outcomes of the traditional approach to analysis and the themes of expanding awareness approach, providing concrete illustrations of the research outcomes that result from the two analytic approaches, and discussing the different insights and utility that each approach provides to our understanding of critical aspects of human experience of phenomena.

The next chapter focuses on one particular context for the use of phenomenographic outcomes, to inform educational interventions using the 'variation theory of learning', which developed from the theoretical assumptions explicated in Marton and Booth's *Learning and Awareness*.

9. Phenomenography and variation theory: The development of complementary traditions

As mentioned in Chapter 2, when Marton and Booth (1997) argued that experience of variation in a dimension of a phenomenon was essential in order to become aware of that dimension (or critical aspect) of the phenomenon, they set the groundwork for what has become known as the 'variation theory of learning'. In brief (and non-theoretical language), this theory asserts that:

1. Educationally desirable understandings of subject matter are marked by awareness of particular critical aspects of the object of learning.

2. So, to achieve an educationally desirable understanding of an object of learning, students' need to discern (or become aware of) these critical aspects.

3. Discernment of the critical aspects requires students to experience variation in those aspects.

4. But some patterns of variation are more likely to be discerned than others.

5. In particular, variation is easier to discern when it occurs against a background of non-variance, or sameness. This means that, in patterns of variation, what is *not* varied is as important as what is varied.

6. Designing learning activities to expose students to particular patterns of variation and invariance in critical aspects of the object of learning maximises the opportunity for students to discern those critical aspects, and thus achieve the desired understanding of the object of learning.

These assumptions enable an analysis of teaching and learning activities in terms of what is made possible for students to learn (or discern) about an object of learning, based on an analysis of the patterns of variation and invariance that students are exposed to during the learning activity. It also enables educational interventions, aimed at improving students' learning by using variation theory to design lesson plans, analyse the enactment of those plans, and evaluate the impact on learning.

Meanwhile, all of this represents a divergence from the traditional scope of phenomenography, and in this way can be described as the development of a new, but complementary tradition, with a strong applied focus. Over time, the variation theory tradition has developed:

- additional theoretical assumptions about what is needed for discernment of critical aspects of an object of learning (Marton et al., 2004; Marton, 2015);

- a distinctive approach to research based on a 'learning study' design (Lo et al., 2004; Pang and Marton, 2003, 2005; Marton and Pang, 2006; Pang and Ki, 2016; Pang and Runesson, 2019); and

- extensive pedagogical applications in school settings and teacher education, also commonly based on a learning study design (Pang and Runesson, 2019; Kullberg and Ingerman, 2022; Kullberg et al., 2024).

This applied focus has meant that, unlike phenomenography, the variation theory tradition encompasses not only a research arm but also an applied arm, with much of the practice of variation theory being focused on pedagogical applications rather than empirical research—though both foci may also be addressed in the one study.

As indicated above, the strong applied focus has been built around one model of intervention in particular, the learning study, which will be described further below. Meanwhile, the practice of learning studies based on variation theory has developed its own adherents, scholarly communities and even a specialised journal, the *International Journal for Learning and Lesson Studies* (jointly focused on publishing research based on variation theory focused 'learning studies' and non-theoretical 'lesson studies'), plus an associated conference hosted by the *World Association for Lesson Studies*. In this sense, variation theory as a tradition has developed as strong ties with the tradition of lesson studies as with the tradition of phenomenography.

This divergence from phenomenography in theory, approach to research, scholarly communities and applied practice has made it possible for some scholars to study and apply variation theory and learning studies with very little insight into the phenomenography tradition, and conversely, for other scholars to study and apply phenomenography with very little insight into the variation theory tradition. The outcome is that there are many researchers using phenomenography without much understanding of the variation theory tradition, and conversely, many using variation theory and learning studies without much understanding of the phenomenography tradition.

Nevertheless, I personally believe it is important for anyone interested in phenomenography, especially with the intention of using phenomenographic research outcomes for educational or developmental purposes, to be aware of the tradition of research and pedagogical application using the variation theory of learning that has developed during the 2000s. This is partially because the two traditions are inevitably theoretically intertwined, and thus shed light on each other, partially because phenomenographic research can be used empirically to inform learning studies and other applications of variation theory, and partially because pedagogical applications of variation theory can be used to enhance the educational implications of phenomenographic outcomes (and most researchers engage in phenomenographic research for educational purposes).

As there are many descriptions of variation theory and applications of the theory in learning studies already in the literature, I will not be focusing on describing the tradition in detail in this chapter, but instead describing how it has developed over time from its phenomenographic roots and highlighting its ongoing relationship with phenomenography, in particular the ways in which the two traditions complement each other.

Three components to the variation theory tradition

One difficulty in describing variation theory and its relationship to phenomenography is that the diversity of developments in variation theory can create confusion when talking about the tradition, because the same term, 'variation theory', can be used to represent quite different aspects of the tradition. In particular, the term can be used to refer to:

1. the theory itself; and/or
2. empirical research based on the theory; and/or
3. pedagogical applications of the theory in teaching and teacher education.

This potential for confusion in what someone is referring to when they use the term 'variation theory' is something I have drawn attention to previously,

> I draw this distinction because, although the tradition as a whole encompasses all three aspects of variation theory, on any one occasion, people referring to variation theory may be referring to just one aspect of the tradition. This can cause confusion for those coming to understand what the term means and when comparing variation theory to other traditions. (Åkerlind, 2018)

In addition, each of the three components of the variation theory tradition can also operate somewhat independently of the others. The theory itself can be discussed without including research or practice. Research can be conducted without necessarily having an impact on practice. Plus, practice can become somewhat divorced from research and theory, in that teachers who are applying variation theory in their lesson designs often do so without a sophisticated understanding of the theory itself or of research using the theory (Pang and Ki, 2016; Durden, 2018; Thorsten and Tväråna, 2023). This is because it takes some time and effort to comprehend the theory in a sophisticated way (even though it is possible to start thinking usefully about teaching and learning in terms of what is and is not being varied, without necessarily understanding the theory in full). Nevertheless, it is not always clear what people are referring to when they use the term 'variation theory'.

This ambiguity in what is meant when people refer to variation theory becomes particularly confusing when trying to compare phenomenography with the variation theory tradition, as I do in this chapter—that is, it makes it difficult to be precise about which aspects of the tradition one is comparing phenomenography to. So, in this chapter I will use the term 'variation theory' to refer to the theory, 'variation theory research' to refer to empirical research using variation theory, 'pedagogical applications of variation theory' (or learning studies) to refer to practical applications in classroom teaching, and 'the variation theory tradition' to refer to all three uses of the term, variation theory.

Turning to a comparison with phenomenography, in contrast to the three components of variation theory, phenomenography has only two comparable components:

1. empirical research; and
2. theoretical assumptions underlying the research.

Theoretical assumptions

With regard to the epistemological and ontological assumptions of phenomenography and variation theory, as described numerous times throughout this book (in particular in Chapter 2 and Chapter 5), phenomenography in the 21st century is underpinned by the theoretical assumptions outlined in *Learning and Awareness* (Marton and Booth, 1997). These are the same theoretical assumptions that underpin the variation theory tradition (though there have since been further theoretical developments in variation theory, described below). In this way, the two traditions are forever theoretically linked.

In addition, Marton and Booth depict 'learning' as a change in awareness, making learning and awareness inherently intertwined. This raises a further point of potential confusion in use of the term, variation theory—i.e., variation theory of what?. Whilst the term 'variation theory' is almost uniformly seen as short for 'variation theory of learning', there is also a 'variation theory of awareness' expounded in Marton and Booth's book, as I have argued previously (Åkerlind, 2018), which also represents a variation theory. The way in which ambiguity in the term 'variation theory' can cause confusion may be illustrated by a conference I recently attended. At one of the sessions, a doctoral student engaged in phenomenographic research introduced her research as underpinned by variation theory. Given the most common usage of the term, I anticipated a research project on the topic of learning. But this turned out not to be so. The student went on to describe variation theory in terms of the implications of experienced variation for awareness, rather than the implications for learning—and this is a perfectly reasonable use of the term 'variation theory'. But the fact that 'variation theory' is typically used as a shorthand for 'variation theory of learning' created a misleading impression in the first instance.

In other words, there is a 'variation theory of awareness' described in *Learning and Awareness*, as well as a 'variation theory of learning'. These are not separate theories, but the same theory, with the variation theory of awareness also able to be applied to learning, on the basis that learning represents a change in awareness. Nevertheless, in this chapter, I will continue to refer to the variation theory of learning by its shorthand, variation theory, because that represents standard practice in the tradition.[1]

Empirical research

In terms of the approach to empirical research taken by the two traditions, although there are differences in method, what is more significant is that they ask different research questions (Pang, 2003; Rovio-Johansson and Ingerman, 2016; Åkerlind 2015, 2018; Kullberg and Ingerman, 2022). Generically, phenomenographic research asks, 'What are the collective range of ways of understanding a particular phenomenon?'. And, in the 21st century, also asks, 'What critical aspects of the phenomenon are discerned (and not discerned) within those ways of understanding?'. Variation theory research then asks, 'What pedagogical design would maximise students' chances of discerning those different critical aspects?'.

So, there is a logical and complementary flow in research foci between the two traditions. This has led to many research studies using variation theory that draw on preceding phenomenographic research into students' understandings of particular subject matter, to help identify the critical aspects of the object of learning that need to be highlighted during pedagogical interventions based on variation

---

1   Nevertheless, it is fair to say that I think it would reduce confusion if standard practice in the tradition changed, and that the tradition started to be routinely referred to in the literature as 'variation theory of learning' rather than just 'variation theory'—in recognition that there is also a variation theory of awareness associated with phenomenography.

theory. (Though there are also other ways of identifying critical aspects that have developed in the tradition, as described below.)

Pedagogical applications

With regard to pedagogical applications, although many researchers conduct phenomenographic research with the explicit aim of subsequently applying the outcomes, the actual process of application lies outside the realm of phenomenography itself. This is in contrast to the variation theory tradition, where application is an inherent part of the tradition. Thus, one very explicit difference between the phenomenographic and variation theory traditions is the focus on direct pedagogical applications of research and theory in the variation theory tradition, but not in the phenomenography tradition.

For those in the scholarly community, the focus on practical implications for teaching and learning in applied situations has become a defining feature of the variation theory tradition. In an open-ended survey I conducted with participants at the 2022 and 2024 phenomenography and variation theory conferences in Stockholm and Uppsala,[2] I asked participants: "What interests you about variation theory?" and "How do you use variation theory?". (The term, variation theory, is here being used to refer to the tradition associated with the theory, not to the theory per se.) Although three different ways of understanding variation theory emerged, all twenty-one responses focused strongly on the applied nature of the tradition, with variation theory variously described as:

1. a practical tool for teaching;
2. an analytical tool for teaching; and
3. a theoretical tool for teaching.

1. A practical tool for teaching—The first way of describing variation theory focuses on the concrete and practical value of the tradition for improving teaching and learning. For example,

---

[2] I would like to thank Malin Tväråna for her assistance in identifying a sample for the survey.

> I'm interested in variation theory because of its direct practical value. Teachers will indeed change their practices of teaching in classrooms when they understand variation theory. I'll use it to improve classroom teaching. (Response 4)

2. An analytical tool for teaching—The second way of describing variation theory focuses on the mechanisms by which the improvements to teaching and learning are made, in terms of identifying critical aspects of the object of learning, particular patterns of variation and invariance of critical aspects, and/or increasing differentiation in students' understanding of the object of learning. Sometimes responses in this category explicitly refer to these ideas as useful for analysing teaching (which then provides an approach to planning, explaining and evaluating teaching), but at other times this is implicit rather than explicit. For example,

> What interests me is how it guides teaching through creating patterns of variation and invariance. I use variation theory to first define the object of learning by its critical aspects for the target group. Then by developing teaching methods where patterns of variation and invariance changes to best lead to learners being able to discern the changed [varied] and unchanged [invariant] aspects [of the object of learning]. (Response 1)

3. A theoretical tool for teaching—It is only in the third way of describing variation theory that the learning theory itself comes to the fore. For example,

> I first learned about variation theory in one of the first courses I took in graduate school. It was the first learning theory that I have ever learned and it caught my attention because of its versatility. It explains how learning occurs and what learning conditions are necessary for learning to occur. In other words, it provides pedagogical reasoning as to why some students learn better and some do not. What is more intriguing is its direct application in teaching. Teaching instructions can be crafted drawing from variation theory which can be useful for teachers, and variation theory can be used to evaluate how effective a lesson is. All of this is obvious in the Learning Study approach. (Response 15)

The distinctive difference between Categories 2 and 3 is that, in Category 2, variation theory is seen as improving teaching by providing a set of theory-informed practices for teachers to follow. In contrast, in Category 3, variation theory is seen as improving teaching by providing a theoretical basis for pedagogical reasoning. So, in Category 3, the focus is on the value of the theory itself for teaching and learning. Whereas, in Category 2, the focus is on the value of the teaching and learning practices that were developed from the theory. In addition, as can be seen from the quote above, the understanding represented by Category 3 is inclusive of that represented by Category 2, making Category 3 the more complex understanding of variation theory.

Some responses in Categories 2 and 3 referred to using variation theory for educational research as well as teaching. However, the emphasis was still on implications for teaching and learning.

Development of the variation theory tradition from its phenomenographic roots

As previously described, variation theory and its implications for learning were first described in Marton and Booth's (1997) *Learning and Awareness*, based on an analysis of the cumulative outcomes of three decades of phenomenographic research on learning. Although the theory had not been given a specific title at this stage, Marton and Booth emphasised the significance for learning of the experience of variation:

> What we are arguing is that it is possible to specify certain conditions that are necessary for learning of the kind we are interested in having take place [defined in quote below]. Whatever teaching method one may use...it must address certain features of the learner's experience—a structure of relevance and a pattern of dimensions of variation—if it is to bring about certain qualities in their learning. (p. 179)

In the following year, Bowden and Marton (1998) published *The University of Learning*, which further developed the implications of variation theory for teaching and learning. Again, the title 'variation theory of learning' was not explicitly used, but was strongly implied (e.g., 'the theory of learning', 'the variation theory').

> What this whole line of reasoning is about is that discernment is a defining feature of learning in the sense of learning to experience something in a certain way. Variation is a necessary condition for effective discernment... When some aspect of a phenomenon or an event varies while another aspect or other aspects remain invariant, the varying aspect will be discerned. (p. 35)

Together these two books formed the departure point for research based on variation theory and for pedagogical applications of the theory to the teaching and learning of disciplinary content or subject matter—though substantial further developments in variation theory continued to emerge over time, as described below.

From pedagogical observations to pedagogical interventions

Early research based on variation theory involved analysing naturally occurring pedagogical situations and documenting the variation in critical aspects of a particular object of learning spontaneously introduced by teachers during a lesson (e.g., Rovio-Johansson, 1999; Runesson, 1999 [as cited in Marton 2015, p. 184, with the original in Swedish]; Marton and Morris, 2002; Marton and Tsui, 2004). A common approach was to focus on different instances of teaching the same subject matter, followed by analysis of student learning outcomes based on the variation students were exposed to in each teaching situation. Such studies demonstrated learning outcomes in line with the variation to which students were exposed.

Having empirically validated the tenets of variation theory and its implications for teaching and learning over a series of studies, the variation theory tradition increasingly expanded its focus to pedagogical applications, thus developing a strong applied focus in addition to its research focus. This move to applied practice was facilitated by major government funding initiatives, initially in Hong Kong when Ference Marton was on a visiting appointment there (Lo et al., 2004), but also in Sweden where Marton was usually located.[3] And by the early 2000s, the primary focus of variation theory research had moved from observing to manipulating pedagogical situations through educational interventions. This took the form of guiding teachers to introduce theoretically desirable patterns of variation and invariance in critical aspects of the object of learning, as described below.

It is important to note, however, that the move to pedagogical interventions continues to include pedagogical observations, with a

---

3   This explains why Sweden and Hong Kong form the primary sites of variation theory research and practice, although it has also spread more broadly.

clear distinction drawn in the variation theory tradition between the 'intended', the 'enacted' and the 'lived' (or experienced) object of learning (Marton et al., 2004). The 'intended object of learning' is what teachers intend for students to learn during a lesson, and is reflected in the lesson plan that has been designed using variation theory. The 'enacted object of learning' reflects the lesson as actually delivered, which is not always the same as planned, and this enacted object of learning can only be determined through pedagogical observation. Meanwhile, it is the enacted, not the intended, object of learning that is most relevant to students' learning. But at the same time, not all students will experience the enacted object of learning in the same way. This leads to the 'lived object of learning', which is what students actually experience about the object of learning during the lesson. This is likely to vary amongst students, and can only be determined through evaluations of student learning after the lesson delivery.

The object of learning is a key concept in the variation theory tradition, so deserves a little explanation. In many ways, the 'object of learning' in the variation theory tradition parallels the 'phenomenon' in the phenomenographic tradition, in that they are each the focus of attention in their respective traditions. And indeed, the object of learning may sometimes be equivalent to a phenomenon, in the sense of representing a particular way of understanding a disciplinary concept or subject matter—but this is not always the case. Objects of learning may also represent a particular critical aspect of a way of understanding, or a particular capability for acting[4] (on the understanding that "powerful ways of acting originate from powerful ways of seeing—Marton and Tsui, 2004, p. 7). The object of learning is often simply defined as 'what is to be learned' in any one lesson, and while this is accurate, it does not make clear that not just the content, but also the nature, of what is to be learned can vary across situations. Kullberg et al. (2024) provide a more meaningful description of what an object of learning may consist of:

---

4   The term 'capability' is used in recognition that, just because one is capable of a particular way of acting, that does not mean that you will choose to engage in that way of acting on every occasion. In addition, just because one is capable of a particular way of understanding in certain situations, does not mean that you will experience that same understanding in every situation.

[An object of learning] may be characterized as a target capability (defined as what a learner is able to do as a result of learning). ... Further, an object of learning can also be characterized as a meaningful whole, as a phenomenon that it is possible to discern and explore... using, for example, phenomenography. (pp. 15–16)[5]

Development of particular patterns of variance and invariance of critical aspects during pedagogical interventions

Marton and Tsui's (2004) *Classroom Discourse and the Space of Learning* marked the first book to be published based on the variation theory of learning, consisting primarily of a collection of educational interventions inspired by variation theory.[6] As described above, the key tenet of variation theory is that, to achieve the desired understanding of subject matter, students' need to discern certain critical aspects of that subject matter. And in order for this discernment to take place, students need to be exposed to variation in those critical aspects.

But it is possible to be exposed to variation without necessarily experiencing, or discerning, that variation. Based on the studies in this book, Marton et al. (2004) were able to identify particular 'patterns of variation' that were regarded as especially effective in making variation in critical aspects visible to students, in particular that variation is more likely to be discerned when it occurs against a background of sameness, or invariance. On this basis, what is not varied in a pedagogical situation becomes as important for students' discernment as what is varied.

Four patterns of variation and invariance were recommended by Marton et al.: contrast, generalisation, separation and fusion.

1. Contrast—this is because, in order to experience something as something, we must experience something else to compare it with.

---

[5] Rovio-Johansson and Ingerman (2016) also provide a useful discussion of different ways of defining the object of learning.
[6] Though many of the examples in Marton and Tsui (2004) showed simplistic understandings of variation theory amongst the teachers involved, in line with my earlier comment that teachers using variation theory do not always have a sophisticated understanding of it.

2. Generalisation—this is because, in order to fully understand something, we must experience varying instances of that thing.

3. Separation—this is because, in order to experience particular critical aspects of a phenomenon, and to be able to separate these critical aspects from other aspects of the phenomenon, we need to experience these aspects varying while other aspects remain invariant.

4. Fusion—this is because, in order to take all of the critical aspects of a phenomenon into account at the same time, they must be experienced as varying simultaneously, in relation to each other.

The order in which these patterns are experienced is also important: contrast needs to precede generalisation; and separation needs to precede fusion.

This initial recommendation of four patterns of variation became refined over time to just three: contrast, generalisation and fusion. I have not seen an explicit explanation of the removal of 'separation' from the list of desirable patterns of variation in the literature, but my understanding is that it is on the basis that the pattern of 'contrast' in and of itself enables 'separation'. That is, the notion of 'separation' relates to the importance of varying each critical aspect separately, or one at a time, in order to help students discern that particular critical aspect, but the mechanism by which each critical aspect is varied is through the pattern of 'contrast'.

As described by Marton and Pang (2006) discernment of a critical aspect requires experiencing variation in that aspect, and this requires experiencing different values along the associated dimension of variation. For example, in order to discern colour as a critical aspect, one must experience different colours, which represent different 'values' along the dimension of colour. In this way, varying two or more values within a critical aspect using the pattern of 'contrast', creates variation along the critical aspect and provides the opportunity for students to become aware of that variation and thus discern the associated critical aspect.

So, whilst separation of the different critical aspects of an object of learning remains an important concept in variation theory, in practice, separation does not require its own pattern of variation, but is achieved through contrast. Kullberg et al. (2024) explain that "Separation of a critical aspect can be made using two patterns of variation, *contrast* or *generalization*" (p. 26, authors' italics), as shown in Table 9.1.

Table 9.1 Patterns of variation and invariance (adapted from Kullberg et al., 2024, p. 26)

		Critical aspect	Other aspects
Separation*	• Contrast	varied	invariant
	• Generalisation	invariant	varied
Fusion		varied	varied

*Separation, in the form of contrast and generalisation, needs to occur for each critical aspect separately, before bringing all critical aspects together in fusion

Another factor in the reduction from four to three recommended patterns of variation is that there was a move away from describing the recommended patterns in conceptual terms (as above) to describing them in more mechanistic terms, i.e., in terms of what was varied and not varied (as seen in Table 9.1), and this shift in focus allowed for only three, not four, patterns of variation.[7]

Meanwhile, the conceptual linkages between the original four patterns of variation helps explain differences in descriptions of practice within the variation theory research literature. Whilst some studies describe desired variation in terms of the original four patterns (contrast, generalisation, separation and fusion—e.g., Marton et al., 2004; Marton and Pang, 2006; Pang and Ki, 2016); others do so in terms of just three patterns (contrast, generalisation and fusion—e.g., Marton, 2015; Kullberg et al., 2024), and yet others, in terms of only the two main patterns of separation and fusion (e.g., Pang and Marton, 2007; Åkerlind et al., 2014). Although this variation in practice may appear confusing

---

7   Although hypothetically there is a fourth pattern—critical aspect 'invariant' and other aspects 'invariant'—this pattern is not recommended by the variation theory of learning because it involves no variation (Marton, 2015; Kullberg and Ingerman, 2022).

on the surface, in fact, all three ways of describing desired patterns of variation are consistent with Table 9.1.

Similarly, many learning studies introduce the pattern of 'contrast' without explicitly introducing subsequent 'generalisation' before moving on to 'fusion'. This is equivalent to those studies that apply just two patterns of variation, separation and fusion, because contrast facilitates separation. In trying to understand this variation in practice, it is important to remember that student experience of an object of learning is not limited to what occurs in the classroom. Students bring different prior experiences with the object of learning to the classroom and may also engage in 'imaginative variation' (imagining varying instances of the object of learning in different scenarios), both during and after the lesson. So, it is often anticipated, at least implicitly, that generalisation of critical aspects may occur spontaneously amongst students once they have discerned the critical aspect through contrast. And because contrast needs to precede generalisation, it is natural that contrast becomes the first point of focus in pedagogical interventions.

Development of the model of 'learning study' for pedagogical interventions

The growing emphasis over the 2000s on using the variation theory of learning to inform educational interventions was accompanied by the introduction of 'learning study' as a key design for interventions and research using variation theory in classroom practice (Lo et al., 2004; Pang and Marton, 2003, 2005; Marton and Pang, 2006; Pang, 2006). The model of 'learning study' was developed from the Japanese model of 'lesson study' (Pang and Marton, 2003, 2005; Lo et al., 2004; Pang 2006; Pang and Lo, 2012; Pang and Runesson, 2019). Both models involve small groups of schoolteachers working together collaboratively to improve the design of individual lessons on particular subject matter. The teachers jointly devise a common lesson plan, then one of them teaches the lesson whilst others observe, and subsequent student learning outcomes are evaluated. The teachers then meet again to collaboratively reflect on the design, enactment and outcomes of the lesson, then use these reflections to develop a revised lesson plan. This is then taught by another teacher from the group, and so the cycle continues, usually for two to three rounds.

But while lesson studies do not adopt any particular theoretical basis to designing and evaluating the lessons, simply using teachers' own sense of professional best practice, learning studies introduce a theoretical underpinning to the model in the form of variation theory, which is used to guide the lesson design, evaluation and revision process. So, unlike lesson studies, learning studies are theoretically based.[8] In this way, learning studies combine all the professional development power of teacher collaborative work and teacher action research (in the same way as lesson studies), but also incorporate the additional power of a basis in learning theory. Over time, the learning study design has come to dominate both research and pedagogical applications of variation theory.

Early learning study research took the form of quasi-experimental studies, comparing the learning outcomes for students in 'experimental' *vs* 'control' (i.e., learning study *vs* lesson study) learning designs. The impact of introducing variation theory into learning design was typically dramatic, for example, 70% of the variation theory group *vs* 30% of the control group achieving the desired understanding of the object of learning (Pang and Marton 2003, 2005). However, the first-order perspective adopted in this approach to research formed a marked departure from the second-order perspective adopted in phenomenographic research.

Whilst this quasi-experimental design to empirical research using learning studies continues as one strand of research, not all learning studies take a first-order perspective. Over time, three different methods for evaluating learning outcomes in learning studies evolved (Pang and Ki, 2016; Pang and Runesson, 2019), with the second method currently the most common:

1. comparison of the learning outcomes from 'experimental' *vs* 'control' teaching situations, along the lines of quasi-experimental studies (as described above);

---

[8] Because the definition of a learning study (in contrast to a lesson study) is that it is theoretically-based, learning studies may also be conducted based on theories other than variation theory, but variation theory is the most common theory used.

2. comparison of learning outcomes between iterative cycles of the learning study (i.e., between each cycle of a teacher delivering the planned lesson), along the lines of action research cycles; and
3. a variant of the learning study approach in which the group of teachers deliver the planned lesson simultaneously, rather than sequentially, and the learning outcomes are compared on the basis of the lesson as enacted, along the lines of design experiments.

Contributing to the professional knowledge of teachers

As already mentioned, much of variation theory research and application are built around a learning study design. Not only does this design have a powerful impact on student learning, but the professional development impact reported by teachers is also substantial, described as adding extra depth to their understanding of the nature of teaching and learning, and also to their understanding of the relevant subject matter (Pang, 2006; Åkerlind et al. 2011, 2014; Rovio-Johanssen and Ingerman, 2016; Pang and Runesson, 2019; Durden, 2020).[9] Consequently, the professional learning benefits to teachers started to become an additional focus of the variation theory tradition, including in teacher education (Pang and Runesson, 2019; Durden, 2020; Kullberg et al., 2024).

A recent outcome of this focus is a book on conducting learning studies using variation theory that is specifically designed for teacher practitioners, Kullberg et al.'s (2024) *Planning and Analyzing Teaching*. In addition to describing learning study as a way to improve students' understanding of particular objects of learning, the authors encourage the collation and wider dissemination of the outcomes of learning studies as a way of developing the professional knowledge of teachers. Documenting the outcomes of learning studies in this way is seen

---

9   Although the impact of learning studies on the sophistication of teachers' understanding (not just students' understanding) of the object of learning is not an explicit aim of learning studies, that it occurs is not surprising from a phenomenographic perspective, which assumes there will be variation in ways of understanding a phenomenon amongst any group—including a group of subject experts.

as providing a cumulative source of development of professional knowledge about the teaching and learning of disciplinary subject matter, in terms of:

- critical aspects of the subject matter that students need to discern to achieve desired understandings;
- powerful patterns of variation and invariance that teachers can introduce into lesson design to help students discern these critical aspects; and
- examples of particular learning activities that can be used to create those patterns of variation.

Although I should also note that, even from its earliest inceptions, learning studies were expected to include documentation and dissemination of outcomes as a step in the process (Lo et al., 2004), to enable professional learning benefits to be shared with other teachers.

Identifying critical aspects of the object of learning in learning studies

Learning study interventions in pedagogical practice have often used a preceding phenomenographic analysis of the relevant object of learning to identify the critical aspects that need to be focused on during the intervention. This may be done by drawing on a pre-existing phenomenographic study relevant to the object of learning, or by analysing interviews or qualitative pre-tests of student understanding of the object of learning as the first stage of the learning study. This approach maintains a methodological, as well as theoretical, link between the phenomenography and variation theory traditions.

However, there is a down-side to doing this, in that grounding learning studies in a preceding phenomenographic analysis also maximises the resources needed to implement the learning study model in schools. As a consequence, less resource-intensive methods of identifying critical aspects have emerged over time, to better encourage spread of the model. For example, critical aspects of learning objects are also commonly identified based on teachers' existing professional knowledge, combined with reflections on learners' responses during learning activities and pre-lesson tests of understanding (Pang and Ki,

2016; Pang and Runesson, 2019; Holmqvist and Selin, 2019; Kullberg et al., 2024). Such methods not only have the advantage of being less resource-intensive than a phenomenographic study, but also being more grounded in the day-to-day practice of teachers. In this way, such methods also better match the professional culture of teachers, by building on teachers' professional subject and didactic knowledge in a way that is likely to enhance uptake of the learning study approach.

At the same time, however, these methods also allow teachers to search for critical aspects without necessarily having a good understanding of the nature of a critical aspect and the epistemological assumptions underlying variation theory (Pang and Ki, 2016; Durden, 2018; Thorsten and Tväråna, 2023). This makes it almost inevitable that critical aspects that are identified by teachers based on their professional knowledge and analysis of learners' responses will be constituted in a less rigorous way than would eventuate from a phenomenographic analysis. As a consequence, the relative value of a teacher-led identification of critical aspects *vs* identification of critical aspects through a phenomenographic study of the object of learning has become a topic of debate in the variation theory literature (e.g., Pang and Ki, 2016; Thorsten and Tväråna, 2023).

Another difference in the way the two traditions identify critical aspects is that variation theory research and practice places a greater emphasis on identifying different values along a critical aspect or dimension of variation than does phenomenographic research. This is clearly illustrated in a study by Holmqvist and Selin (2019), where a phenomenographic analysis and a variation theory analysis were undertaken on the same data and with respect to the same phenomenon, thus allowing a direct comparison of the outcomes (see Tables 9.2 and 9.3)

Table 9.2 Outcomes of an analysis of the concept of 'learning' using phenomenography (adapted from Holmqvist and Selin, 2019, p. 6)

Ways of experiencing 'learning'	Critical aspects of 'learning'
A: Experiencing something new	Extended skills
B: Something you do	Process
C: An advantage for future challenges	Investment

D: A knowledge object that is acquired	Object
E: A relationship between requirements for learning	Causal relationship
F: Judging what learning is	Attributes

Table 9.3 Outcomes of an analysis of the concept of 'learning' using variation theory (adapted from Holmqvist and Selin, 2019, p. 7)

Critical aspects of 'learning'	Features/values of critical aspects
The learner	• skills • abilities • pre-knowledge
Learning activities	• brain processes • memorising • listening • taking notes • repetition • practicing
Sources of learning	• teacher • school • friends • places/ persons outside school • internet • quiz • homework • learning materials • methods
Forms of content/ knowledge	• facts • information • activity • mistakes

Outcome of learning	<ul><li>development</li><li>performance</li><li>smartness</li><li>widening knowledge</li><li>access to higher education</li><li>improved future</li><li>future employment</li></ul>

The outcomes of the phenomenographic analysis (Table 9.2) show discernment of a different critical aspect of learning associated with each qualitatively different way of experiencing the concept of learning. But different values of each critical aspect are not specified. In contrast, the outcomes of the variation theory analysis (Table 9.3) identify a number of specific values for each critical aspect. These values represent the ways in which that critical aspect can be experienced as varying. In addition, unlike the phenomenographic analysis, the critical aspects of the concept of learning have been identified without explicitly linking each critical aspect to a specific way of experiencing learning.

So, based on the comparison provided in the Holmqvist and Selin study, at this point in the development of the two traditions, phenomenographic analysis places less emphasis on identifying the different values of each critical aspect, but more emphasis on linking the different critical aspects to different ways of experiencing than do analyses based on variation theory. This is consistent with common practice across learning studies more broadly, where it is not unusual for critical aspects to be identified by noting what is spontaneously being varied (and not varied) by students in pre-tests and classroom interactions, without necessarily clarifying the relationship between these critical aspects and specific ways of understanding the object of learning. At the same time, there is a focus on identifying different values along each critical aspect, which may then be used in lesson design to form a 'contrast' with each other and thus provide the opportunity for students to discern variation in that critical aspect.

The greater focus on identifying the different values of a critical aspect in variation theory research and practice has also led to a change in terminology. Initially in the variation theory literature, critical aspects were commonly also referred to as critical features (e.g., Marton et al., 2004). But in his 2015 book on *Necessary Conditions of Learning*, Marton selected the word 'feature' to be used to refer to a 'value' of a critical aspect (rather than to the critical aspect itself). This change in terminology may be a source of confusion for some phenomenographers, because an 'aspect' of a phenomenon has commonly also been referred to as a 'feature' of a phenomenon in the phenomenographic literature. Nevertheless, to maintain consistency between the phenomenography and variation theory traditions, and reduce potential confusion for readers of the two literatures, I think it is desirable for phenomenographic research to follow the same terminology for the values of a critical aspect as that used in variation theory research and reserve the word 'feature' for different values of a critical aspect.

Variation theory in higher education

So far, variation theory based learning studies have primarily been undertaken in school rather than higher education settings, with a few exceptions (e.g., Rovio Johansson and Lumsden, 2012; Rovio-Johansson, 2013; Åkerlind et al., 2011, 2014). Why is this? There is an obvious potential for variation theory to be applied in higher education (Bowden and Marton, 1998; Marton and Trigwell, 2000; Åkerlind, 2015). Plus, there are many people interested in phenomenography within higher education, so one would expect that the potential to extend that interest to learning studies and the variation theory of learning would also be present. So, why has it not happened? As someone who has tried to extend interest in phenomenography to interest in variation theory and learning studies in higher education (and so far largely failed), I have a perspective on this.

Schools have a common (often national) curriculum that runs across institutions, irrespective of the individual teachers involved. But this is not the case in higher education, where individual teachers typically have the power to set their own curriculum for the courses they teach (even if within certain parameters). This makes finding groups of teachers who are able to work on a common object of learning much easier in school education than in higher education. In addition, for teachers to dedicate time to actively engage in their own professional development as a teacher is well-accepted at school level, but much less so in higher education. Particularly in research universities, expectations of professional development in teaching are relatively low, with professional development in research much more highly valued. This makes institutional support for and teacher willingness to engage in resource-intensive approaches to teaching development much harder to find in a higher education than a school context.

Airi Rovio-Johansson is one of the few other researchers who has conducted learning studies in higher education (e.g., Rovio-Johansson, 2013; Rovio-Johansson and Lumsden, 2012), and she draws similar conclusions in Rovio-Johanssen and Ingerman (2016). Here, they describe a methodological obstacle to the cyclical nature of learning studies in higher education, in that it is possible to go through one round of collaborative lesson design, implementation, review and revision, but not the additional rounds normally expected in learning studies.[10]

> However, in a bachelor programme, there are consecutive courses, and the order can't be changed. Students move on to the next course. From the teachers' perspective, there is no possibility to finish the learning study cycle in the way it is done for instance in the compulsory school. In order to apply the learning study cycle according to the learning study model, in higher education, there is a need for several methodological as well as contextual time adjustments. (p. 266)

I experienced the same difficulty with my own learning study in higher education (Åkerlind et al., 2011, 2014), where a second round was definitely needed in order to implement what teachers had learned from the first round; yet another round was not possible for another twelve months, and this was then not possible due to funding limitations.

The relationship between the phenomenography and variation theory traditions

Despite the differences between the phenomenography and variation theory traditions that I have described in this chapter, the two traditions continue to complement and enhance each other in many ways, as I

---

10 At least two, hopefully three, rounds are regarded as desirable (Marton and Pong, 2013).

will describe further below. But before I describe my own view of the relationships between them, I would like to describe how others see the relationships, based both on what is written in the literature and on responses to a small survey that I conducted. It is clear from both sources that there is not one universal view of the relationship between the two traditions (as any phenomenographer would expect), though there are some agreed upon elements.

Views from the research community

As part of the open-ended survey of participants at the phenomenography and variation theory conferences I described above, I also asked, "How would you describe the relationship between phenomenography and variation theory?". I received twenty-one responses to the question, amongst which four inclusively expanding ways of understanding the relationship were evident:

1. variation theory developed from phenomenography;
2. variation theory has a theoretical focus, while phenomenography has a methodological focus;
3. variation theory has an applied focus that phenomenography does not have; and
4. variation theory focuses on variation 'within' ways of experiencing, while phenomenography focuses on variation 'between' ways of experiencing.

1. Development from phenomenography—The first way of understanding the relationship focuses on the historical connection between the two traditions, in that phenomenography both pre-dates variation theory and also provided the foundational research from which variation theory developed. For example:

> Phenomenography is where the variation theory comes from. In other words, variation theory is drawn from phenomenography. (Response 8)

> VT developed later, as part of the work of trying to tease out the learning theory involved in phenomenography. (Response 17)

2. *Theoretical vs methodological focus*—The second way of understanding the relationship contrasts the two traditions as having different, but complementary, foci. For example:

> Phenomenography is methodological whereas variation theory is theoretical in nature. (Response 15)

> I see VT as providing a theoretical framework for the development of phenomenographic work. ... I see them as developing together and separately, with contributions to be made in their respective domains of theoretical and methodological advancement of the field of studying variation in human experiences. (Response 3)

3. *Applied pedagogical focus*—The third way of understanding the relationship positions variation theory as providing something additional to phenomenography, in terms of its usefulness for guiding classroom teaching. For example:

> I also see Variation Theory as phenomenography implemented in the classroom. A powerful toolbox for teachers to consider when planning their teaching... (Response 6)

> Variation theory also provides theoretical tools for practitioners (not only researchers) to design and analyze and improve teaching and students' learning. (Response 16)

4. *Variation within and between ways of experiencing*—The fourth way of understanding the relationship again draws a contrast between the two traditions in a complementary way, with phenomenography seen as unpacking variation 'between' ways of experiencing, whilst variation theory unpacks variation 'within' a way of experiencing, in terms of different critical aspects that are discerned within particular ways of experiencing something. For example:

> Phen is about variation between ways of understanding. VT within ways. (Response 10)

> Whereas phenomenography is interested in finding the different ways that a phenomenon can be experienced, VT is concerned with the internal structure of the phenomenon and how that can be used to help reveal critical and necessary conditions for learning... (Response 12)

Phenomenography studies variations in the ways people experience a given phenomenon, while variation theory focuses on "what is a way of experiencing a phenomenon" and the distinctions between different ways of experiencing. (Response 14)

Although different words are being used in these quotes, the underlying meaning of the words are all strongly related. I have grouped them into one category because a focus on the 'internal structure' (or internal horizon) of a way of experiencing a phenomenon, on 'what is a way of experiencing' and on 'necessary conditions for learning' all involve a focus on identifying the variation 'within' a way of experiencing, in terms of the dimensions of variation, or critical aspects, of a phenomenon that need to be discerned in order to experience something in a certain way. Additional ways of describing this focus that were seen in the survey responses included that variation theory focuses on 'what makes it possible for people to experience something' and on 'what should be learned'.

> **Conceptual aside:**
>
> **Notions associated with a focus on variation within a way of experiencing**
>
> The phrases used in the survey responses representing Category 4 are also commonly seen in the variation theory literature, i.e., that the variation theory tradition focuses on:
>
> - variation within a way of experiencing;
> - the internal horizon (or structure) of a way of experiencing;
> - what is a way of experiencing;
> - what makes it possible to experience something;
> - necessary conditions for learning; and
> - what should be learned.
>
> On the surface, it is not obvious how all of these notions are conceptually related, so I will unpack that here. As described in Chapter 5, an analysis of the 'variation within a way of experiencing' highlights different critical aspects of the phenomenon that are discerned within different ways of experiencing it. The set of critical aspects (including the ways in which they relate to each other and to the phenomenon as a whole) constitute the 'internal horizon', or structure, of each specific way of experiencing. In this sense, it is the discernment of particular critical aspects of a

> phenomenon (and the relations between those critical aspects) that defines 'what a way of experiencing is'.
>
> Meanwhile, discernment of a critical aspect occurs through the experience of variation along that aspect (or dimension) of the phenomenon, and it is this variation that explains 'what makes it possible to experience something'. So, 'necessary conditions for learning' consist of exposure to variation along each of the critical aspects that learners need to discern in order to experience an object of learning in the desired way. This means that 'what should be learned' are the critical aspects needed to experience the learning object in a particular way.
>
> In this sense, a specific way of experiencing may be defined in terms of what critical aspects of a phenomenon are discerned and focused on simultaneously, different ways of experiencing may be explained in terms of different critical aspects of the phenomenon that are discerned and focused on simultaneously, and what is to be learned may be described in terms of particular critical aspects of the object of learning that need to be discerned and focused on simultaneously.[11]
>
> This is why I have said that all these phrases indicate, as a minimum, awareness of variation within a way of experiencing. With more data (or more detailed data) further distinctions in ways of understanding the relationship between phenomenography and variation theory might become apparent within this grouping of responses, but with these data I think it is appropriate to group them together into one category.

The different ways of seeing the relationship between phenomenography and variation theory that emerged from the survey are also reflected in the literature, as I will describe below. But there is a fifth way of understanding the relationship (which accords with my own way of understanding) that I will also present.

Views from the literature

Whilst everyone agrees that the variation theory tradition arose out of the phenomenographic tradition (in line with the first way of describing the relationship represented in my survey), this may be understood as

---

11 Hence, the intense focus of the variation theory tradition on identifying and discerning critical aspects of an object of learning.

simply a chronological development, in the sense of phenomenography preceding variation theory chronologically, rather than as the two traditions sharing common epistemological foundations or a shared knowledge interest. When thought of as a chronological connection, the shared foundations can be seen as merely historical and of little relevance to how variation theory is practiced today. Whilst when thought of as an epistemological connection, the traditions can be seen as having the potential to inform each other. So, simple statements in the literature that variation theory arose out of phenomenography can be understood in different ways.

Some authors go on to explain that variation theory arose from the analysis of decades of phenomenographic research on learning (e.g., Kullberg and Ingerman, 2022). However, the focus on phenomenographic research in such descriptions allows for a distinction to be drawn between empirical research (associated with phenomenography) on the one hand and theoretical assumptions (associated with variation theory) on the other. This distinction is commonly expressed in the literature and is fundamental to the second way of describing the relationship represented in my survey, where the phenomenography tradition is seen as primarily methodological and the variation theory tradition as primarily theoretical in nature.

In line with this view, because the variation theory tradition developed directly from the analyses in Marton and Booth's (1997) book on *Learning and Awareness*—a book that can be seen as primarily about learning (e.g., Kullberg and Ingerman, 2022), even though it is also about phenomenography—this has led to some authors describing the theoretical components of the book as more relevant to the variation theory tradition than to the phenomenography tradition (e.g., Rovio-Johansson and Ingerman, 2016; Pang and Ki, 2016). This reflects the view that the phenomenography tradition continues to be fundamentally an empirically based approach, whilst the variation theory tradition is theoretically based.

Whilst I agree that the foundations of phenomenography are empirical, and the foundations of variation theory theoretical, phenomenography has since developed strong theoretical underpinnings, and the practice of variation theory strong empirical elements. For instance, the lesson study model that is so common in applications of variation theory is more empirically than theoretically grounded. (That is, whilst variation theory brings a theoretical basis to the enactment of the lesson study model as a learning study, the model itself is not theoretically based.) So, this distinction is really only applicable to the starting point of the two traditions, not to the breadth of ways in which they are practiced today.

The third way of understanding the relationship between the phenomenography and variation theory traditions focuses on the ways in which variation theory is applied in the classroom. There is no doubt that this is indeed a central difference between the two traditions, especially since development of the learning study model. In principle, distinguishing between the two traditions on this basis does not require any assumptions about how related or unrelated they are theoretically, but in practice, this distinction commonly still builds upon the second way of understanding the relationship (as seen in the survey responses), with phenomenography seen as more empirically focused and variation theory as more theoretically focused.

The fourth way of understanding the relationship places the focus of difference on an interest in variation between ways of experiencing *vs* within ways of experiencing. This is reflected in early descriptions of the difference between phenomenography and variation theory, starting with a key paper by Ming Fai Pang in 2003 on *Two Faces of Variation*. Pang describes the two traditions as linked by a common focus on variation, but on different aspects (or 'faces') of variation. Pang describes traditional phenomenography as descriptive and methodologically oriented, with research that asks, "What are the different ways of experiencing [a] phenomenon?" (p. 2), and I would add, 'How are these ways of experiencing related to each other?'. This focus on variation that constitutes collective experience, is described as representing the 'first face of variation' in the phenomenographic tradition (i.e., the variation between different ways of experiencing).

He contrasts this with the extension to phenomenography represented by the variation theory tradition (at that early point still referred to as 'new phenomenography') which asks, "What is a way of experiencing a phenomenon?" and "How do different ways of experiencing something evolve?" (p. 3). This focus on variation that constitutes a specific way of experiencing, in terms of the critical aspects or dimensions of variation discerned, is described as representing the 'second face of variation' (i.e., variation within a way of experiencing). This includes theoretical questions about what it means to say someone is experiencing something in a particular way. And in a pedagogical situation, these theoretical questions have implications for the practical questions of 'What is to be learned?' and 'What are necessary conditions for learning to take place', because "What critical [aspects] the learner discerns and focuses on simultaneously characterises a specific way of experiencing that phenomenon" (p. 6).

An underlying perspective evident in much of the literature as well as all four ways of understanding the relationship between phenomenography and variation theory represented in my survey is that the phenomenographic tradition is regarded as continuing largely unchanged from its beginnings. From this perspective, the publication of *Learning and Awareness* is seen as initiating the variation theory tradition, but being largely irrelevant to phenomenography. This perspective is represented visually in Figure 9.1.

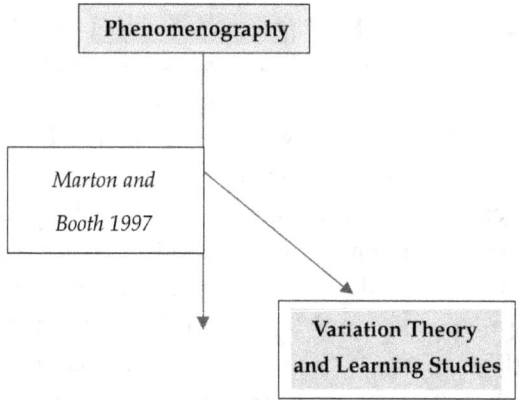

Fig. 9.1 One view of the relationship between the phenomenography and variation theory traditions, in which *Learning and Awareness* is seen as having had no impact on phenomenography

However, it is obvious from my frequent references throughout this book to 21st-century phenomenography, that I disagree with this perspective (see Chapters 2 and 5 in particular). The understanding represented in Figure 9.1 is no doubt reinforced by the fact that pre-21st century approaches to phenomenography are still being practiced and published in the 2000s. However, as one of the cohort of doctoral students engaged in phenomenographic research at the time *Learning and Awareness* was published, I am very aware of the ways in which we attempted to incorporate the ideas in the book into our practice of phenomenography, and the resulting changes in approaches to phenomenographic research that took place during the 2000s that I have described throughout this book.

So, I would now like to present a fifth view of the relationship between phenomenography and variation theory (my own view), which is that *Learning and Awareness* was as influential on the phenomenography tradition as on the variation theory tradition, that Marton and Booth outlined not just a 'variation theory of learning' but also a 'variation theory of awareness' in their book, with the variation theory of awareness going on to underpin future developments in the phenomenography tradition, and the variation theory of learning going on to underpin future developments in the variation theory tradition. This perspective is represented visually in Figure 9.2.

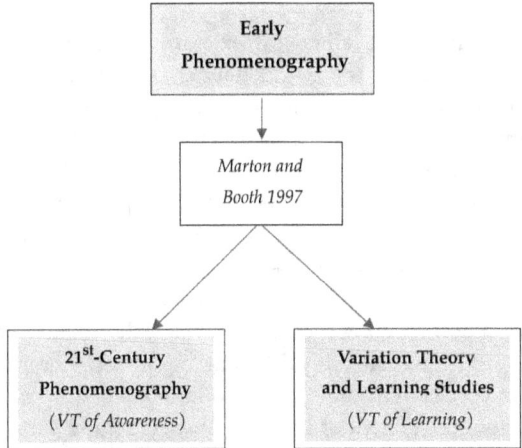

Fig. 9.2 An alternative view of the relationship between the phenomenography and variation theory traditions, in which *Learning and Awareness* is seen as having had a profound impact on phenomenography

From this perspective, both variation theory and phenomenography (as it has developed during the 21st century) share common theoretical foundations based in *Learning and Awareness*, plus a common interest in identifying variation within ways of experiencing, as well as what is needed to move from a less complex to a qualitatively more complex way of experiencing. This way of understanding the relationship between phenomenography and variation theory may also be seen in the literature, in that any researcher who has ever used phenomenographic research to identify the critical aspects of different ways of experiencing a phenomenon is, at least implicitly, expressing this way of experiencing the relationship between the two traditions, because they are focusing on variation within as well as between ways of experiencing (see Chapter 5). I have also explicitly asserted this relationship in my own learning studies and discussions of the relationship between phenomenography and variation theory (Åkerlind, 2008, 2018; Åkerlind et al., 2011, 2014).

Lastly, indications of this view of the relationship between phenomenography and variation theory was also evident in one response to the survey described above, initially obscured by the ambiguity of the term, variation theory. Usually, the term is taken to refer to the variation theory of learning, but in this case, I think the respondent is referring to what I have called the variation theory of awareness, which they describe as 'variation theory in phenomenography'.

> Phenomenography is the empirical examination of the variations in how people think about the world, with the goal of identifying and characterizing the qualitatively different ways of experiencing a specific phenomenon. Variation theory in phenomenography further organizes the results of a research study into a two-dimensional outcome space, which articulates the aspects or specific features of a phenomenon that individuals are aware of and pay attention to, as well as the variations or distinctions in how each of these aspects are experienced by different individuals. Together across multiple aspects, the outcome space represents a hypothesis based on a set of logically related descriptions that define the qualitatively different ways of experiencing the phenomenon by different individuals. While outcome space existed as a concept before the advent of variation theory, I think variation theory helps operationalize the idea of an outcome space into something more structured. (Response 9)

In this quote, the respondent distinguishes between phenomenography and 'variation theory in phenomenography' in a similar way to which I have distinguished between phenomenography of the 1970s–1990s and phenomenography of the 21st century throughout this book. So, instead of being a description of the difference between the phenomenography and variation theory of learning traditions, as it initially appeared, I think this response is a description of the difference between phenomenography before and after incorporation of the theory of variation that was presented in *Learning and Awareness*. This response provides a further example of the ambiguity of the term, variation theory.

Meanwhile, if I were to add this way of understanding the relationship between phenomenography and variation theory to my list of ways of understanding presented above, it would be:

5. variation theory is underpinned by a variation theory of learning, while phenomenography is underpinned by a variation theory of awareness.

The relationship in summary—complementary theoretical, applied, empirical and educational relationships

The four ways of understanding the relationship between phenomenography and variation theory represented in the survey tended to focus on differences between the two traditions. However, the fifth way of understanding places as much emphasis on commonalities as differences, with both traditions seen as sharing a common theoretical foundation in the variation theory of discernment outlined in *Learning and Awareness* and a common interest in identifying variation within ways of experiencing, as well as what is needed to move from a less complex to a qualitatively more complex way of experiencing.

At the same time, there are also differences, but I would describe these as complementary differences, allowing the two traditions to address different aspects of a mutual knowledge interest in the role of variation in human experience. As stated by respondent 3 in the survey,

> I see them as developing together and separately, with contributions to be made in their respective domains... of the field of studying variation in human experiences. (Response 3)

So, the complementary differences between the phenomenography and variation theory traditions can also be seen as complementary contributions to a larger field or knowledge interest. I would group the complementary foci of phenomenography and variation theory into five areas in particular: (1) theoretical; (2) applied; (3) empirical; and (4) educational, including (5) the level of education where each tradition makes its greatest contribution.

Theoretical focus—As I have argued previously, the theory of variation and discernment outlined in *Learning and Awareness* presents not only a 'variation theory of learning', the underpinning of the variation theory tradition, but also a 'variation theory of awareness', which is of great relevance to the phenomenographic tradition. So, I see phenomenography in the 21st century as sharing a foundational theoretical relationship with the variation theory tradition, in terms of their shared epistemological assumptions. It should be noted, however, that the variation theory tradition has since developed further theoretical assumptions, in the form of different patterns of variation and different perspectives on the object of learning (as described above).

In addition, both 21st-century phenomenography and the variation theory tradition focus on identifying variation *within* a way of experiencing, in terms of identifying the dimensions of variation, or critical aspects, discerned within each way of experiencing. In phenomenographic research, this within-category variation is then used to further elucidate its traditional focus on variation *between* ways of experiencing (variation at the collective level), and what critical aspects need to be discerned in order to move from one way of experiencing to a qualitatively different way (as described in Chapter 2 and Chapter 5). This shared analytic framework enables the critical aspects of phenomena identified in phenomenographic research to potentially be used within learning studies whenever there is a matching object of learning.

Applied focus—Although phenomenography commenced with an applied interest, in the sense of a desire not just to understand "why are some people better at learning than others" (Marton, 1994, p. 4424), but to use that knowledge to improve teaching and learning (as described in Chapter 2), applications of the outcomes of phenomenographic research in the classroom have always represented an additional step separate from phenomenography itself. In contrast, applications in the classroom are inherent to the way the practice of the variation theory tradition has developed, in particular the large emphasis on learning studies. So, it is generally acknowledged that the variation theory tradition has a stronger applied focus than the phenomenography tradition.

Empirical focus—Empirically, phenomenography has maintained its initial focus on investigating human experience from a second-order perspective. In contrast, the applied focus in variation theory research has meant that second-order perspectives focused on the experience of students have become intermingled with first-order perspectives focused on demonstrating the pedagogical effectiveness of learning studies. So, unlike phenomenographic research, both second- and first-order perspectives can be seen in variation theory research.

Educational focus—Whilst variation theory research and practice is entirely focused on education, phenomenographic research is not. Although phenomenography arose in an educational setting and has most commonly been used to research educational topics, there has also always been a strand of pure knowledge interest, with phenomenographic research also being undertaken to better understand human collective awareness (as described in the next chapter). As a consequence, phenomenographic research is undertaken in fields outside education and has the potential to inform social science research more broadly (also discussed in the next chapter).

Level of education—Even within the field of education, the phenomenography and variation theory traditions make their main contributions at different levels of education. Internationally, phenomenography is better known amongst researchers in higher education than in school education, whereas for variation theory it is the opposite. This is not due to an inherent difference between the two traditions, but to historical and cultural reasons.

Historically, the first phenomenographic studies happened to be conducted with university students. Further, these early studies provided a basis for the distinction between deep and surface approaches to learning that subsequently became famous in higher education (Marton and Säljö, 1976). This had a major impact on higher education research and pedagogical practice, especially in Australia, New Zealand and the United Kingdom. As described by Biggs and Tang (1999), "this series of studies struck a chord with ongoing work in other countries; in particular with that of Entwistle in the UK and Biggs in Australia" (p. 61), which probably also explains the particular popularity of phenomenography in the UK and Australia (just as the Hong Kong and Swedish government funding initiatives described above explain the particular popularity of variation theory and learning study in Hong Kong and Sweden.)

The spread of variation theory, in contrast, was facilitated by government funding initiatives in school education (Lo et al., 2004; Kullberg and Ingerman, 2020). These initiatives were focused on curriculum reform at primary and secondary school level, and not tertiary or university level. They also occurred at a time when interest in Japanese lesson study was spreading internationally, and the connection of variation theory to the lesson study model through the creation of learning studies then formed part of this spread (Pang and Runesson, 2019). Meanwhile, lesson study was also primarily associated with school education, not higher education.

To conclude this chapter, I summarise the complementary foci I have discussed in Table 9.4, below.

Table 9.4 Complementary foci of the phenomenography and variation theory traditions

Phenomenography tradition	Variation theory tradition
Focus on experience of phenomena that make up the world	Focus on experience of learning objects in educational settings
Relevant to education and broader social sciences	Relevant to education only
Particularly popular in higher education	Particularly popular in school education
Empirically derived, with subsequent theoretical developments	Theoretically derived, with subsequent empirical developments
Underpinned by a variation theory of awareness (in the 2000s)	Underpinned by a variation theory of learning (since inception)

Generic research questions: • What are the collective range of ways of experiencing a particular phenomenon? • What critical aspects of the phenomenon are discerned (and not discerned) within each way of experiencing it?'	Generic research questions: • What are educationally critical aspects of the object of learning? • What pedagogical design would maximise students' chances of discerning those critical aspects?
More pure knowledge interest, with a focus on description (though researcher may have an applied intention)	More applied knowledge interest, with a focus on pedagogical interventions
Second-order perspective to research, focused entirely on phenomena and learning as experienced	First and second-order perspectives to research, including measurements of impacts on learning
Potential to inform learning studies, through identification of critical aspects associated with different ways of understanding the learning object	Potential to increase the impact of phenomenographic research on educational practice, through applying the outcomes in learning studies

Chapter summary

This chapter describes the tradition of 'variation theory' research and practice that arose out of phenomenographic research. Originating in theoretical descriptions of the role of variation in discernment outlined in *Learning and Awareness*, a 'variation theory of learning' was developed, with an associated tradition of researching and applying the theory in the classroom. Over time, these empirical and pedagogical applications of variation theory became strongly based in the model of 'learning studies', developed from the better-known model of 'lesson study'.

The chapter also describes the ways in which the phenomenography and variation theory traditions differ from and complement each other. Whilst views of the relationship between the two traditions vary, I have argued that they have a complementary relationship marked by similarities and differences in the areas of theoretical, applied, empirical and educational foci. In particular, they are underpinned by common theoretical assumptions about the role of variation in discernment and experience, derived from Marton and Booth's (1997) *Learning and Awareness*. These common assumptions mean that phenomenographic research has the potential to inform the identification of critical aspects of objects of learning, which can then be utilised in learning studies. Meanwhile, learning studies have the potential to maximise the educational impact of phenomenographic research, through pedagogical interventions based on the outcomes of that research.

Having strongly focused on phenomenography's contribution to teaching and learning in this chapter, in the next and final chapter of this book, I look beyond phenomenography's usefulness for educational research and consider what it has to offer the broader social sciences. Whilst phenomenography is best known within the field of education, there has always been an additional strand of 'pure' phenomenographic research designed to investigate human collective awareness of significant social phenomena. In Chapter 10, I describe phenomenographic research that lies outside the educational arena, and the potential of phenomenography to make a greater contribution to other fields of research.

10. Phenomenography and collective awareness: The potential of phenomenography to contribute to the broader social sciences

As described in Chapter 2, phenomenography initially developed in the context of research in education. The earliest topics of research investigated the process of student learning and variation in student understanding of disciplinary content or subject matter. Since then, phenomenography's potential to inform education and pedagogy has continued to be the most common driver of phenomenographic research, and with the development of variation theory (see Chapter 9), the relevance of phenomenography for educational research and educational applications was further reinforced. Indeed, phenomenography is often described as an 'educational' research approach.

However, in this dominant focus on the implications of phenomenography for education, the potential of phenomenography to contribute to other social sciences has been backgrounded. But, as highlighted in Chapter 6, from its inception there have always been two purposes proposed for phenomenographic research:

- improvement of teaching and learning; and
- insight into humanity's collective understanding of the world.

Phenomenography and collective awareness

Ference Marton introduced the notion of collective understanding, or collective awareness, of the world in his first paper on phenomenography in 1981. He referred to the notion as 'collective mind', that is, the "complex of possible ways of viewing various aspects of the world" (Marton, 1981a, p. 197).[1]

> This collective intellect can thus be seen as a structured pool of ideas, conceptions and beliefs underlying the possible interpretations (or possible constructions) of reality and it is enhanced steadily, as new possibilities are continually added to those previously available. (Marton, 1981a, p. 198)

Whilst the aim of phenomenographic research in education is typically to provide insights that will help students move from one way of thinking to a qualitatively 'better' way, the aim of research into collective mind is simply to understand other people's ways of thinking, not to change their ways of thinking:

> What has not been realized sufficiently is that the characterization of distinctly different ways that people understand various phenomena (for example, political power, the concept of number, or inflation) is of interest in itself. ... It is a goal of phenomenography to discover the structural framework within which various categories of understanding exist. Such structures (a complex of categories of description) should prove useful in understanding other people's understandings. (Marton, 1986, pp. 33–34)[2]

Marton proposed describing the world, not in terms of the most common ways of experiencing it, or even the 'best' ways of experiencing it, but in terms of the ways in which it is *possible* for us to experience it:

> We should put all findings together which concern the experience (conception) of, for instance, time (or power or learning or justice) irrespective of whether the studies from which they originate stem from pre-school children in Massachusetts, Samoan aborigines, medieval writings or the daily life in a London suburb. (Marton, 1981b, p. 168)

---

[1] This is not to imply that an ultimate description of human ways of understanding the world can ever be achieved, because new forms of understanding are inevitably introduced into human society, or collective understanding, at different points in time. And whilst the current range of ways of understanding a phenomenon can be described for a particular group, additional ways of understanding may not just develop over time, but also co-exist at the same time in different social and cultural contexts.

[2] A very similar quotation can also be found in Marton, 1988, pp. 180–182.

The importance of investigating collective awareness was further developed in Bowden and Marton (1998). In particular, they discuss the value of learning on the collective level, and the importance of "expanding, widening and transforming the collective mind" (p. 5). They also introduce the notion of 'collective consciousness', defined as the degree of our awareness of others' ways of thinking ("regardless of whether or not we are convinced by, or appropriate, their ways of seeing", p. 14). They attribute clear benefits from using phenomenographic research to enhance collective consciousness:

> By becoming aware of other people's ways of seeing various phenomena one's understanding is enriched and therefore becomes more powerful. (Bowden and Marton, 1998, p. 190)

As Marton has previously argued, "[phenomenographic] categories of description, make other people's ideas about the world more comprehensible to us" (1981b, p. 166) and "...[when people] become conscious of the fact that there are different ways of thinking. This is a very fundamental insight" (1986, p. 46). In other words, becoming aware of other people's ways of seeing a phenomenon enables us to understand our own way of seeing as just *one* way amongst a multitude of ways. Without this awareness, we tend to assume that there is only one way of seeing a phenomenon, that this is what the phenomenon is really like, and that everyone else sees (or at least should see) the phenomenon in the same way we do.

Bowden and Marton describe phenomenographic research outcomes as inevitably reflecting our 'collective cultural heritage' with respect to the phenomenon, in that any outcome space can be expected to reflect the historical and social development of different ways of understanding the phenomenon over time—"collective mind cuts across and comprises cultural differences distributed in time and space" (p. 5). Indeed, Marton has long assumed a cultural-historical 'layering' to collective understanding:

> Traces of societies of the past as well as different physical, regulative and scientific ways of arranging our existence today in actual fact reflect the ways in which we think or have thought about the world around us. Society embodies conceptions. (Marton, 1984, p. 65)

This assumption opens up opportunities for historical or cultural studies of variation in ways of understanding significant phenomena in different cultures, social groups or time periods. Just as Marton emphasised the potential of phenomenography to inform our understanding of educational phenomena, he also envisaged phenomenography as a way to inform our understanding of historical, social and cultural phenomena:

> ...in the same way we can formulate meaningful questions about the conception of reality dominant in a particular epoch, a particular culture, or in a particular society. (Marton, 1981a, p. 187)

Consequently, Marton, Svensson and others envisaged potential applications of phenomenography in disciplines such as history, cultural studies and psychology.

> Such research would be of interest to those studying developmental psychology and the psychology of learning. Sociologists and anthropologists would be interested in learning why certain perceptions are more prevalent in one culture than in another. (Marton, 1986, p. 33)

> Describing conceptions may be said to be an interdisciplinary field of research. In several disciplines there is a wide interest in people's conceptions. ... For instance, they have been parts of describing memory and cognitive development in psychology, a part of describing learning and teaching in education, a part of describing cultures and subcultures in anthropology and ethnography and a part of describing historical persons, situations and developments within the field of history. (Svensson and Theman, 1983, p. 2)

Marton initially referred to research on collective understanding as 'pure phenomenography' (Marton, 1986, 1988, 1994), to distinguish it from phenomenographic research with an educational focus.

> There is a pure phenomenographic 'knowledge interest' that transcends the educational context. By describing the different ways in which individuals can experience, or understand, the world around them, they are characterizing the world as it appears to them, which is tantamount to characterizing 'the collective mind' encompassing the different ways in which people are capable of making sense of the world. (Marton, 1994, p. 4429)

Early examples of phenomenographic research in this vein include studies of social concepts in community settings, such as political power (Theman, 1983, cited in Svensson and Theman, 1983) and different understandings of competence in the workplace, such as car engine optimisation (Sandberg, 1994). And such 'pure' phenomenographic research has continued over the years, even though less frequently than educationally-related phenomenographic research, including studies of policy development, management and professional work (e.g., Sandberg, 2001; Dall'Alba, 2002; Åkerlind and Kayrooz, 2003; Reid et al., 2006; Åkerlind, 2008b; Sin et al., 2011; Värk and Reino, 2018; Röing et al., 2018, Kettunen et al., 2020; Kettunen and Tynjälä, 2021; Yu and Åkerlind, 2024; Kettunen 2024).

But, despite this early and continuing interest in collective understanding and the pure phenomenographic knowledge interest, at this point in the development of phenomenography, its potential to contribute to our understanding of the world through application in social science disciplines other than education is still a largely untapped resource. So, the next section focuses on the neglected potential of 'pure phenomenography', or what one might call the 'phenomenography of collective consciousness',[3] to contribute to disciplines beyond education.

Phenomenography and sociocultural perspectives on human experience

One limitation on phenomenography's potential to contribute to broader social science research is its silence on the socially mediated nature of human experience. Given the significance of social theory in much social science research, it is important to clarify the potential and the limitations of phenomenography in this regard. First, let me say that phenomenographers do not deny the socially mediated nature of human experience:

> Learning takes place through ... how people do things together, how they handle their tools, how they become more and more parts of the particular context and how this particular context becomes more and more their own. ... Against the background of this line of reasoning,

---

3   In contrast to the 'phenomenography of learning' (Marton, 1992).

> taking the single individual unaided doing a task on her own... lacks ecological validity (Marton and Trigwell, 2000, p. 384)

> ...when conceptions are expressed not by persons but by man-made [sic] artifacts. The law system may, for instance, tell us a great deal about prevalent ideas in a certain society, and how we build new cities may very well reflect our way of stratifying the life-world. (Marton, 1988, p. 63)

By focusing research on human experience at a collective, not individual, level phenomenography automatically focuses its outcomes at the level of a particular social group with certain social characteristics and socially mediated experiences of the world. It is just that phenomenography does not go on to actively explore the social nature of experience, because the research aim is on description of difference, not explanation of difference. In other words, the aim of phenomenography is to describe the range of ways of experiencing the same phenomenon that can occur within a particular social group, and how these different ways of experiencing build on each other in a developmental way—not to investigate potential external causes of, or influences on, the different ways of experiencing.

To the extent that phenomenography explores 'causes' of different ways of experiencing, it is at a theoretical level. That is, from a phenomenographic perspective, the socially mediated nature of human experience of phenomena would be seen as lying in the ways that the social relationships and sociocultural environment experienced by humans in different social groups creates a situation in which they are more or less likely to be exposed to particular patterns of variation (and invariance) in phenomena, and thus to discern different aspects of those phenomena (as per Chapter 5).

Whilst the background assumption of many phenomenographers may be that different ways of experiencing the same phenomena arise from different cultural and historical layerings in discernment of different aspects of the phenomenon, the socio-historical background to these layerings of meaning (or discernment) are not directly explored in phenomenography. However, that does not mean that other researchers cannot use phenomenographic research to do so. For example, much of the variation theory research discussed in Chapter 9 makes use of phenomenographic outcomes to explore learning in non-phenomenographic ways. Plus, phenomenography is already being used concomitantly with other theoretical and methodological frameworks, including sociocultural frameworks. For example, in a review of phenomenography by Tight (2016), he describes phenomenography being combined with activity theory, ethnography, grounded theory and knowledge space theory. Phenomenography has also been integrated with discourse analysis (Wan and Leung, 2021), narrative analysis (de Búrca, 2024), practice theory (Warner, 2018) and Heidegger's ways of being-in-the-world (Sandberg and Pinnington, 2009).

To illustrate, in a study of students' experience of their learning environment, Berglund (2005) used phenomenography to look at variation in experience of learning, and activity theory to look at the role of context in the experience of learning. Activity theory was used to synthesise related phenomenographic outcome spaces into a holistic picture, by mapping different categories of description to different components of the activity system.

In a study of safety in anaesthesia, Warner (2018) simultaneously drew on phenomenography, practice theory and sociomateriality. She investigated how safety emerges in the course of anaesthetists' everyday working practices, and argued that phenomenography is a useful method for practice-based research.

> If one is to account for how practices are made intelligible in their doing and how practices act in the design of social life, I suggest that one must look to a research method based upon a relational epistemology, like phenomenography, that recognises the entwinement of humans and nonhumans in the social world. (pp. 55–56)

In a study of conceptions of curriculum leadership in facilitating curriculum change in schools, Wan and Leung (2021) used a phenomenographic framework to gather interview data, but in analysing the transcripts, they combined phenomenography with a focus on different linguistic aspects of the transcripts, including text analysis (i.e., vocabulary, grammar), discourse practice (i.e., text production, text distribution) and social practice (i.e., nature of social practice within a larger community).

As a final example, in a study of the practice of law in a corporate law firm, Sandberg and Pinnington (2009) used Heidegger's 'existential ontology' of how self, others and tools co-constitute human ways of being-in-the-world as an analytic framework.

Interviews and field observations were undertaken and first analysed phenomenographically, to identify different ways of practicing law. The same data were then re-analysed with a focus on understandings of self and work, involvement of 'others' and the use of 'tools' in the different ways of practicing law, in line with the three dimensions of Heidegger's ontology. The different analyses were then combined through an integrative analysis of how the different ways of practicing law initially identified through the phenomenographic analysis reflected a particular self-understanding, understanding of work, and involvement of others and tools.

Potential applications of phenomenography in the broader social sciences

Once we start thinking beyond the boundaries of educational research, we can envisage ways in which phenomenographic methodology may be useful for other fields of research. For example, in historical research, phenomenography could facilitate investigation of changing understandings of significant social phenomena at different historical time periods. As described by Marton (1981a) when talking about the history of science,

> The 'authorized' conception... [is] a special case among the varying conceptions science itself has held during its history. A conception of a certain aspect of reality accepted as the scientifically correct view is not something given, something which is to stand for all time... Historically, there have been other dominant conceptions no longer taken as correct and it is not unreasonable to think there will be others in the future. The scientifically accepted conceptions of today thus appear as a section in time as well as a special case of the variation in people's commonsense conceptions of the same aspect of reality which exists at the same point in time.... Commonsense conceptions held by today's laymen [sic] and judged wrong by science frequently turn out to be identical to conceptions accepted previously in history as scientifically valid ways of thinking. (p. 185)

Although he is talking about historical changes in scientific concepts here, the same would apply to other social phenomena.

The focus on collective ways of understanding a phenomenon could also be of value in social and cultural studies. As described in Marton (1984),

> The most fundamental images of our world are always taken for granted and they are mostly not present in individual consciousness, but they are reflected in the way we organize our society, how we build our cities, how we separate or unite nature and the man-made [sic] world, for instance. In the future psychology will of necessity deal with such culturally sedimented layers of the experience of mankind. (p. 45)

> ...only then can we see all the taken-for-granted conceptions embodied in contemporary society as well as in traces of the past. (p. 6)

In addition, pure phenomenography can be used to guide policy development at organisational, national and international levels. An example is Kettunen's (2024) study of Finnish national policy on career guidance in schools, based on an analysis of policy documents and legislation. As described by Kettunen,

> This research also demonstrates how a conceptual framework grounded in [phenomenographic analysis of] empirical data (Kettunen et al., 2023) can be used to assess the development of [policy] systems, both nationally and internationally. The hierarchical structure of the themes and categories can help policymakers and other stakeholders to deepen their understanding of critical factors that may play an important role in the development of a [policy] system. (p. 81)

Phenomenography has also been used to enhance our understanding of humans at work, in terms of variation in how different professional occupations are experienced, and the perceived nature of competence, expertise and success in these professions. It is now well accepted that professionals' performance at work is related to their ways of understanding their work (Sandberg, 2001; Larsson et al., 2004; Dall'Alba and Sandberg, 2006; Sandberg and Pinnington, 2009). For example, Sandberg (2001) found that Volvo testing engineers understood their work in three distinct ways, what he called 'sequential', 'interactive' and 'customer' focused engine optimizers.

> The differences amongst [the three] groups explained many of the variations in how individual engineers carried out their jobs. ... Strikingly, all [participants] agreed that customer optimizers were the

most effective at their work, and all thought the sequential optimizers were the least capable. But the reasons given for these assessments differed, depending on how the individual defined the job. When I asked sequential optimizers, for instance, why they thought the customer optimizers were so good, they explained it in terms of their own understanding of the job [not in terms of what customer optimizers thought was important in the job] ...if people don't recognize or value the attributes that really determine success, how easy will it be for them to acquire those attributes? (p. 27)

In this way, phenomenography provides a methodology for investigating how people make sense of their professional work, for example, in law (Reid et al., 2006; Sandberg and Pinnington, 2009), accounting (Sin et al., 2011); career guidance counselling (Värk and Reino, 2018; Kettunen et al., 2020); academia (Åkerlind 2004, 2008a; Bowden et al., 2005); nursing (Sjöström and Dahlgren, 2002; Whitfield et al., 2023); medical practice (Dall'Alba, 2002; Yu and Åkerlind, 2024); and various other health professions (Röing et al., 2018). Such research can usefully inform professional education, but also human resource recruitment and management.

> Using such descriptions ...may increase our effectiveness in managing professional competence in organizations and enable us to educate people more effectively in becoming professionals. (Sandberg and Pinnington, 2009, p. 1164)

In addition, phenomenographic research is being used to inform professional development in various professions, for example, academia (Åkerlind, 2005e, 2007, 2008c), medical practice (Yu, 2019) and career guidance (Kettunen and Tynjälä, 2022).

Phenomenographic research has also been used to investigate particular features of different occupations, for example,

> service quality in marketing (Schembri and Sandberg 2011); environmental responsibility in outdoor education (Hales and Watkins 2004); plagiarism in academic work (Ashworth et al. 1997); clinical reasoning in physiotherapy (Hendrick et al. 2009); domestic violence (McCosker et al. 2003), and smoking cessation during pregnancy (Abrahamsson et al. 2005). (Warner, 2018, p. 92)

To which list I would add other examples, such as being a healthcare professional with a family member in hospital (Carlsson et al., 2016), curriculum leadership in schools (Wan and Leung, 2021) and career management skills in career guidance (Kettunen et al., 2020).

Phenomenography is also growing in popularity as an approach to research in healthcare.

> [I]n health care research, it is essential to recognize the qualitatively different ways phenomena are experienced and understood. Recognition can have an important impact on health care, health maintenance, clinical practice, theory and education. Central to improving health care and developing any discipline is identifying the ways in which phenomena are understood and experienced by practitioners, patients, institutions and society. (Barnard et al., 1999, p. 212)

In a search of PubMed, PsycINFO, Scopus and Web of Science databases, Yu (2019) found 286 references that combined 'medic' with phenomenography. Whitfield et al. (2023) found almost 200 phenomenographic studies on nursing published since 2002. And in a MEDLINE search, Warner (2018) found 62 references to the use of phenomenography in healthcare research. These studies include accounts of the experiences of both practitioners and patients in clinical practice settings.

In terms of organisational development, the outcomes of phenomenographic research could be used to inform studies of collective consciousness (degree of awareness of other people's ways of seeing) within different institutions and organisations. A high degree of collective consciousness indicates that the organisation should be able to handle situations in which different views are present in more effective ways.

> ...in order to make sense of how people handle problems, situations, the world, we have to understand the way in which they experience the problems, the situations, the world, they are handling or acting in relation to. ... You cannot act but in relation to the world as you experience it. (Marton, 1988, p. 178)

Different degrees of collective consciousness could thus be associated with more and less harmonious and innovative workplaces, plus work satisfaction and productivity.

Phenomenographic research can also be used to inform community and public policy debate by clarifying what issues need to be considered in the debate. For example, in debate about the role of academic freedom in universities, in the context of increasing government concern with accountability of academic performance, Åkerlind and Kayrooz (2003) explain,

> To date, this debate has been muddied by a lack of clarity as to what academic freedom means and as to which interpretation any one party in a debate is using. Further, there is often little awareness that different interpretations of academic freedom exist. For example, in a debate about a recent discussion paper on the future of universities, the two key contributors clearly spoke from different understandings of academic freedom (Kinnear, 2001). One contributor discussed academic freedom from the perspective that it should involve a complete absence of constraints; the other saw academic freedom as involving an absence of constraints, but with clear academic responsibilities. ... This provides a valuable opportunity to clarify where any disagreement between different debaters lies and precisely which aspects of academic freedom are regarded as most under threat due to the current changes in the higher education system. (p. 342)

In this way, a high degree of collective consciousness can also reduce miscommunications and assist in negotiation and conflict resolution within organisations and communities. As Bowden and Marton (1998) argue,

> [When we are] aware of some of the ways in which something appears to others ..., we have an interpretive framework for making greater sense of whatever the others may say about the shared object of attention. (p. 189)

A final point

Ideologically, an interest in undertaking phenomenographic research into collective awareness and using that to enhance collective consciousness encourages a certain ethical stance.

> This is a shared world, a collective world, the joint capability of humankind to experience the world. As our shared world comprises all the ways in which we can think about reality, we are all contributing to it. ... [this position] has ethical implications as a consequence. It cannot be separated from respect for seeing other people's ways of seeing the world. Even if certain ways of seeing certain phenomena are indeed more powerful than others in certain contexts, all the different ways of

conceiving the world have to have bestowed upon them equally genuine interest and respect. (Bowden and Marton, 1998, p. 208)

As described by Marton (1981b),

> [there are] two distinctly different ways of dealing with [differences in] human thinking. In the first we aim at understanding other persons' understanding, we try to find out what their premises are, in which way they have perceived the situation and the problem. ... [In the second] we start by establishing whether or not there is a correspondence between another person's way of reasoning and what we believe to be the correct way of reasoning. (p. 162)

The common outcome of this second way of viewing human difference is to account for views that do not agree with our own in terms of failures in the person (or community, culture, race, etc.). But phenomenographic research supports and encourages the first way of viewing human difference, that differences in human understanding and action arise from differences in perceptions of the world, rather than differences in the nature of people(s).

In a world riven by racism, discrimination, religious persecution, civil conflicts, wars and other forms of misunderstanding, miscommunication and intolerance, a phenomenographic research program aimed at expanding collective consciousness of key and contentious social issues has much to offer the world, in terms of helping to understand and relate different ways of experiencing the world, and explicating the logical relationship between ways of acting and ways of understanding.

> [B]y learning about how the world appears to others, we will learn what the world is like, and what the world could be like. (Marton and Booth, 1997, p. 13)

Chapter summary

Phenomenography is primarily known as a methodology for educational research. But there has always been a strand of 'pure' phenomenographic research that investigates variation in understanding of socially significant phenomena entirely for the insight provided into humanity's collective understanding of the world. This chapter explores the neglected potential of phenomenography to contribute to broader social science research and to develop the degree of 'collective consciousness' in different organisations, societies and communities. To aid in the uptake of phenomenographic research in social sciences beyond education, the chapter also outlines phenomenography's implicit position on the socially-mediated nature of human experience, and presents a number of examples of studies that have integrated phenomenographic research with social and practice theories.

References

Åkerlind, G. (2003a) *Growing and Developing as an Academic: Implications for Academic Development, Academia and Academic Work.* (PhD thesis) University of Sydney, Australia. (Subsequently published as Åkerlind, 2011.)

Åkerlind, G. (2003b) Growing and developing as a university teacher—variation in meaning. *Studies in Higher Education, 28*(4), 375–390. http://dx.doi.org/10.1080/03075070601099416

Åkerlind, G.S. (2004) A new dimension to understanding university teaching. *Teaching in Higher Education, 9*(3), 363–376. http://doi.org/10.1080./1356251042000216679

Åkerlind, G.S. (2005a) Variation and commonality in phenomenographic research methods. *Higher Education Research and Development, 24*(4), 321–334. http://doi.org/10.1080/07294360500284672 (Subsequently republished as Åkerlind, 2012.)

Åkerlind, G.S. (2005b) Learning about phenomenography: Interviewing, data analysis and the qualitative research paradigm. In J. Bowden and P. Green (Eds), *Doing Developmental Phenomenography*, Melbourne: RMIT University Press, 63–73.

Åkerlind, G.S. (2005c) Phenomenographic methods: A case illustration. In J. Bowden and P. Green (Eds), *Doing Developmental Phenomenography*, Melbourne: RMIT University Press, 103–127.

Åkerlind, G.S. (2005d) Ways of experiencing being a university researcher. In J. Bowden and P. Green (Eds), *Doing Developmental Phenomenography*, Melbourne: RMIT University Press, 145–155, accompanied by Appendix B: Interim stages of the analysis of ways of experiencing being a university researcher, 171–177.

Åkerlind, G.S. (2005e) Academic growth and development—How do university academics experience it?. *Higher Education, 50*, 1–32. https://doi.org/10.1007/s10734-004-6345-1

Åkerlind, G.S. (2007) Constraints on academics' potential for developing as a teacher—Variation in meaning. *Studies in Higher Education, 32*(1), 21–37. https://doi.org/10.1080/03075070601099416

Åkerlind, G.S. (2008a) An academic perspective on research and being a researcher: An integration of the literature. *Studies in Higher Education*, 33(1), 17–32. https://doi.org/10.1080/03075070701794775

Åkerlind, G.S. (2008b) A phenomenographic approach to developing academics' understanding of the nature of teaching and learning. *Teaching in Higher Education*, 13(6), 633–644. https://doi.org/10.1080/13562510802452350

Åkerlind, G.S. (2008c) Growing and developing as a university researcher. *Higher Education*, 55, 241–254. https://doi.org/10.1007/s10734-007-9052-x

Åkerlind, G. (2011) *Growing and Developing as an Academic: Implications for Academic Development and Academic Practice*, Saarbrucken: Lambert Academic Publishers.

Åkerlind, G.S. (2012) Variation and commonality in phenomenographic research methods. *Higher Education Research and Development*, 31(1), 115–127. https://doi.org/10.1080/07294360500284672

Åkerlind, G. (2015) From Phenomenography to Variation Theory: A review of the development of the Variation Theory of Learning and implications for pedagogical design in higher education. *HERDSA Review of Higher Education*, 2, 1–29.

Åkerlind, G. (2018) What future for phenomenographic research? On continuity and development in the phenomenography and variation theory research tradition. *Scandinavian Journal of Educational Research*, 62, 949–958. https://doi.org/10.1080/00313831.2017.1324899

Åkerlind, G. (2022) Critique of the article, 'Theoretical foundations of phenomenography: a critical review'. *Higher Education Research and Development*, 42(6), 1299–1308. https://doi.org/10.1080/07294360.2022.2142535

Åkerlind, G. (2024a) Common misunderstandings of phenomenographic research in higher education. *Higher Education Research & Development*, 43(1), 1–16. https://doi.org/10.1080/07294360.2023.2218804

Åkerlind, G. (2024b) Why should I be interested in phenomenographic research? Variation in views of phenomenography amongst higher education scholars. *Higher Education* (Epub ahead of print). https://doi.org/10.1007/s10734-024-01270-6

Åkerlind, G. (2024c) Different understandings of the nature of 'structural relationships' in phenomenographic research: views of educational researchers. *International Journal of Social Research Methodology* (Epub ahead of print), 1–15. https://doi.org/10.1080/13645579.2024.2366830

Åkerlind, G.S., Bowden, J. and Green, P. (2005) Learning to do phenomenography: A reflective discussion. In J. Bowden and P. Green (Eds), *Doing Developmental Phenomenography*, Melbourne: RMIT University Press, 74–100.

Åkerlind, G.S. and Kayrooz, C. (2003) Understanding academic freedom: The views of social scientists. *Higher Education Research and Development*, 22(3), 327–344. https://doi.org/10.1080/0729436032000145176

Åkerlind, G.S., McKenzie, J. and Lupton, M. (2011) *A Threshold Concepts Approach to Curriculum Design: Supporting Student Learning through Application of Variation Theory*, NSW, Australia: Australian Learning and Teaching Council.

Åkerlind, G.S., McKenzie, J. and Lupton, M. (2014) The potential of combining phenomenography, variation theory and threshold concepts to inform curriculum design in higher education. In J. Huisman and M. Tight (Eds) *Theory and Method in Higher Education Research II. International Perspectives in Higher Education Research, Vol. 10*, Bingley: Emerald Publishing Group Ltd., 227–247.

Andersson, S.O., Lundberg, L., Jonsson, A., Tingström, P. and Dahlgren, M.A. (2013) Interaction, action, and reflection: How medics learn medical care in the Swedish Armed Forces. *Military Medicine*, 178(8), 861–866. https://doi.org/10.7205/MILMED-D-13-00048

Ashwin, P., Blackie, M., Pitterson, N., and Smit, R. (2023) Undergraduate students' knowledge outcomes and how these relate to their educational experiences: A longitudinal study of chemistry in two countries. *Higher Education*, 86, 1065–1080. https://doi.org/10.1007/s10734-022-00962-1

Ashwin, P., Abbas, A., and McLean, M. (2014) How do students' accounts of sociology change over the course of their undergraduate degrees?. *Higher Education*, 67, 219–234. https://doi.org/10.1007/s10734-013-9659-z

Ashworth, P. and Lucas, U. (1998) What is the 'world' of phenomenography?. *Scandinavian Journal of Educational Research*, 42(4), 415–431.

Ashworth, P. and Lucas, U. (2000) Achieving empathy and engagement: A practical approach to the design, conduct and reporting of phenomenographic research. *Studies in Higher Education*, 25(3), 295–308. https://doi.org/10.1080/713696153

Barnard, A., McCosker, H. and Gerber, R. (1999) Understanding technology in contemporary surgical nursing: a phenomenographic examination. *Nursing Inquiry*, 6(3), 157–166.

Berglund, A. (2005) *Learning Computer Systems in a Distributed Project Course*. (PhD thesis) Acta Universitatas Upsaliensis, Sweden.

Biggs, J. and Tang, C. (1999) *Teaching for Quality Learning at University*, New York: McGraw Hill, SRHE and Open University Press.

Booth, S. (1992) *Learning to Program: A Phenomenographic Perspective*. (PhD Thesis) Acta Universitatis Gothoburgensis 89:1992, Sweden.

Bowden, J. (1994a) The nature of phenomenographic research. In J. Bowden and E. Walsh (Eds) *Understanding Phenomenographic Research: The Warburton*

Symposium, Melbourne: RMIT University Press, 1–16. (Republished as Bowden, 2000a.)

Bowden, J. (1994b) Experience of phenomenographic research: A personal account. In J. Bowden and E. Walsh (Eds) *Understanding Phenomenographic Research: The Warburton Symposium*, Melbourne: EQARD, RMIT University Press, 44–55. (Republished as Bowden, 2000b.)

Bowden, J. (1996) Phenomenographic research: Some methodological issues. In G. Dall'Alba and B. Hasselgren (Eds) *Reflections on Phenomenography: Toward a Methodology?* (Goteborg Studies in Educational Sciences 109), Gothenburg: Acta Universitatis Gothoburgensis, 49–66.

Bowden, J. (2000a) The nature of phenomenographic research. In J. Bowden and E. Walsh (Eds) *Phenomenography*, Melbourne: RMIT University Press, 1–18.

Bowden, J. (2000b) Experience of phenomenographic research: A personal account. In J. Bowden and E. Walsh (Eds) *Phenomenography*, Melbourne: RMIT University Press, 47–61.

Bowden, J. (2005) Reflections on the phenomenographic team research process. In J. Bowden and P. Green (Eds) *Doing Developmental Phenomenography*, Melbourne: RMIT University Press, 11–31.

Bowden, J., and Green, P. (Eds) (2005) *Doing Developmental Phenomenography*, Melbourne: RMIT University Press.

Bowden, J., and Green, P. (2010) The voice of the researched in qualitative research. In J. Higgs, N. Cherry, R. Macklin and R. Ajjawi (Eds) *Researching Practice: A Discourse on Qualitative Methodologies* (Practice, Education, Work and Society 2), The Netherlands: Brill Publishers, 123–132.

Bowden, J., Green, P., Barnacle, R., Cherry, N. and Usher, R. (2005) Academics' ways of understanding success in research activities. In J. Bowden and P. Green (Eds) *Doing Developmental Phenomenography*, Melbourne: RMIT University Press, 128–144.

Bowden, J., and Marton, F. (1998) *The University of Learning*, London: Kogan Page. (Subsequently reprinted as Bowden and Marton, 2003.)

Bowden, J., and Marton, F. (2003) *The University of Learning*, London: Routledge.

Bowden, J., and Walsh, E. (Eds) (1994) *Understanding Phenomenographic Research: The Warburton Symposium*, Melbourne: RMIT University Press. (Subsequently republished as Bowden and Walsh, 2000.)

Bowden, J., and Walsh, E. (Eds) (2000) *Phenomenography*, Melbourne: RMIT University Press.

Brauer, S., Kettunen, J., Levy, A., Merenmies, J. and Kulmala, P. (2023) The educational paradigm shift—a phenomenographic study of medical teachers' experiences of practices. *BMC Medical Education, 23*(29), 1–10. https://doi.org.10.1186/s12909-023-04013-w

Carlsson, B. (1999) *Ecological Understanding—A Space of Variation*. (PhD thesis) Luleå University of Technology, Sweden.

Carlsson, E., Carlsson, A., Prenkert, M. and Svantesson, M. (2016). Ways of understanding being a healthcare professional in the role of family member of a patient admitted to hospital. A phenomenographic study. *International Journal of Nursing Studies, 53*, 50–60. https://doi.org/10.1016/j.ijnurstu.2015.10.004

Collier-Reed, B. I. (2006) *Pupils' Experiences of Technology: Exploring Dimensions of Technological Literacy*. (PhD thesis) University of Cape Town, South Africa.

Collier-Reed, B. I. and Ingerman, Å. (2013) Phenomenography: From critical aspects to knowledge claim. In J. Huisman and M. Tight (Eds), *Theory and Method in Higher Education Research. International Perspectives in Higher Education Research, Vol. 9*, Bingley: Emerald Publishing Group Ltd, 243–260.

Collier-Reed, B. I., Ingerman, Å. and Berglund, A. (2009) Reflections on trustworthiness in phenomenographic research: Recognising purpose, context and change in the process of research. *Education as Change, 13*(2), 339–355. https://doi.org/10/1080/16823200903234901

Cope, C.J. (2004) Ensuring validity and reliability in phenomenographic research using the analytical framework of a structure of awareness. *Qualitative Research Journal, 4*(2), 5–18.

Cutajar, M. (2014) *Qualitative Differences in Post Compulsory pre-University Maltese Students' Accounts of their Network Learning Experiences*. (PhD thesis) Lancaster University, UK.

Cuyvers, K., Donche, V. and Van den Bossche, P. (2016) Learning beyond graduation: exploring newly qualified specialists' entrance into daily practice from a learning perspective. *Advances in Health Sciences Education, 21*, 439–453. https://doi.org/10.1007/s10459-015-9640-y

Dahlgren, L. O. and Fallsberg, M. (1991) Phenomenography as a qualitative approach in social pharmacy research. *Journal of Social and Administrative Pharmacy, 8*, 150–156.

Dahlin, B. (2007) Enriching the theoretical horizons of phenomenography, variation theory and learning studies. *Scandinavian Journal of Educational Research, 51*(4), 327–346. https://doi.org/10.1080/0031.3830701485437

Dall'Alba, G. (1994) Reflections on some faces of phenomenography. In J. Bowden and E. Walsh (Eds), *Phenomenographic Research: Variations in Method*, Melbourne: RMIT University Press, 73–88. (Subsequently republished as Dall'Alba, 2000.)

Dall'Alba, G. (1996) Reflections on phenomenography—an introduction. In G. Dall'Alba and B. Hasselgren (Eds), *Reflections on Phenomenography. Towards a Methodology?* (Goteborg Studies in Educational Sciences 109), Göteborg: Acta Universitatis Gothoburgensis, 7–17.

Dall'Alba, G. (2000) Reflections on some faces of phenomenography. In J. Bowden and E. Walsh (Eds), *Phenomenography*, Melbourne: RMIT University Press, 83–101.

Dall'Alba, G. (2002) Understanding medical practice: different outcomes of a pre-medical program. *Advances in Health Sciences Education, 7*, 163–177. https://doi.org/10.1023/A:1021194117367

Dall'Alba, G. and Hasselgren, B. (1996) (Eds), *Reflections on Phenomenography. Towards a Methodology?* (Goteborg Studies in Educational Sciences 109), Göteborg: Acta Universitatis Gothoburgensis.

de Búrca, S. (2024) *How Do Transformative Experiences in a 'Design-for-good' Pedagogy Enable Ethical Responsibility in Undergraduate Designers?*. (PhD thesis) University of Kent, UK.

Denzin, N.K. (2009) The elephant in the living room: or extending the conversation about the politics of evidence. *Qualitative Research, 9*(2), 139–160. https://doi.org/10.1177/1468794108098034

Denzin, N.K. and Lincoln, Y.S. (Eds)(2000) [1994] *Handbook of Qualitative Research*, Beverly Hills, CA: Sage Publications.

Daly, S.R. (2008) *Design across Disciplines*. (PhD thesis) Purdue University, USA.

Dortins, E. (2002) Reflections on phenomenographic process: Interview, transcription and analysis. *Quality Conversations: Research and Development in Higher Education, 25*, 207–213.

Durden, G. (2018) Improving teacher learning: variation in conceptions of learning study. *International Journal for Lesson and Learning Studies, 7*(1), 50–61. https://doi.org/10.1108/IJLLS-09-2017-0041

Durden, G. (2020) Qualitative differences in beginner teachers' knowledge of pupils' understandings: Evidence from learning study and implications for teacher education. *Journal of Education for Teaching: International Research and Pedagogy, 46*(1), 99–116. https://doi.org/10.1080/02607476.2019.1708630

Entwistle, N. (1991) Approaches to learning and perceptions of the learning environment. *Higher Education, 22*, 201–204.

Entwistle, N. [1984] (1997) Approaches to learning. In F. Marton, D. Hounsell and N. Entwistle (Eds), *The Experience of Learning (2nd edition)*, Edinburgh: Scottish Academic Press, 39–58.

Entwistle, N. (1997) Introduction: Phenomenography in higher education, *Higher Education Research and Development, 16*(2), 125–126.

Feldon, D.F., Maher, M.A., Hurst, M. and Timmerman, B. (2015) Faculty mentors', graduate students', and performance-based assessments of students' research skill development. *American Educational Research Journal*, 52(2), 334–370. https://doi.org/10.3102/0002831214549449

Feldon, D.F. and Tofel-Grehl, C. (2018) Phenomenography as a foundation for mixed models research. *American Behavioral Scientist*, 62(7), 887–899. https://doi.org/10.1177/0002764218772640

Forbes, H. (2011) Clinical teachers' conceptions of nursing. *Journal of Nursing Education*, 50(3), 152–157. https://doi.org/10.3928/01484834-20100930-06

González, C. (2011) Extending research on 'conceptions of teaching': Commonalities and differences in recent investigations. *Teaching in Higher Education*, 16(1), 65–80. https://doi.org/10.1080/13562517.2010.507302

Green, P. (2005) A rigorous journey into phenomenography: from a naturalistic inquirer stand point. In J. Bowden and P. Green (Eds), *Doing Developmental Phenomenography*, Melbourne: RMIT University Press, 32–46.

Green, P. and Bowden, J. (2009) Principles of developmental phenomenography. *Malaysian Journal of Qualitative Research*, 2(2), 52–70.

Guba, E. (1981) Criteria for assessing the trustworthiness of naturalistic inquiries. *Educational Communication and Technology Journal*, 29(2), 75–91.

Guba, E.G. and Lincoln, Y.S. (1994) Competing paradigms in qualitative research. In N.K. Denzin and Y.S. Lincoln (Eds), *Handbook of Qualitative Research*, Beverly Hills, CA: Sage Publications, 105–117.

Hajar, A. (2020) Arab sojourner expectations, academic socialisation and strategy use on a pre-sessional English programme in Britain. *Pedagogies: An International Journal*, 15(3), 221–239. https://doi.org/10.1080/1554480X.2019.1696200

Hajar, A. (2021) Theoretical foundations of phenomenography: A critical review. *Higher Education Research & Development*, 40(7), 1421–1436. https://doi.org/10.1080/07294360.2022.2142535

Harris, L.R. (2011) Phenomenographic perspectives on the structure of conceptions: The origins, purposes, strengths, and limitations of the what/how and referential/structural framework. *Educational Research Review*, 6(2), 109–124. https://doi.org/10.1016/j.edurev.2011.01.002

Hasselgren, B. and Beach, D. (1997) Phenomenography—A 'good-for-nothing-brother' of phenomenology?. *Higher Education Research and Development*, 16, 191–202.

Higgs, J., Cherry, N., Macklin, R. and Ajjawi, R. (Eds) (2010) *Researching Practice: A Discourse on Qualitative Methodologies* (Practice, Education, Work and Society 2), Rotterdam: Brill Publishers.

Hella, E. (2008) Variation in Finnish students' understanding of Lutheranism and its implication for religious education: a phenomenographic study. *British Journal of Religious Education*, 30(3), 247–257. https://doi.org/10.1080/01416200802170185

Holmqvist, M. and Selin, P. (2019) What makes the difference? An empirical comparison of critical aspects identified in phenomenographic and variation theory analyses. *Palgrave Communications*, 5(71), 1–8. https://doi.org/10.1057/s41599-019-0284-z

Hyrkäs, K., Koivula, M., Lehti, K., and Paunonen-Ilmonen, M. (2003). Nurse managers' conceptions of quality management as promoted by peer supervision. *Journal of Nursing Management*, 11(1), 48–58. https://doi.org/10.1046/j.1365-2834.2003.00345.x

Jarrett, K.L. (2016). *A Phenomenographical Inquiry into Experiences of Using Game Based Approaches among Physical Education Teachers in England and Australia*. (PhD thesis) University of Canterbury, New Zealand.

Johansson, B., Marton, F. and Svensson, L. (1985) An approach to describing learning as change between qualitatively different conceptions. In L. West and A. Pines (Eds), *Cognitive Structure and Conceptual Change*, Orlando, FL: Academic Press, 233–258.

Kettunen, J. (2024) Finnish lower secondary career education through a systems lens. *Nordic Journal of Transitions, Careers and Guidance*, 5(1), 73–85. https://doi.org/10.16993/ njtcg.85

Kettunen, J., Lee, J. and Vuorinen, R. (2020) Exploring Finnish guidance counselors' conceptions of career management skills. *SAGE Open*, 10(4), 1–10. https://doi.org/10.1177/2158244020968778

Kettunen, J. and Tynjälä, P. (2022) Bridging the gap between research and practice: Using phenomenographic findings to develop training for career practitioners. *International Journal for Educational and Vocational Guidance*, 22, 247–262. https://doi.org/10.1007/s10775-021-09483-2

Khan, M., Abdou, B., Kettumen, J. and Gregory, S. (2019) A phenomenographic study of students' conceptions of mobile learning: An example from higher education. *Sage Open*, 9(3), 1–17. https://doi.org/10.1177/2158244019861457

Ki, W. and Marton, F. (2003) *Learning Cantonese Tones*. Paper presented at the biennial conference of the European Association for Learning and Instruction, Padova, Italy.

Killam, L., Akerind, G., Lock, M., Camargo-Plazas, P. and Luctkar-Flude, M. (2024) Healthcare students' experiences of learner-educator cocreation of virtual simulations: A phenomenographic study. *Simulation in Healthcare* (Epub ahead of print), 1–8. https://doi.org/10.1097/SIH.0000000000000806

Kullberg, A. and Ingerman, Å. (2022) Researching conditions of learning—phenomenography and variation theory. In *Oxford Research Encyclopedia of Education*, Oxford: Oxford University Press, 1–21. https://doi.org/10.1093/acrefore/9780190264093.013.17708

Kullberg, A., Ingerman, Å. and Marton, F. (2024) *Planning and Analyzing Teaching using the Variation Theory of Learning* (WALS-Routledge Lesson Study Series), London: Taylor and Francis Group.

Kvale, S. (1996) *InterViews: An Introduction to Qualitative Research Interviewing*, California: SAGE Publications.

Lamb, P., Sandberg, J. and Liesch, P. (2011) Small firm internationalisation unveiled through phenomenography. *Journal of International Business Studies*, 54(2), 1–22. https://www.jstor.org/stable/29789452

Larsson, J. and Holmström, I. (2007) Phenomenographic or phenomenological analysis: does it matter? Examples from a study on anaesthesiologists' work. *International Journal of Qualitative Studies on Health and Well-being*, 2(1), 55–64. https://doi.org/10.1080/17482620601068105

Light, G. and Calkins, S. (2015) The experience of academic learning: uneven conceptions of learning across research and teaching. *Higher Education*, 69, 345–359. https://doi.org/10.1007/s10734-014-9779-0

Lo, M., Marton, F., Pang, M. and Pong, W. (2004) Toward a pedagogy of learning. In F. Marton and A. Tsui (Eds), *Classroom Discourse and the Space of Learning*, Hillsdale, NJ: Lawrence Erlbaum, 189–225.

Lupton, M. (2004) *The Learning Connection. Information Literacy and the Student Learning Experience*, Blackwood, Australia: AusLib Press.

Lupton, M. (2008) *Information literacy and learning*. (PhD thesis) Queensland University of Technology, Brisbane, Australia.

Marton, F. (1981a) Phenomenography—Describing conceptions of the world around us. *Instructional Science*, 10, 177–200.

Marton, F. (1981b) Studying conceptions of reality—A metatheoretical note. *Scandinavian Journal of Educational Research*, 25(4), 159–169.

Marton, F. (1984) Towards a psychology beyond the individual. In K.M.J. Lagerspetz and P. Niemi (Eds) *Psychology in the 1990s*, Amsterdam: Elsevier, 45–72.

Marton, F. (1986) Phenomenography—A research approach to investigating different understandings of reality. *Journal of Thought*, 21, 28–49.

Marton, F. (1988) Phenomenography: Exploring different conceptions of reality. In D. Fetterman (Ed.), *Qualitative Approaches to Evaluation in Education: The Silent Revolution*, New York: Prager, 177–205.

Marton, F. (1992) The phenomenography of learning: A qualitative approach to educational research and some of its implications for didactics. *Learning and Instruction*, 2, 601–616.

Marton, F. (1994a) Phenomenography. In T. Husen and T. Postlethwaite (Eds), *International Encyclopedia of Education*, Oxford: Pergamon Press, 4424–4429.

Marton, F. (1994b) On the structure of awareness. In J. Bowden and E. Walsh (Eds), *Understanding Phenomenographic Research: The Warburton Symposium*, Melbourne: RMIT University Press, 89–100. (Subsequently republished in Bowden and Walsh, 2000.)

Marton, F. (1996) Cognosco ergo sum: Reflections on reflections. In G. Dall'Alba and B. Hasselgren (Eds), *Reflections on Phenomenography: Toward a Methodology?* (Goteborg Studies in Educational Sciences 109), Gothenburg: Acta Universitatis Gothoburgensis, 163–138.

Marton, F. (2015) *Necessary Conditions of Learning*, New York and London: Routledge.

Marton, F. and Booth, S. (1997) *Learning and Awareness*, Hillsdale, NJ: Lawrence Erlbaum Ass.

Marton, F., Dall'Alba, G. and Beaty, E. (1993) Conceptions of learning. *British Journal of Educational Research*, 19, 277–300.

Marton, F. and Morris, P. (Eds) (2002) *What Matters? Discovering Critical Conditions of Classroom Learning*, Gothenburg: Acta Universitatis Gothoburgensis.

Marton, F. and Pang, M. (2006) On some necessary conditions of learning. *Journal of the Learning Sciences*, 15(2), 192–220. https://doi.org/10.1207/s15327809jls1502_2

Marton, F. and Pang, M. (2013) Meanings are acquired from experiencing differences against a background of sameness, rather than from experiencing sameness against a background of difference: Putting a conjecture to the test by embedding it in a pedagogical tool. *Frontline Learning Research*, 1(1), 24–41. https://doi.org/10.14786/flr.v1i1.16

Marton, F. and Pong, W.Y. (2005) On the unit of description in phenomenography. *Higher Education Research and Development*, 24, 335–348. https://doi.org/10.1080/07294360500284706

Marton, F., Runesson, U. and Tsui, A. (2004) The space of learning. In F. Marton and A. Tsui (Eds), *Classroom Discourse and the Space of Learning*, Hillsdale, NJ: Lawrence Erlbaum, 3–40.

Marton, F. and Säljö, R. (1976) On qualitative differences in learning. I: Outcome and Process. *British Journal of Educational Psychology*, 46, 4–11.

Marton, F. and Säljö, R. [1984] (1997) Approaches to learning. In F. Marton, D. Hounsell and N. Entwistle (Eds), *The Experience of Learning* (2nd edition), Edinburgh: Scottish Academic Press, 39–58.

Marton, F. and Svensson, L. (1979) Conceptions of research in student learning. *Higher Education*, 8471–8486.

Marton, F. and Trigwell, K. (2000) Variato est mater studorum. *Higher Education Research and Development*, 19(3), 381–395. https://doi.org/10.1080/07294360020021455

Marton, F. and Tsui, A. (Eds) (2004) *Classroom Discourse and the Space of Learning*, Hillsdale, NJ: Lawrence Erlbaum.

Mimirinis, M. (2018) Qualitative differences in academics' conceptions of e-assessment. *Assessment and Evaluation in Higher Education*, 44(2), 233–248. https://doi.org/10.1080/02602938.2018.1493087

Mimirinis, M., Ventouris, A. and Wright, E. (2023) Variation in Black students' conceptions of academic support. *British Educational Research Journal*, 50(1), 241–259. https://doi.org/10.1002/berj.3921.

Moroz, J. (2021) Questioning the phenomenological foundations of Marton's research approach. *Przegląd Badań Edukacyjnych (Educational Studies Review)*, 35(2), 309–324. https://doi.org/10.12775/PBE.2021.045

Nelson, C.D. (2012) *Applying Phenomenography to Development Aid: Should We Recognise and Embrace Complexity in Aid Practice?*. (PhD thesis) University of Technology Sydney, Australia.

Ozkan, B.C. (2004) Using NVivo to analyze qualitative classroom data on constructivist learning environments. *The Qualitative Report*, 9(4), 589–603. http://www.nova.edu/ssss/QR.QR9-4/ozkan.pdf

Paakkari, L. (2012) *Widening horizons: A phenomenographic study of student teachers' conceptions of health education and its teaching and learning*. (PhD thesis) University of Jyväskylä, Finland.

Paakkari, L., Tynjal, P. and Kannas, L. (2010) Student teachers' ways of experiencing the objective of health education as a school subject: A phenomenographic study. *Teaching and Teacher Education*, 26(4), 941–948. https://doi.org/10.1016/j.tate.2009.10.035

Pang, M. (2003) Two faces of variation: On continuity in the phenomenographic movement. *Scandinavian Journal of Educational Research*, 47(2), 145–156. https://doi.org/10.1080/00313830308612

Pang, M.F. (2006) The use of learning study to enhance teacher professional learning in Hong King. *Teacher Education*, 17(1), 27–42. https://doi.org/10.1080/10476210500527915

Pang, M.F. and Ki, W.W. (2016) Revisiting the idea of 'critical aspects'. *Scandinavian Journal of Educational Research*, 60(3), 323–336. https://doi.org/10.1080/00313831.2015.1119724

Pang, M.F. and Lo, M.L. (2012) Learning study: helping teachers to use theory, develop professionally, and produce new knowledge to be shared. *Instructional Science*, 40, 589–606. https://doi.org/10.1007/s11251-011-9191-4

Pang, M.F. and Marton, F. (2003) Beyond 'lesson study'—Comparing two says of facilitating the grasp of economic concepts. *Instructional Science*, 31, 175–194. https://doi.org/10.1023/A:1023280619632

Pang, M. F. and Marton, F. (2005) Learning theory as teaching resource: Enhancing students' understanding of economic concepts. *Instructional Science*, 33, 159–191, https://doi.org/10.1007/s11251-005-2811-0

Pang, M.F. and Runesson, U. (2019) The learning study: Recent trends and developments. *International Journal for Lesson and Learning Studies*, 8(3), 162–169.

Patrick, K. (2002) Doing history. In F. Marton and P. Morris (Eds), *What Matters? Discovering Critical Conditions of Classroom Learning*, Gothenburg: Acta Universitatis Gothoburgensis, 93–112.

Prosser, M. (1994) Some experiences of using phenomenographic research methodology in the context of research in teaching and learning. In J. Bowden and E. Walsh (Eds), *Phenomenographic Research: Variations in Method*, Melbourne: RMIT University Press, 31–43. (Subsequently republished as Prosser, 2000.)

Prosser, M. (2000) Some experiences of using phenomenographic research methodology in the context of research in teaching and learning. In J. Bowden and E. Walsh (Eds), *Phenomenography*, Melbourne: RMIT University Press, 34–46.

Prosser, M. and Trigwell, K. (1999) *Understanding Learning and Teaching: The Experience in Higher Education*, Buckingham: SRHE and Open University Press.

Prosser, M., Trigwell, K. and Taylor, P. (1994) A phenomenographic study of academics' conceptions of science learning and teaching. *Learning and Instruction*, 15, 217–231.

Ramsden, P. (1985) Student learning research: retrospect and prospect. *Higher Education Research and Development*, 4(1), 51–69.

Reid, A., Nagarajan, V. and Dortins, E. (2006) The experience of becoming a legal professional, *Higher Education Research & Development*, 25(1), 85–99, https://doi.org/10.1080/13600800500453220

Richardson, J. (1999) The concepts and methods of phenomenographic research. *Review of Educational Research*, 69(1), 53–82.

Röing, M., Holmström, I.K., and Larsson, J. (2018) A metasynthesis of phenomenographic articles on understandings of work among healthcare professionals. *Qualitative Health Research*, 28(2), 273–291, https://doi.org/10.1177/1049732317719433

Rotar, O. (2024) The reflective practice framework for phenomenographic data analysis. *Systemic Practice and Action Research*. https://doi.org/10.1007/s11213-024-09677-z

Rovio-Johannson, A. (1999). *Being Good at Teaching: Exploring Different Ways of Handling the Same Subject in Higher Education*. (PhD thesis) Acta Universitatis Gothoburgensis, Gothenburg, Sweden.

Rovio-Johansson, A. (2013) An application of Variation Theory of Learning in higher education. In M. Tight and J. Huisman (Eds), *Theory and Method in Higher Education Research. International Perspectives in Higher Education Research* (*Vol. 9*), Bingley: Emerald Publishing Group, 261–279.

Rovio-Johansson, A. and Ingerman, Å. (2016) Continuity and development in the phenomenography and variation theory tradition. *Scandinavian Journal of Educational Research, 60*(3), 257–271. https://doi.org/10.1080/00313831.2016.1148074

Rovio-Johannson, A., and Lumsden, M. (2012) Collaborative production of pedagogical knowledge: enhancing students' learning. *Journal of Applied Research in Higher Education, 4*(1), 72–83.

Säljö, R. (1981) Learning approach and outcome: Some empirical observations. *Instructional Science, 10*(1), 47–65.

Säljö, R. (1996) Minding action—Conceiving of the world versus participating in social practices. In G. Dall'Alba and B. Hasselgren (Eds), *Reflections on Phenomenography. Towards a methodology?* (Goteborg Studies in Educational Sciences 109), Gothenburg: Acta Universitatis Gothoburgensis, 19–33.

Säljö, R. (1997) Talk as data and practice — A critical look at phenomenographic inquiry and the appeal to experience. *Higher Education Research and Development, 16*, 203–212.

Sandberg, J. (1994) *Human Competence at Work: An Interpretive Perspective*. (PhD thesis) Göteborg University, Sweden.

Sandberg, J. (1996) Are phenomenographic results reliable? In G. Dall'Alba and B. Hasselgren (Eds), *Reflections on Phenomenography: Toward a Methodology?* (Goteborg Studies in Educational Sciences 109), Gothenburg: Acta Universitatis Gothoburgensis, 129–140. (Subsequently republished as Sandberg, 1997.)

Sandberg, J. (1997) Are phenomenographic results reliable?. *Higher Education Research and Development, 16*, 203–212.

Sandberg, J. (2001) Understanding competence at work. *Harvard Business Review, 79*(3), 24–27.

Sandberg, J. (2005) How do we justify knowledge produced within interpretive approaches? *Organizational Research Methods, 8*(1), 41–68. https://doi.org/10.1177/1094428104272000

Sandberg, J. and Pinnington, A. (2009) Professional competence as ways of being: An existential ontological perspective. *Journal of Management Studies, 46*(7), 1138–1170. https://doi.org/10.1111/j.1467-6486.2009.00845.x

Sin, S. (2010) Considerations of quality in phenomenographic research introduction. *The International Journal of Qualitative Research Methods, 9*(4), 305–319. https://doi.org/10.1177/160940691000900401

Sin, S., Reid, A. and Dahlgren, L.O. (2011) The conceptions of work in the accounting profession in the twenty-first century from the experiences of practitioners. *Studies in Continuing Education*, 33(2), 139–156. https://doi.org/10.1080/09639284.2012.661604

Sjöström, B. and Dahlgren, L.O. (2002) Applying phenomenography in nursing research. *Journal of Advanced Nursing*, 40(3), 339–345. https://doi.org/10.1046/j.1365-2648.2002.02375.x

Stoffels, M., van der Burgt, S., Stenfors, T., Daelmans, H., Peerdeman, S. and Kusurkar, R. (2021) Conceptions of clinical learning among stakeholders involved in undergraduate nursing education: A phenomenographic study. *BMC Medical Education*, 21(520), 1–12. https://doi.org/10.1186/s12909-021-02939-7

Stolz, S. (2020) Phenomenology and phenomenography in educational research: A critique. *Educational Philosophy and Theory*, 52(10), 1077–1096. https://doi.org/10.1080/00131857.2020.1724088

Straub, J. and Maynes, N. (2021) Rigorous phenomenography: A conceptual model. *Journal of Studies in Education*, 11(2), 71–86. https://doi.org/10.5296/jse.v11i2.18496

Svensson, L. (1997) Theoretical foundations of phenomenography. *Higher Education Research and Development*, 16(2), 159–172.

Svensson, L. and Theman, J. (1983) *The Relation between Categories of Description and an Interview Protocol in a Case of Phenomenographic Research*, Research Report 1983:02, Department of Education, University of Goteborg.

Täks, M., Tynjälä, P. and Kukemelk, H. (2016) Engineering students' conceptions of entrepreneurial learning as part of their education. *European Journal of Engineering Education*, 41(1), 53–69. https://doi.org/10.1080/03043797.2015.1012708

Thorsten, A. and Tväråna, M. (2023) Focal points for teaching the notion of critical aspects. *Scandinavian Journal for Educational Research*, 68(6), 1–14. https://doi.org/10.1080/00313831.2023.2228817

Tight, M. (2016) Phenomenography: The development and application of an innovative research design in higher education research. *International Journal of Social Research Methodology*, 19(3), 319–338. https://doi.org/10.1080/13645579.2015.1010284

Töytäri, A., Piirainen, A., Tynjälä, P., Vanhanen-Nuutinen, L., Mäki, K. and Ilves, V. (2016) Higher education teachers' descriptions of their own learning: A large-scale study of Finnish Universities of Applied Sciences. *Higher Education Research & Development*, 35(6), 1284–1297. https://doi.org/10.1080/07294360.2016.1152574

Trigwell, K. (1994) A phenomenographic study of phenomenography. In J. Bowden and E. Walsh (Eds), *Understanding Phenomenographic Research:*

The Warburton Symposium, Melbourne: RMIT University Press, 56–72. (Subsequently republished as Trigwell, 2000.)

Trigwell, K. (2000) A phenomenographic study of phenomenography. In J. Bowden and E. Walsh (Eds), *Phenomenography*, Melbourne: RMIT University Press, 19–33.

Trigwell, K. and Prosser, P. (2020) *Exploring University Teaching and Learning*, London: Springer Nature for Palgrave MacMillan.

Uljens, M. (1996) On the philosophical foundations of phenomenography. In G. Dall'Alba and B. Hasselgren (Eds), *Reflections on Phenomenography: Toward a Methodology?* (Goteborg Studies in Educational Sciences 109), Gothenburg: Acta Universitatis Gothoburgensis, 103–128.

Värk, A. and Reino, A. (2018) Meaningful solutions for the unemployed or their counsellors? The role of case managers' conceptions of their work. *British Journal of Guidance & Counselling*, 46(1), 12–26, https://doi.org/10.1080/03069885.2017.1370692

Walsh, E. (1994) Phenomenographic analysis of interview transcripts. In J. Bowden and E. Walsh (Eds), *Phenomenographic Research: Variations in Method*, Melbourne: RMIT University Press, 17–30. (Subsequently republished as Walsh, 2000.)

Walsh, E. (2000) Phenomenographic analysis of interview transcripts. In J. Bowden and E. Walsh (Eds), *Phenomenography*, Melbourne: RMIT University Press, 19–33.

Wan, S.W. and Leung, S. (2021) Integrating phenomenography with discourse analysis to study Hong Kong prospective teachers' conceptions of curriculum leadership. *Cambridge Journal of Education*, 52(1), 91–116. https://doi.org/10.1080/0305764X.2021.1946484

Wardak, D., Huber, E. and Zeivots, S. (2023) Towards a conceptual framework of professional development: A phenomenographic study of academics' mindsets in a business school. *International Journal for Academic Development*, 1–16. https://doi.org/10.1080/1360144X.2023.2183403

Warner, K. (2018) *Safety Matters: The Relations of Safety in Anaesthesia.* (PhD thesis) University of New South Wales, Australia. https://doi.org/10.26190/unsworks/20332

Webb, G. (1997) Deconstructing deep and surface: Towards a critique of phenomenography. *Higher Education*, 33(2), 195–212. https://doi.org/10.1023/A:1002905027633

Whitfield, M., Mimirinis, M., Macdonald, D., Klein, T. and Wilson, R. (2023) Phenomenographic approaches in research about nursing. *Global Qualitative Nursing Research*, 10, 1–10. https://doi.org/10.1177/23333936231212281

Wilson, A., Howitt, S., Holloway, A., Williams, A. and Higgins, D. (2021) Factors affecting paramedicine students' learning about evidence-based practice: A phenomenographic study. *BMC Medical Education*, 21(45), 1–12. https://doi.org/10.1186/s12909-021-02490-5

Yu, S.V. (2019) *From Conceptions to Capacity: Conceptualising the Development of Medical Practitioners' Sense of Being a Doctor and Developing as a Doctor, with Implications for Medical Education.* (PhD thesis) Australian National University, Australia.

Yu, S.V. and Åkerlind, G.S. (2024) Being a doctor: From treating individual patients to maximising community health and social justice. *Health Care Analysis*, 32, 224–242. https://doi.org/10.1007/s10728-024-00484-0

Index

21st-century phenomenography 3, 8, 10, 12–13, 19, 23–25, 29–30, 33, 66, 82, 99, 134, 154, 177, 183, 215–216, 240–242, 244

analytic guidelines 3, 133–134, 136, 138–139, 152, 159, 173, 181, 199

analytic strategies 76–77, 83, 87–90, 133

applied focus 212, 220, 234, 244–245. *See also* variation theory of learning

Ashworth, Peter 172, 174

aspects (of phenomena) 13, 32, 56, 63, 77, 79–81, 85, 89, 108, 155, 170, 178, 182, 184–186, 209–210, 223, 236–237, 244. *See also* critical aspects; *See also* part-whole structure

awareness 1–2, 4–6, 8, 13–14, 20–25, 27–33, 38–39, 42, 44, 46, 48–49, 51, 53–64, 66, 73–74, 75, 78–83, 85–90, 95, 99–102, 108, 113, 135, 149, 150, 153–155, 163–165, 169, 170–172, 174, 177–178, 182–198, 204, 206–211, 215–216, 237, 241–246, 248–249, 251, 259, 260. *See also* collective awareness; *See also* expanding awareness; *See also* experience; *See also* ways of experiencing

Berglund, Anders 255

Booth, Shirley 2–3, 11, 23, 29, 33, 38, 69, 71, 76, 78, 80–82, 97, 172, 175, 183, 185–186, 210–211, 215, 219, 238, 241, 248

Bowden, John 7, 92, 101, 109, 115, 124, 130, 139, 152, 166, 168, 174, 251, 260

categories of description 19, 25, 43, 55–56, 61–62, 64, 86, 95, 103, 135, 139, 146, 149–150, 152–154, 156–158, 160, 169, 177, 193–194, 199, 201–205, 207–208, 250–251, 255

collective awareness 4, 6, 14, 83, 89, 101, 102, 245, 248, 249, 251, 260. *See also* collective consciousness; *See also* collective mind

collective consciousness 251, 253, 259–262

collective experience 59, 60, 67, 77, 78, 88–89, 101, 103, 154, 179–181, 192, 209, 239. *See also* ways of experiencing

collective mind 101, 249–252

Collier-Reed, Brandon 136, 143, 157

communicative credibility 163, 176, 182. *See also* credibility of research outcomes

context 4, 10, 40, 47, 56, 59, 60, 64, 68, 73, 76–78, 88, 90, 96, 99, 103, 106, 111, 130, 137–138, 140, 142, 144, 169, 176, 180–181, 187, 210, 250, 253, 255. *See also* relevance structure

credibility of research outcomes 139, 161, 163, 175–179, 182. *See also* research rigour; *See also* trustworthiness (of research procedures)

critical aspects 5–6, 13, 23–24, 30–33, 35, 38, 42–44, 52–53, 56–59, 63, 65–68, 82–84, 86–87, 89–90, 99–100, 133, 135–136, 147–149, 151–152, 154–156, 158, 160, 169, 170–171, 176–180, 182–189, 191, 194–196, 209–212, 216–218, 220–225, 228–232, 235–237, 239, 242, 244, 247, 248. *See also* aspects (of phenomena); *See also* dimensions of variation; *See also* part-whole structure; *See also* variation within ways of experiencing

Dahlgren, Lars-Owe 15, 134, 156
Dall'Alba, Gloria 152
data analysis 7, 12, 19, 25, 37, 41–42, 45, 91–92, 95, 102, 104, 131, 133, 136, 163, 165–166, 170, 178, 181–182, 184, 187, 193, 263
data generation 3, 12, 42–43, 52, 91–93, 102, 106, 131, 165, 169, 172–173, 182. *See also* interview; *See also* survey
devil's advocacy 153, 163, 168
dialectical relationship between meaning and structure 55, 61–63, 65, 67, 69, 74–76, 85, 87–90, 95, 170, 202, 209
dialogic consensus 163, 166. *See also* devil's advocacy; *See also* research rigour
dimensions of variation 5, 13, 82, 150, 158, 175, 183–196, 198, 200, 203, 205, 207–210, 219, 236, 240, 244. *See also* critical aspects
discernment 7, 21, 30–32, 57, 66, 79, 87, 106–107, 136, 148, 180, 183, 187–191, 194–195, 201–203, 205–206, 209–210, 212, 219, 222–223, 231, 236–237, 243–244, 247, 254
Doing Developmental Phenomenography 92, 124

Eaton, Lance 93
empirical research 2–4, 6, 9, 12, 14–15, 18, 23, 28, 30, 33, 35, 40, 44, 49, 58, 60, 65, 86, 88–89, 139, 212, 214–216, 226, 238, 242–244, 246–247, 257. *See also* logical relationship; *See also* structural relationship
epistemology 1, 4–5, 8–9, 11–13, 18, 23, 32–33, 41, 46, 48–49, 56, 66, 69, 71, 73–74, 76–77, 79, 85–91, 97, 133, 161–163, 173, 179, 180, 182, 215, 229, 238, 244, 255. *See also* ontology
expanding awareness 5, 13, 24, 28, 32, 53, 56, 63, 100, 155, 171, 182–187, 191–198, 206–210. *See also* inclusive hierarchy
experience 1–2, 5–6, 9, 12–14, 16–22, 26, 30, 36–37, 40, 48–49, 52–54, 56, 59, 60, 64, 67, 71–90, 92, 94–101, 103, 106–108, 110, 111, 113, 117–118, 122, 126, 131, 133, 138, 143, 154–155, 163–164, 166, 170, 173–175, 179–181, 183, 185, 187, 192, 207–211, 219, 221–223, 225, 236, 237, 239, 243, 245–246, 248, 250, 252–255, 257, 259–260, 262. *See also* awareness; *See also* ways of experiencing
external horizon 72, 79, 169. *See also* internal horizon

Fallsberg, Margareta 134, 152, 156
feature 152, 230, 232. *See also* value
figure-ground structure 73, 80–81, 83, 88–90, 170–171. *See also* structure

Green, Pamela 92, 114, 116, 124, 130, 139, 152, 166

hierarchy 19, 25, 28–29, 38, 42, 45, 48, 53–55, 58, 60–69, 85–86, 88, 136, 139, 154, 170, 175, 177–178, 191, 202, 205, 257. *See also* inclusive hierarchy; *See also* phenomenographic hierarchy; *See also* structure
Holmqvist, Mona 229–231
'how' aspect 21, 22, 72, 75. *See also* structural aspect; *See also* 'what' aspect
human experience. *See* experience

inclusive hierarchy 38, 45, 53, 62, 95, 177. *See also* hierarchy; *See also* expanding awareness
Ingerman, Åke 136, 143, 157, 222, 233
internal horizon 72, 79, 83, 89, 169, 236. *See also* external horizon

interpretive awareness 153, 163, 164–165, 169, 172, 174, 182. *See also* trustworthiness (of research procedures)
interpretive research 12, 17, 161–163
interview 7, 12, 25, 35–36, 41, 43, 68, 91–93, 99, 103–105, 108–119, 121–125, 129–131, 136–138, 141–143, 150, 173, 176, 179, 228, 255
  conduct of interview 117, 130–131
  interview design 92, 104, 108, 111, 129–130, 138
  transcription of interview 130–131

Kettunen, Jaana 197, 257
Killam, Laura 93, 157
Kullberg, Angelika 221, 224, 227

Learning and Awareness 2–5, 8–9, 11–13, 23, 30, 33, 38, 69, 71, 73–74, 80, 86, 183, 186, 210, 215–216, 219, 238, 240–241, 243–244, 247–248
learning study 212–213, 215, 225–229, 231–233, 239, 242, 244–248
logical relationship 184, 193, 261
longitudinal study 102–104
Lupton, Mandy 155

Marton, Ference 2–3, 7–8, 11, 15–16, 20, 23, 29, 33, 38, 69, 71, 76, 78, 80–82, 96–98, 101, 103, 110, 122, 137, 139, 155, 172, 174–175, 183, 185–190, 210–211, 215, 219–223, 232, 238, 241, 248–249, 251–252, 256–257, 260–261
methodology 2–7, 9–12, 14–15, 18–19, 23–25, 33, 36–40, 42–49, 51–52, 58–60, 67, 71, 78, 90–92, 100, 102–103, 107, 131, 133, 158–159, 161–162, 177, 182, 216, 218–219, 226, 228–230, 255–256, 258, 261

non-dualism 73, 84–85, 88, 90, 96–97, 163, 174–175, 181
NVivo 146–147

object of learning 211–212, 216, 218, 220–222, 224–229, 231–232, 237, 244, 246–247
object of study 11, 33, 72–73, 84, 91–95, 98, 111, 131, 141, 160, 166, 169, 177
ontology 8, 11, 23, 33, 71, 84, 96–97, 174, 215, 255–256
outcome space 13, 20, 28, 30, 41–42, 47, 55–56, 62, 65, 83, 85–86, 103–104, 136, 139, 143, 154–155, 159, 167–170, 175, 177–179, 182–183, 188–189, 191–196, 198–199, 202, 205–206, 208–209, 242, 251, 255

Paakkari, Leena 197
Pang, Ming Fai 223, 225, 239
part-whole structure 18, 29, 31, 52, 54–57, 61, 63–66, 69, 83–85, 88–90, 95, 100, 133, 155, 169–171, 191, 196, 205
patterns of variation and invariance 180, 211–212, 218, 220, 222–225, 228, 244, 254
  contrast 222, 224–225
  fusion 222–224
  generalisation 222–225
  separation 222–224
pedagogy 5, 13, 25, 38–39, 41, 44–47, 51, 58, 82, 212–222, 225–226, 228, 235, 240, 245, 247–249
phenomenographic hierarchy 29. *See also* hierarchy
phenomenology 17–18, 26, 74, 79, 172
Pong, Wing Ming 98, 155, 187–190
pool of meanings 7, 135–138, 142–144. *See also* whole of transcript
Prosser, Mike 7, 145, 152–153

qualitative difference 5, 11, 18, 21, 23–25, 28, 30, 33, 35, 37–38, 45, 54, 58–59, 61, 75, 78, 80, 82, 86, 95, 99, 149, 152, 158, 169, 183, 193, 231, 242, 244, 259
qualitative research 16, 67, 160–162, 169, 178–179, 266

referential aspect 22, 75
relational perspective 84, 86, 96, 107, 158, 163–165, 173–176, 182, 255. *See also* non-dualism
relevance structure 78
research question 10, 28, 30, 32–33, 46, 72, 91, 93, 99–100, 102, 111, 131, 161–162, 164, 182, 216, 247
research rigour 12, 52, 91–92, 139, 148, 153, 161–163, 172, 174, 178, 182
role of researcher 163–164, 174, 182, 195
Rovio-Johansson, Airi 8, 222, 233

Säljö, Roger 15
sample 28, 31, 35–38, 43, 45–46, 52–53, 60, 64, 67–68, 78, 84, 89, 91–92, 103–108, 124, 131, 144, 148, 162, 171, 176, 180, 217
Sandberg, Jorgen 130, 255
second-order perspective 16, 102–103, 226, 245, 247
sociocultural perspective 253–256
structural aspect 22, 75–76, 79, 88, 90, 133
structural relationship 4, 11, 19–20, 29, 35–36, 38, 40, 45–46, 49, 51–61, 63–69, 88–89, 95, 100, 136, 148, 157, 159, 169–172, 178, 182, 184, 209
structure 1–2, 4, 11, 13, 18–20, 23–24, 28–29, 32–33, 40, 43–44, 46, 51–52, 54–58, 60–69, 72–76, 78–80, 83, 85–90, 95, 100, 108, 136, 151, 154, 158–159, 169–171, 183, 191, 202–203, 205, 209, 219, 235–236, 250, 257
survey 4, 11, 36–37, 43, 52–53, 58, 60–61, 63, 68, 92–93, 104, 110–113, 169, 170–171, 217, 234, 236–240, 242–243. *See also* data generation
Svensson, Lennart 15, 118, 122, 130, 141, 252

Theman, Jan 118, 130, 141
transferability (of research outcomes) 106–107, 180

Trigwell, Keith 7, 35, 82, 254
trustworthiness (of research procedures) 12, 19, 77, 161, 163, 172, 178, 182
Tsui, Amy 221–222

value 223, 230–232. *See also* feature
variation between ways of experiencing 235, 239, 242, 244. *See also* variation within ways of experiencing
variation theory of awareness 5, 215–216, 241–244, 246
variation theory of learning 5, 8, 71, 210–211, 213, 215–216, 219, 222, 224–225, 232, 241–244, 246–247
variation within ways of experiencing 235–237, 239, 240–244. *See also* variation between ways of experiencing

Wan, Sally Wai-Yan 255
Warner, Kerry 255
ways of experiencing 2, 19–20, 23, 29, 40, 43, 53–55, 57, 60, 62, 64–66, 69, 75–78, 80–81, 83–88, 90, 93, 95, 97–98, 100, 102–104, 106–108, 111–112, 133, 138–139, 143, 148, 157, 160, 167, 169, 176, 180–181, 184–194, 196, 198–199, 208–210, 229, 231, 234–237, 239, 241–244, 247, 250, 254, 261
ways of understanding 4, 10–11, 15, 21, 23–26, 28–33, 35, 37–40, 42–49, 51, 53–55, 57, 66–67, 77, 95, 98, 100, 110, 158, 160, 169, 172, 180, 187, 191, 197, 216–217, 227, 231, 234–235, 237, 240, 243, 247, 250–252, 257, 261
'what' aspect 22, 72, 75. *See also* 'how' aspect; *See also* referential aspect
Whitfield, Martha 259
whole of transcript 7

Yu, Suet Voon 146–148, 259

About the Team

Alessandra Tosi was the managing editor for this book.

Adèle Kreager proof-read this manuscript and compiled the index.

Jeevanjot Kaur Nagpal designed the cover. The cover was produced in InDesign using the Fontin font.

Cameron Craig typeset the book in InDesign and produced the paperback and hardback editions. The main text font is Tex Gyre Pagella and the heading font is Californian FB.

Cameron also produced the PDF and HTML editions. The conversion was performed with open-source software and other tools freely available on our GitHub page at https://github.com/OpenBookPublishers.

Jeremy Bowman created the EPUB.

Raegan Allen was in charge of marketing.

This book need not end here...

Share

All our books — including the one you have just read — are free to access online so that students, researchers and members of the public who can't afford a printed edition will have access to the same ideas. This title will be accessed online by hundreds of readers each month across the globe: why not share the link so that someone you know is one of them?

This book and additional content is available at
https://doi.org/10.11647/OBP.0431

Donate

Open Book Publishers is an award-winning, scholar-led, not-for-profit press making knowledge freely available one book at a time. We don't charge authors to publish with us: instead, our work is supported by our library members and by donations from people who believe that research shouldn't be locked behind paywalls.

Join the effort to free knowledge by supporting us at
https://www.openbookpublishers.com/support-us

We invite you to connect with us on our socials!

BLUESKY	MASTODON	LINKEDIN
@openbookpublish.bsky.social	@OpenBookPublish@hcommons.social	open-book-publishers

Read more at the Open Book Publishers Blog
https://blogs.openbookpublishers.com

You may also be interested in:

Phenomenology and the Philosophy of Technology
Bas de Boer and Jochem Zwier (Eds)

https://doi.org/10.11647/obp.0421

Science as Social Existence
Heidegger and the Sociology of Scientific Knowledge
Jeff Kochan

https://doi.org/10.11647/obp.0129

Forms of Life and Subjectivity
Rethinking Sartre's Philosophy
Daniel Rueda Garrido

https://doi.org/10.11647/obp.0259

www.ingramcontent.com/pod-product-compliance
Lightning Source LLC
Chambersburg PA
CBHW050207240426
43671CB00013B/2241